WIN, LOSE OR DIE

STUART BARKER

WIN, LOSE OR DIE

*Inside the Lethal Sport of Motorcycle
Road Racing and the Isle of Man TT*

First published in the UK in 2026 by Blink Publishing
An imprint of Bonnier Books UK
5th Floor, HYLO, 105 Bunhill Row,
London, EC1Y 8LZ

A CIP catalogue record for this book is available from the British Library.

Hardback ISBN: 978-1-78512-896-7
Trade Paperback ISBN: 978-1-78512-897-4
Paperback ISBN: 978-1-78512-898-1

Also available as an ebook and an audiobook

1 3 5 7 9 10 8 6 4 2

Design and Typeset by Envy Design Ltd
Printed and bound in Great Britain by CPI (UK) Ltd, Croydon CR0 4YY

At Bonnier Books UK, we are committed to publishing sustainably.
Find out more here: bonnierbooks.co.uk/sustainability

Every reasonable effort has been made to trace copyright holders of
material reproduced in this book, but if any have been inadvertently
overlooked the publishers would be glad to hear from them.

The authorised representative in the EEA is
Bonnier Books UK (Ireland) Limited.
Registered office address:
Block B, The Crescent Building
Northwood, Santry
Dublin 9, D09 C6X8, Ireland
compliance@bonnierbooks.ie

www.bonnierbooks.co.uk

For Wullie Fulton and Yvonne Fulton.
In thanks for taking me to all those races.

CONTENTS

PROLOGUE

Isle of Man TT Course, Wednesday 30th May, 2018

It was a beautiful golden early summer's evening as riders set off from the Isle of Man TT grandstand to complete some crucial practice laps. The first race of the 2018 TT was only three days away; time was of the essence.

Steve Mercer was among the first group of riders to take to the infamous 37.73-mile public roads course, widely regarded as the most dangerous racing circuit on earth. A hugely experienced rider, it was Mercer's ninth TT and, after struggling to get his Jackson Racing Honda Fireblade dialled in earlier during practice week, he finally felt he had a set-up that would stand him in good stead come the races themselves. 'Up until the Wednesday practice session, I had been struggling a bit with set-up, but I reverted to my 2016 settings that night and the bike felt great,' Mercer recalls. 'It was a really nice bike to ride, so I was really looking forward to race week.'

Mercer set off from the paddock along with Ivan Lintin, Dan Cooper, James Cowton and Daley Mathison. Around ten minutes later, on the approach to the very bumpy and tree-lined Churchtown section of the course, Mercer spotted red flags being displayed, meaning the session had been stopped – red flags are never good news at the world's most dangerous sporting event, and they wouldn't prove to be in this case. Mercer and the other riders pulled over to the side of the road to await further instructions. There had been a crash at Churchtown, and the resultant debris had blocked the road. There was no way through.

'While I was stopped at the roadside with a few other riders, I managed to borrow a phone and called my wife Caroline in the paddock to let her know that I was okay. I told her to let the partners of the other riders know that we were all okay, and we would be back in the paddock in about ten minutes,' Mercer explains. 'Unfortunately, before she got a chance, she was called up to the race office.'

Dan Kneen, the local Manx hero who had been edging ever closer to taking his first TT win and was a hot favourite to finally take a victory in 2018, had lost his life in the crash. He was just 30 years old.

At this point, the other riders were unaware of the extent of the tragedy that had just unfolded, and with the wreckage from the crash preventing them from completing the lap and getting back to the paddock, Mercer and the others were instructed to turn around and return the way they had come. 'Because the track was blocked, the marshals told us to turn our bikes around and to ride back towards the paddock in the wrong direction on the course,' Mercer says.

The riders obliged, but what happened next would change Steve Mercer's life forever.

'We were just cruising back, doing about 25–30mph and, as I got to Ballacrye, I saw this car coming round the corner towards us, and it was broadside – it was absolutely on the pipe. I just had time to think *Fuck!* and, in the time it took to blink, I saw the car's bumper right in front of my face and knew I had to get off the bike. So I tried to jump off the bike, but as I did so, the bike's handlebar caught my leg and almost tore it off. I flew over the handlebars and hit the screen of the car, then flew off into a field and completely wiped out the scaffolding for the TV camera.'

An official car had been sent out onto the course and was rushing towards Dan Kneen's crash site at around 100mph. Mercer had no time to react and no chance of avoiding the car. Hideously injured, his life hanging by a thread, he struggled to comprehend what had just happened. 'It was a beautiful summer's evening, and I was lying on my back, looking up at the sky, with this horrible ringing sound in my ears, as if I had just come out of a nightclub,' he says. 'I lay there thinking, Oh, my God as I relived the crash about a thousand times, wondering what had happened, and knowing that I was in really bad shape.'

One of the other returning riders, Daley Mathison, witnessed the collision and rushed to Mercer's aid. 'Daley stopped his bike, jumped over a stile and came to try to help me,' Mercer explains. 'He was sat on the grass next to me. I didn't know it at the time, but Daley later told me that he was holding my leg because, with every beat of my heart, blood was pumping out of it. My right femur had exploded, and my leg was only being held on by a thin strip of skin. The femoral artery had been ruptured, too, and I had punctured my lung, so I couldn't breathe. I couldn't speak either, because I had paralysed my vocal cords. Eventually, I passed out.'

Mercer slipped into the merciful darkness of unconsciousness; his body so traumatised it simply shut down, the pain too great to endure. When he finally came round, it would be to a very different life.

CHAPTER 1

THE RUSH

'Road racing's a lot more dangerous. If you fall off at a short circuit you'll fall into a gravel trap. On a road course you'd be straight into trees and walls. It's just about whether you enjoy that sort of thing or whether you don't.'
MICHAEL DUNLOP

'Why do I prefer road racing to short circuit racing?' Guy Martin ponders. 'Because if you get it wrong it's gonna kill you. I'm not a fatalist or anything, but that's what I like about it. If it was safe I wouldn't do it. It's that simple.'

Martin is the most successful Isle of Man TT rider never to win a race. Now a much-loved TV presenter, he has largely retired from racing, but when he does have the occasional outing it's at an Irish road race rather than at a more glamorous British championship event. 'I chuck a bike in the back of me van on a Thursday night, catch the ferry, qualify Friday afternoon, race on the Saturday then be back home in time for work on Monday,' he says. 'I love doing that. You don't get much time on the bike, but it's great just talking shite all weekend with some mates. And those Irish national road-race meetings are some of the best tracks in the world, for my money. That's what makes it worthwhile, because it takes a lot of faffing about and money for the ferry and time off work, but riding those circuits makes it all worthwhile.'

Martin isn't the only rider who prefers riding flat out on real-world roads rather than on much safer short circuits, with all their air fences, gravel traps and run-off areas. Ryan Farquhar carved out a whole career racing on the roads and never showed much interest in short circuits. 'It's just the buzz you get from it,' he said before retiring in 2015. 'It's a different type of riding and it's more jumps and bumps. I would get bored riding round short circuits all the time. Obviously there is still speed involved, but it's just a different thing. I just get a far bigger buzz out of the jumps and going past lamp posts and things. It's better craic too. In road racing, everybody seems to be more down to earth. The teams in British Superbike paddocks are full of guys that are all hairdos and sunglasses, whereas road racing's not really like that.'

The most successful Isle of Man TT racer of all time, Michael Dunlop, points out another difference between road racing and circuit racing. 'Road racing's a lot more dangerous,' he says. 'If you fall off at a short circuit, you'll fall into a gravel trap. On a road course you'd be straight into trees and walls. It's just about whether you enjoy that sort of thing or whether you don't.'

Michael's father, Robert Dunlop, was also a helpless addict to the thrills of road racing. 'Like most riders I am very selfish,' he admitted. 'We sacrifice everything for the thrill of racing. There's no substitute for it – from the riders' point of view and the spectators.' Robert Dunlop lost his life to the sport in 2008.

'Pure' road racing, 'real' road racing; whatever you choose to call it, it's simply to distinguish this branch of racing from short circuit racing. Once upon a time, every circuit was a 'roads' circuit. Before the conversion of airfields (like Silverstone or Snetterton) or parkland venues (like Cadwell Park and Oulton Park) into short circuits, and before multi-million-pound purpose-built circuits were constructed (the now-defunct Rockingham is the only example in the UK, though they proliferate abroad) all motorcycle road races were held on real-world, everyday roads, with real-world, everyday hazards.

Road racing could not be further removed from the multi-million-pound, glitzy, glamorous world of MotoGP – the pinnacle of motorcycle racing. Paddocks are often muddy fields, team transport and sleeping accommodation is usually a van or caravan, and money is always short on all fronts. Riders' children play in the paddock, while their dads risk their lives at ferociously high speeds around some of the most dangerous courses on earth. There's little in the way of prize money on offer and sponsors are hard to come by, so most riders pay for everything themselves. Road racing is more usually a way to lose money than to make it. Michael Dunlop is the biggest star in the sport, but despite winning four TT races in 2025, his total prize money from that event was just £52,500. Compared to Max Verstappen's $46-million wages for a season of Formula 1 racing, it's peanuts.

But road racers don't race for money – they race for the sheer rush of it, and it's a rush that cannot be replicated in any other way. Skimming stone walls at speeds of over 200mph on bumpy, treacherous public roads offers a buzz like nothing else on earth, and riders queue up like junkies to get their fix.

Although he eventually became the highest-paid motorcycle racer in history in his day, five-time world champion Geoff Duke insisted money was always a secondary factor for him. Speaking of modern-day MotoGP racing before he passed away in 2015, Duke said, 'It's much more financially rewarding for today's stars, but I can honestly say that I raced because I loved doing it, not because of what I was going to get paid. Money was a secondary thing for me. The main consideration was the thrill, the challenge and the competitiveness of the racing itself.'

Duke also felt that modern circuits were boring compared to the old-school road circuits he used to race on. 'To some extent I've lost interest in world championship racing now because it's so different that I can't really relate to it,' he said. 'There is a "sameness" about all the circuits that I find dull. There's so much run-off that a rider can afford to ride near the limit in the knowledge that, if he does fall off, he's probably not going to hurt himself. I never had that luxury. I still keep an interest in bike racing, but nothing like as much as I did, because it's so different now. Chalk and cheese is the best description of it, really. The circuits are entirely different and look much the same to me. They're not so challenging as the circuits I rode on. And that's what I loved about racing – the challenge. The more challenging it was, the better I liked it. I mean, places like the Nürburgring (a 14-mile road circuit in Germany which used to host a round of the world championship), it was certainly on a par with the TT. I loved the TT, but the Nürburgring probably was my favourite. And places like Spa-Francorchamps in Belgium (another road circuit); I loved the fast, sweeping bends there where I could make up a lot of time.'

There's a great variation in the size and prestige of road races. Events like the Isle of Man TT and the North West 200 draw massive crowds and enjoy global television coverage. Held on an 8.97-mile course that joins the towns of Portrush, Portstewart and Coleraine on the North Antrim coast, the North West 200 is Northern Ireland's biggest outdoor sporting event, attracting over 100,000 spectators each May. With its long straights, the 'Triangle' course (so named because it follows a rough triangular shape) sees riders jostling in a pack at speeds well over 200mph.

The Isle of Man TT, by contrast, is a race against the clock, with riders starting alone at ten-second intervals to attack the notoriously dangerous 37.73-mile course. But most road races feature mass starts, and that means upwards of 40 bikes and riders starting at the same time, or in two waves. With so many bikes racing so close, the opening few corners of a mass-start road race can be mayhem, but the spectacle and the thrill is undeniable. As society becomes ever more risk-averse, road racing is now being seen as something of a last stand against health-and-safety culture, with its evermore intrusive laws, restrictions and regulations. Road racing proudly flies in the face of this culture, and it stands in its own way as a last bastion of freedom – a defiant V-sign to the very laws that seek to constrain human beings from partaking of any kind of dangerous pursuit.

Once a rider gets a taste of road racing it's very hard for them to turn back because the rush is so much greater than racing on a short circuit. Australian racer David Johnson is one such rider. 'The TT has become the centre of my racing year now – I don't even want to do short circuits anymore,' he says. 'I had always classed myself as a short circuit rider, but now I'm getting classed as a roads guy. The roads are definitely more of a thrill to ride.'

Davey Todd is a double British Superstock champion and currently races in the British Superbike Championship but, for him, there's no rush like the roads. 'It's hard to put down into words why I love the TT so much,' he muses. 'It's more of a feeling; the feeling I get there is like nothing else. I've raced in pretty much every discipline of motorcycle sport, and I love them all, but as soon as I did the TT I knew it was different – it was just better than everything else. In fact, it's sort of spoiled everything else a little bit for me!'

While Todd acknowledges that road racing, and the TT in particular, offers a far greater adrenaline rush than circuit racing, he also admits that the risk factor is part of the appeal. 'You experience the highest emotions and the lowest emotions that you'll ever have racing a bike,' he says. 'The risk factor and the dangers are the biggest you'll ever face too. And the challenge – I mean, learning the course and trying to win a TT? I don't think there's anything harder to do. It's certainly the hardest thing I've ever done in my life. All the studying and learning – everything that's entailed in racing the TT – is the biggest challenge I've ever had.

It's the biggest thrill and the biggest adrenaline rush too. Sitting on the grid at the TT is the craziest pre-race nerves you will ever get. When I go to a British Superbike race after the TT I could probably fall asleep on the grid! I try to get myself all wound up for the race, but I can't. I just feel very flat after the extreme emotions of the TT.'

Ultimately, it's the reward that riders get from road racing that keeps them coming back, despite the dangers. There's simply no other sport on earth that can give competitors such a hit, as TT winner James Hillier acknowledges. 'Obviously road racing is dangerous, but the way I see it I take some risks for a couple of weeks a year and the return it gives me is huge,' he explains. 'Not financially, but personally, and you can't put a price on that. A lot of people think that TT riders lead a glamorous lifestyle, but that's not the case. We don't do it for the money – we do it because we love it. It's tricky to explain how I cope with the dangers. I don't want to grow old and regret things that I didn't do. What do you do in life? Do you sit around wishing you'd done stuff, or do you get out there and do it?'

Racing on the roads requires a different riding style to racing on short circuits, and the number one rule is not to crash. While short circuit riders are skating on the very limit of physics and adhesion at every corner – because they can afford to crash, thanks to all the gravel traps, air fences and other safety measures in place at such events – road racers don't have that luxury, so they have to adjust their riding styles accordingly. 'One of the easiest ways to crash is when you're trail-braking into the corners,' says 11-time North West 200 winner Glenn Irwin. 'On short circuits you go into the corners leaned over and you're still applying the front brakes. You don't want to do that in road racing because you really don't want to crash. So, you do your hard braking when you're upright and don't try to gain time on corner entry – or I certainly don't anyway. Instead, you gain time on the exits onto the straights. You're safer and faster concentrating on your exits and respecting your entries.'

The late Steve Hislop was outstanding on both short circuits and road circuits and knew just how differently the two disciplines needed to be ridden. 'It may not be obvious to the casual observer that there's such a difference between the two disciplines but, believe me, there is,' he said. 'Road racing is about stamina; it's about ignoring the dangers and not being afraid to clip brick walls and brush hedges, and it's about nursing the bike over extremely bumpy and taxing roads. On short circuits, it's a flat-out sprint from the start over a relatively short distance and you're bunched up tight with 30 other riders, literally leaning on each other. Also on short circuits, you're leaning the bike over more, decking everything out on the absolute limits of adhesion. Because there's more run-off space you can afford to ride that bit harder, too, because crashing is safer than on the roads. I suppose it's like the difference between a 10,000-metre cross-country run and a 100-metre sprint, and there are not many athletes who excel at both of those disciplines.'

Until the 1970s, the Motorcycle Grand Prix world championships used to take in several rounds that were essentially road races: circuits like the original Nürburgring in Germany, Imatra in Finland and Spa-Francorchamps in

Belgium. But the greater dangers they presented meant they were eventually dropped from the calendar, as five-time world champion Geoff Duke explained: 'Grand Prix riders used to have to race on road circuits as well as purpose-built circuits, but the manufacturers put a stop to that because they didn't want to risk their riders getting hurt and missing out on world championships. I didn't think the dangers of road circuits were that much greater, because you rode according to the type of circuit you were on.'

Top privateer road racer James McBride, now retired, paradoxically felt that fast road circuits were actually safer than short circuits. 'The sustained high speeds at the TT felt safer to me,' he says. 'I used to thrive on high-speed circuits rather than stop-and-go circuits, which I was never that great at, probably because I was quite heavy as a rider. I was never too fond of being on the side of the tyres and cracking open the throttle because it's so easy to high-side [when a rear tyre breaks traction and slides, then regains traction, grips, and throws the rider off the "high" side of the bike]. I'd much rather be going through a fifth-gear right-hander and feeling what the tyres are doing at speed. The gyroscopic effect keeps the bike in line at speed, to a degree. But if you come out of the hairpin at Pembrey (a short circuit in Wales) at about 20mph you can so easily high-side and break a rib or two.'

For experienced roads campaigners like Peter Hickman, riding round the TT course is almost a serene experience. 'You're not fighting with other riders like you do on a short circuit, so it's just more relaxing – like a very, very fast Sunday run!' he says. 'I always take a couple of steps back at the TT and just chill out a bit. You're still riding at 100 per cent, but it's a different 100 per cent compared to short circuits.'

One of Hickman's great rivals, Dean Harrison, agrees. 'When you're riding a road course, it's not as intense as a short circuit race,' he says. 'In British Superbikes you're going absolutely mental for 18 laps – you're aggressive, and attacking it and on the point of crashing in every single corner. The TT is more chilled because you're out there on your own and there's no one to use as a reference point. Having said that, everyone's riding as fast as they possibly can. People think we only ride at 99 per cent but believe me, if we did then somebody would ride at 100 per cent and win all the time!'

Not all riders feel the same way. Double TT winner Cameron Donald doesn't share Hickman and Harrison's opinion that road racing is more relaxed than short circuit racing – in fact, he believes the very opposite. 'Road racing is a lot more hard work, and a lot more stressful than short circuit racing,' he says. 'Just mentally, the strain of racing on the roads, to me, is harder. Riding at your limit on either kind of circuit is extremely difficult, but the extra demands of the dangers involved and the sheer speeds – the roads are *so* much faster – it's a different ball game. And somewhere like the North West 200, where you've got five races in a day, it just takes so much out of you. But that's why good results are so much more satisfying.'

While some riders, Michael Dunlop among them, focus almost exclusively on road racing, others would never dream of riding at 200mph between stone walls and prefer to stick to short circuit racing. Some riders switch quite happily between the two disciplines, though most say the transition can be challenging. 'Switching from short circuits to road racing is very easy, but switching back the other way is hard,' Peter Hickman says. 'It takes me a full practice session in British Superbikes to get back up to speed on the short circuits. You're braking a lot later and cornering a lot harder, and you're just more on the edge and a lot closer to crashing all the time. It's a much faster way of riding than you do on the roads. The speeds are higher at the TT, but the actual way you take each turn is a lot faster in BSB.'

Davey Todd has no problem making the transition. 'You definitely have to ride the roads different to how you ride the circuits,' he admits. 'Some riders struggle making that transition, but I've got no problem with it. Don't get me wrong, it's not easy, but I focus really hard on being competitive in both disciplines because not many people can do both competitively.'

One common mistake that many people make when watching a road race is to assume that the riders must be fearless, but double British Superbike champion and TT racer Josh Brookes insists that's not the case. 'Of course we feel fear,' he says. 'If you're not afraid at the TT you're not going to be alive for very long. Every rider feels fear – it's just about how you manage it. We control it with experience and knowledge of what we're doing. No one goes out and rides a 135mph lap on their very first outing. It's a process – you spend years of learning and understanding motorcycles, and years of learning and understanding race craft, and then you spend years learning the TT course. So, we all get scared, but it's how you control it. You need to understand what kind of moments and situations cause that fear, because then you can understand how to manage those variables. You get to a point where you either have to line up on the grid or go home – you either accept what you're about to do or you don't do it. No one's forcing us to be there.'

Brookes insists it's not bravery that makes a good road racer, it's having the knowledge and experience. 'We're professionals, we know what we're doing, and that breeds confidence,' he says. 'This is our job. If you asked a photographer to electrically wire a house, of course they're not going to know what they're doing. In the same way, if you took a TT rider and asked them to do something they didn't know about or understand they wouldn't be nearly as brave or bold as they are on a bike. Like public speaking – a TT racer might take every risk imaginable at very high speeds, but if you asked them to give a public speech they would probably be more terrified of that! So it's not like we can just turn off fear by choice in any given situation. We do what we do out on the TT course through training and experience. Look at astronauts – the reason they're happy to blast off into space is because that's all they know, it's all they've trained for. To them, sure, there's a risk involved, but there's always risks in life – every time you drive your car there's a risk. We all know it but we're all willing to accept certain risks in life, otherwise we'd all be smothered in bubble wrap and cotton wool.'

Only once a rider has the required knowledge and experience can they then control a racing motorcycle on normal public roads at such high speeds. 'For the average person, to blast off into space would be suicide, and the same would go for the average person trying to do what we do at the TT,' Brookes continues. 'But with the right experience and knowledge of racing a motorbike you can manage those risks and lessen them. Like, I might have finished second in the Senior TT, and have lapped the TT course at 134mph, but that doesn't mean I would do an open water dive with a great white shark! Not without all the relevant training and experience so that I understood the characters of the sharks and all the other variables.'

Even the late, great Joey Dunlop (a 26-time TT winner) wasn't fearless. As strange as it might sound for a man who was as comfortable skimming stone walls at 180mph as he was sat in front of the fire in his own armchair, Dunlop was terrified of flying. World-renowned sports photographer and former official Honda Britain team photographer Don Morley remembers that 'I quite literally had to hold Joey's hand on flights just to reassure him. He was totally petrified of aeroplanes and was absolutely incapable of saying a word for the duration of the flight. That's why he drove to all the races in his van whenever he could.'

Fear usually disappears once a road race begins. As soon as it's underway, the riders are fully concentrated, focused and committed to what they're doing and don't think about the dangers – until they get a graphic reminder. Road-racing veteran Michael Rutter says the worst thing about racing on the roads is 'seeing things that you don't want to see. When you're riding past an incident you end up looking and then wish you hadn't. When I was younger, I could just put those things straight out of my mind and get on with riding, but it becomes harder to do that as you get older. I was one of the first on the scene after Guy Martin's crash at Ballagarey during the 2010 TT when his bike exploded in a wall of flames. It was horrific. Guy was lying in the road, not moving, and there were flames and smoke everywhere. For the next five miles my head was gone, and it was really difficult to concentrate; but if you don't then you're putting yourself in danger, so you *have* to move on.'

Having a scary moment or a near miss out on track is another way riders get reminded of the dangers they're facing. Like all road racers, Michael Dunlop is adept at the art of compartmentalising his fears, in other words ignoring them; locking them out of his stream of consciousness for the duration of the race. 'I've had a good few scares, but I never really fret about it, I just get on with the job,' he says. 'I've never sat down and thought about it and went, *Oh shit, that was a big one!* I mean, I *have* had big ones, but you just have to put them out of your mind straight away.'

Road racers also need to be able to accept the consequences should things go wrong. Contrary to what many people think, they're not madmen, nor do they have a death wish. Quite the opposite, in fact: they're very calm, measured and methodical and are in full possession of the facts. The difference between them and most other people is that they're prepared to accept the risks in return for the thrill and sense of satisfaction they get from racing on the roads. 'I know a motorbike will get you in the end,' TT legend John McGuinness readily admits. 'It might not be this year or next, but it will happen eventually. I've been with guys who are no longer with us, like Lee Pullen,

David Jefferies, Mick Lofthouse . . . If you don't think about the bad things that could happen then you've got something wrong with you. When I'm getting ready for the TT, I wash the cars, put the finances straight, stuff like that, because you never know.'

McGuinness made his TT debut in 1996, and even the death of his roommate didn't put him off. 'I shared a room with Mick Lofthouse at my first TT, and he got killed in practice,' he says. 'You'd think that would put you off for life, but I suppose bike racers are just not right in the head.'

The camaraderie among TT racers is powerful, as Lofthouse showed. Operating on a shoestring budget for his first TT, McGuinness had a van but no accommodation until a chance meeting with Lofthouse. 'I arrived in Douglas at about six o'clock in the morning, so nothing was open and there was nowhere to park up the truck,' McGuinness says. 'I saw Mick Lofthouse and asked where he was staying, and he told me the Monaville Hotel. So, I parked up there and slept until about 9am, when Mick came out and woke me up and invited me in to get a bit of breakfast. I ended up staying in a box room with Mick free of charge for the whole TT. Blagged the whole thing.'

Yet before the racing even began there was an empty room at the Monaville. Lofthouse was killed during practice. McGuinness witnessed the aftermath of his friend's fatal accident. 'I came across Mick's crash, saw the bike lying in the middle of the road and thought, *What am I doing? Why am I doing this?*'

Seven years after making his TT debut, McGuinness lost his great friend David Jefferies at the 2003 event.

'I considered quitting after David was killed,' he says. 'I spoke to his mum, Pauline, and said, "I think that's me finished. I'm done," and she said, "No, you can't do that, you've got to ride." She was the strongest person in the paddock. You've got obligations with sponsors and teams, but at the end of the day your head's not on a chopping block at the TT – you don't *have* to race. You only do it because you want to do it.'

McGuinness wanted to do it so much that he was back on a bike the very next day. Now 53 years old, he continues to race at the TT, and he always has a word with his old friend David Jefferies when he passes the spot where he lost his life. 'Every time I go past there, I always have a little word with myself, and I'm the same where Mick Lofthouse was killed,' he says. 'I say a lot of strange things to myself. Every time before a race I pray to all the lads who have gone.'

Despite all his years of experience, McGuinness is still at a loss to explain how road racers do what they do. 'I don't know how we do it, really – how we somehow manage to switch off to all the deaths. We're kind of brought up that way as Brits – the old stiff upper lip thing. I remember a foreign rider got killed at the TT and his mate went straight home and said he'd never come back, and you can't really blame him for that, but here I am – ready for more. I can't explain it.'

It's not that road racers *don't* think about the dangers of the sport – they very much do – but, like a well-trained soldier, they accept those dangers and redeploy to the front lines, ready to take their chances. Road specialist Ryan

Farquhar retired in 2016 after his uncle Trevor Ferguson was killed at the Manx Grand Prix (the amateur version of the TT, held on the same course), but when he was still racing he admitted to often thinking about his fallen friends and rivals. 'Every day when I'm working on the bikes I think about races that I've done and the riders that I've raced against and try to work out how I'll beat them in certain circumstances, and it always comes up – riders like Richard Britton, Darran Lindsay, Owen McNally, Joey Dunlop, Martin Finnegan . . . Riders that I've had good races with and got to know, and they're not here now. It is sad, but they were like me – they knew the risks but thought it was never going to happen to them. I believe it'll not happen to me, but I might be next – you never know.'

Top privateer Paul 'Moz' Owen is another rider who, despite losing a great friend, carried on, such is the lure of road racing. When New Zealand rider Paul Dobbs was killed at the TT in 2010, Owen stopped, laid down his own bike, and ran to help, but there was nothing he could do. For his selfless actions, Owen was awarded that year's 'Spirit of the TT' award but, despite his loss, he raced on. 'Packing it in goes through your mind every time someone gets killed and you think, *I've had enough, I can't do this anymore*,' he says. '*It could have been me, and I've got a wife and a kid sat at home.* I went and saw Dobbsy's wife then went and sat in the back of my van and cried my eyes out. Then the boys in my team came to see me and said, "What do you want to do? Shall we pack the stuff away?" and I said, "No. We've got a Superbike there, and you've been struggling all week trying to get it ready. And if I don't get straight back on a bike now then I never will." I knew Dobbsy wouldn't have wanted me to stop.'

But the greater the risk, the greater the reward, and for every road racer risks are worth taking, just for the outlandish feeling and sheer euphoria the sport gives them. 'Road racing is a far bigger thrill than racing on short circuits, simply because you're on real-life public roads that are used by normal traffic every day of the year, so to be going through a 30mph zone at 180mph just feels so *bad!*' says Manx rider Conor Cummins. 'It's like the naughty little kid in you that's not gone away. The first lap I ever did of the TT was unbelievable, even though I was behind a travelling marshal, it was just such a bizarre feeling.'

TT winner Lee Johnston couldn't believe his luck when he was first let loose on the TT course. 'I spent the whole time waiting for a policeman to jump out in front of me and stop me,' he says of the first few laps he completed. 'I just couldn't believe that you were allowed to do that – to have that much fun.'

Conor Cummins believes that road racing is a much more exciting experience than short circuit racing for spectators too. Speaking of spectating at the TT he says, 'You can get much closer to the action. Where else in the world would you be able to sit within a few inches of a race bike coming past at 180mph? It's more personal, too, because it's easy to get to meet and interact with the riders. You don't have a chance of doing that at a MotoGP race. And it's free. Okay, you have to pay to get to the Isle of Man, but once you're there the racing is free. There's not many top-class sports [that] can boast that.'

Because the TT only happens once a year, it takes riders a few laps to adjust to the sustained high speeds encountered on the Mountain course (so-called because part of it runs over the shoulder of Snaefell mountain), and the first few laps can be a frightening experience. Michael Rutter again: 'On the first day of practice I'm always petrified because everything's flashing past you at such speed. But by the end of race week, instead of feeling you're doing 190mph, you feel like you're doing 90mph because you just get used to it. That means you have more time to think about things, so that's when the mind can start wandering and I'll sometimes think things like, *Oh, it's a really nice day, I think we'll have a barbecue tonight.* It depends how you're doing in the race, though. If you're challenging for the win then you concentrate 100 per cent, but if you're further down the order, your mind can wander.'

Crashing on road circuits is never a good idea and, even if a rider is lucky enough to get away with it, the mental effects can linger. Four decades after retiring from racing, seven-time TT winner Mick Grant still has nightmares. 'I had a dream just the other night,' he says. 'I was racing round the TT Course and I got both wheels in the gutter somewhere near Bishopscourt, but luckily I woke up before I went over the handlebars. I ran too wide around the corner and was fully in the gutter and just thought, *Oh shit, here we go!* I used to pride myself on being really accurate round the TT course and can only remember that happening for real on one occasion – going up May Hill in Ramsey on the Suzuki XR69. I was right up on the pavement, which was very unusual for me.

Racing was such a huge part of my life, so I still have nightmares about crashing.'

Not all road races are equal. Some riders are quite happy to take part in some events, but not others. Barry Sheene loved racing at Oliver's Mount in Scarborough (a very dangerous parkland course) but hated the TT. Ian Simpson was perfectly comfortable at the TT, the North West 200 and the Ulster Grand Prix, but drew the line at the smaller Irish national road races, considering them just 'too risky'. In the 1980s, Gary Lingham was happy to ride flat out at the North West and the Ulster Grand Prix but never felt comfortable at the TT, even though he raced there – technically speaking, at least. In reality, he just rode around, then pretended to have a mechanical problem. 'I loved the North West and the Ulster, but I never wanted to ride at the TT, even though I did,' Lingham says. 'In 1980 I got a ride with Derry's Racing, and they wanted me to do the TT. I went to the Isle of Man and did a few laps but it just wasn't my cup of tea. I don't think I ever completed a race at the TT because I never had any intention of really attacking it. The bikes were too fast and too light and too dangerous for the course, and we were losing too many people.'

An added danger at the TT is the length of the races. A six-lap Superbike race involves riding flat out for 226 miles. 'The sheer mileage increases the odds of something going wrong,' Lingham continues. 'A six-lap TT is the equivalent of doing about ten normal road races, so I usually made sure I had a problem with my bike and had to pull out of the races. So, did I do the Isle of Man TT? Not really. It's more accurate to say I went there, then hit the kill switch after about half a lap! I lost Derry's support because of an interview I did to that effect.'

Lingham was happier contesting shorter road races, even though they were still fraught with danger. 'The North West and the Ulster Grand Prix were shorter races and, for me, much more enjoyable, even though I witnessed John Newbold and Tom Herron being killed at the North West,' he says. 'You're just not putting your life on the line for the same amount of time that you are at the TT. I've watched documentaries about the current guys at the TT, and with the speed they're doing now the bikes are all out of shape everywhere.'

Some riders, Michael Rutter among them, are equally happy on both the short circuits and the roads and don't have a preference. 'I'd say it's about 50–50 for me,' he says. 'It's brilliant to go and do things like the TT, the North West and Macau and then come back to British Superbikes where you have to ride at 150 per cent all the time. Road racing is just completely different. Everything about it is different – from when you walk into the paddock to when you drive home.'

Learning the 37.73-mile TT course is also a very different experience to learning a short circuit, as 11-time winner Steve Hislop explained, shortly before losing his life in a helicopter crash in 2003. 'The TT is different to learn compared to short circuits because it's got well over 300 corners and you need to know where every one of them goes, where every bump is, every drain cover and every rise in the road. You need to find the quickest, but safest, lines to take, as well as knowing where all the damp patches tend to linger after it has rained. You must know where the wind is likely to get under the bike and lift it or blow you sideways, you must know your braking points for every corner on different types of machine, and you've got to know what gear to be in for them all, too, so that you get the optimum revs, grip and drive. On top of that there's cambers to learn – both converse and adverse – and loads of little tricks to gain time, like using kerbs or bus stops to run wide, meaning you can take certain corners faster. And when you've learned all that, you need to find out how you can go quicker still by shaving off fractions of a second each lap. In short, it's the most difficult and demanding course in the world to learn and you never, ever stop learning it. There's never been and never will be a perfect lap of the TT.'

Steve Hislop came closer than most to setting a perfect lap of the TT. He was the first man to post an average lap speed of 120mph back in 1989, and for many he was the greatest TT rider of all time. Like so many others before and after him, Hislop quickly became addicted to the unique thrills that road racing offered. 'The buzz of riding the Mountain course was every bit as awesome as I'd hoped for,' he said of his Manx Grand Prix debut in 1983. 'Racing flat out on real roads without worrying about tractors, coppers or anything coming the other way is an amazing thrill and that's what attracts riders to the TT, year after year, despite the dangers.'

In fact, the most dangerous parts of the TT course proved to be Hislop's favourites. 'I loved being in among the trees, hedges and stone walls,' he admitted. 'It was fantastic racing between them at such high speeds, and that's where I always made time up on the other guys who maybe backed off a little through those parts. Those sections took a lot more learning as well, which is more pleasurable in the end because it's more of a challenge and very rewarding when you get it right.'

It has often been said that if someone invented the concept of road racing today there's no way it would be allowed to happen. But attitudes towards risk and danger – indeed, death itself – were markedly different at the turn of the 20th century, when motorcycle road racing first began.

*

There's clearly something about road racing that gets in the blood. Despite the dangers, the crashes, the injuries, the financial hardships, the time, the effort, the heartbreak and the pain, riders are drawn back time and time again to get the rush that only racing a bike at 200mph between houses and hedges can give them.

It has been said, only half-jokingly, that motorcycle racing was invented when the second motorcycle was built. As soon as there were two motorcycles in existence, then racing was inevitable. Back then, of course, there were no purpose-built racetracks with acres of run-off areas, gravel traps, air fencing and super smooth surfaces, there were only real-world roads, as used by the general public; or, at least, those lucky enough to own a car or a motorcycle.

The first production motorcycle – a Hildebrand & Wolfmüller – was sold in Germany in 1894 and, one year later, the first known motorcycle race took place on the roads between Paris and Madrid – a distance of over 1,000 miles.

It was chiefly a race for automobiles, but motorcycles were also permitted. In the early days of the combustion engine, the race was considered an almost otherworldly spectacle, and it attracted over three million spectators along the route. How many of those spectators were killed is not recorded, but out-of-control automobiles caused the deaths of so many that the race was abandoned. It was clear from the outset that racing combustion engine vehicles on public roads was a very dangerous thing to do, and that remains true to this day.

For this reason, the British authorities refused to pass any Act that would allow UK mainland roads to be used for racing. Indeed, such was the concern about the dangers of automotive vehicles that the entire British mainland was covered by a 20mph blanket speed limit.

Car and motorcycle races continued on the Continent, though, and as their popularity increased, British petrolheads wanted to stage their own events. The Isle of Man – which is a Crown dependency but has its own parliament (Tynwald) and largely makes its own laws – provided the solution.

The secretary of the Automobile Club of Great Britain (now known as the RAC), Julian Orde, was keen to stage a car race somewhere within the British Isles. Fortunately, he happened to be a cousin of the Governor of the Isle of Man, Lord Raglan. Raglan was a fan of the motorsport events that were being held on the Continent and he quickly persuaded the Manx authorities of the potential benefits of staging similar events on the island. The Manx parliament agreed to allow its roads to be used for racing and, with the decision having been made in principle, the matter was passed over to Tynwald to make it legal. At a special public sitting on 5th May, Tynwald passed the 1904 Road Closure Act. Thanks to a parliament founded by the Vikings some 900 years earlier, the legislation, which would eventually allow for the Isle of Man TT races to take place, was ratified.

Unlike the races on the Continent, this event was for motorcycles only and, with the staging of the first TT in 1907, motorcycle road racing as we know it today was born.

To this day, the Isle of Man is the Mecca of motorcycle road racing, but the sport's heartland has always been Northern Ireland. When Ireland was partitioned on 3rd May, 1921, the north gained its own parliament and was free to make its own decisions – just like the Isle of Man authorities – regarding the closure of public roads for racing purposes.

Two men in particular lobbied hard for the Act to be passed. One was Harry Ferguson, famous for being the first man in Ireland to build and fly an aeroplane. As the owner of a well-known garage in Belfast, Ferguson was one of the key figures behind the passing of the Road Races Act in 1922 by the Northern Ireland parliament, enabling motorcycle and car races to take place on the province's roads. This Act led to the creation of some of the world's most famous road races, including the North West 200 and the Ulster Grand Prix.

Another keen supporter of the Act – and the man who finally saw it through – was the Marquess of Londonderry. He introduced it on 18th May, 1922, and the Act gained King George V's assent on 10th June. From that point on, the people of Northern Ireland were free to apply for road closure orders to run races, and they were queuing up to do so.

Some enthusiasts didn't even bother waiting for the Act to be passed. In 1921, the year before it was passed, members of the Temple Motorcycle & Athletic Club in County Down had staged what was Ireland's first ever motorcycle road race, the Temple 50. Held on 3rd September, the race saw ten gallant pioneer riders lining up to take part in a 12-lap, 25-mile race. Dubbed the 'Temple 25 Miles Open Handicap Race', it was won by a 20-year-old local called Thomas Graham Lindsay on his 2 ¾ Imperial J.A.P machine.

He couldn't have known it then, but Lindsay had created a piece of motorcycling history by becoming the first winner of a road race in Ireland. Before long, only football would be a more popular sport in the country – the Irish very quickly became obsessed by road racing and would produce many of its greatest champions.

The now-defunct Ballydrain 60 was also held before the road-closing order was passed but, just like the organisers of the Temple 50, those behind the Ballydrain asked for, and got, the cooperation of the local authorities, who all spotted a great commercial opportunity and were keen to help, even though the event was technically illegal.

The first Ulster Grand Prix was all above board when it was held on the 20.5-mile Clady circuit on 14th October, 1922. But while the Ulster Motorcycle Club had permission to close the roads for race day, they didn't bother for practice, as Graham Walker (father of Formula 1 commentator Murray Walker and a former motorcycle racer) recalled.

'The roads were closed for the race, but they were wide open for practice, to an amazing assortment of wheeled vehicles, with a variety of livestock, ranging from herds of cows to dogs, pigs and chickens as additional hazards.'

Over the last 100 years and more, road racing has retained much of its original character. There may be glitzy race transporters and hospitality areas in the paddock at the Isle of Man TT and the North West 200, but that's only because they're the two biggest events on the road-racing calendar. Most races are still organised by local clubs, have very limited paddock infrastructure and take place on startlingly narrow country roads. Yet, even at the TT, the challenges that face the riders remain very much the same as those that faced the early pioneers. Roads may be closed for practice sessions now, and loose chickens and pigs are not usually a problem, but riders do occasionally have to deal with wildlife and pets straying onto the roads – and walls and houses don't get any softer with the passing of time. Today's riders face just as many hazards as their predecessors did, the only difference being that they're travelling at much, much higher speeds. That means riders have less time to react when things go wrong, and while safety measures have improved dramatically over the decades, the increased speed of the bikes, year on year, means the danger level remains high. But for many riders the temptation to race flat out on real-world roads is too great. Short circuit racing is one thing, road racing is altogether different, and in order to get the rush they crave from it the competitors are willing to accept the risks and take their chances on some of the most fearsome courses in the world. And they don't come much faster or more fearsome than the North West 200 – one of the greatest road races on earth.

CHAPTER 2

THE TRIANGLE

*'I was so desperate for a win that if someone had said
"Eat some dogshit for luck" I'd have done it.'*
CARL FOGARTY

When it's kissed by the sun and fragranced by a salty sea breeze, there's no finer place in the world to watch a road race than on the North Antrim coast in Northern Ireland.

The North West 200 course covers a distance of 8.97 miles and runs between the towns of Coleraine, Portrush and Portstewart. The section between Portrush and Portstewart – known as the coast road – is particularly spectacular, following the contours of the Atlantic coastline with views across the vast expanse of water towards Scotland.

The riders, of course, do not have time to appreciate the spectacular views on offer, but for spectators there's nowhere better to witness the heart-stopping sport of road racing. And, at the North West 200, the racing is truly heart-stopping.

Unlike at the Isle of Man TT, where riders set off

individually and race against the clock, races at the North West are mass starts, just as they are in MotoGP, the World Superbike Championship or the British Superbike Championship. That means upwards of 50 riders jostling side-by-side at speeds of well over 200mph, desperately trying to slipstream one another to gain another precious few miles per hour. The bikes may be set off in two waves, but the effect is still astonishing. And all this through towns, under a railway bridge, along the swooping coast road, atop the cliffs and out into the countryside for those epic 200mph slipstreaming battles.

Road races with mass starts aren't to everyone's liking. John McGuinness is cautious of the added dangers. 'I'm not mega keen on mass-start road races,' he says. 'I like a bit of space around me when it comes to the roads because we all know what happens when it goes wrong – it can be pretty big.'

Known as 'the Triangle' because of its approximate shape, the North West course has been adjusted over the years to account for the ever-increasing speeds of the bikes. Several chicanes have been added (at Mather's Cross, Magherabuoy and Juniper Hill) to slow the bikes down ahead of particularly fast and dangerous corners. The effect of these chicanes is evident in the lap times. Before any were added, Irish rider Tom Herron lapped the course at 127.63mph way back in 1978. The current lap record of 124.79mph was set by Peter Hickman in 2022. But those figures belie the speed of modern Superbikes: today's riders are approaching top speeds of 210mph, so if they didn't have to negotiate three chicanes their average lap speeds would be far, far higher than what Herron managed over four decades ago. The North West 200 is fast. Seriously fast. Nowhere else can a Superbike be held flat out in sixth gear for so long, with squadrons of other bikes in close company, mile after mile after mile, engines screaming in protest with nothing left to give, but still being urged on by their riders – faster, faster, faster. No amount of power is enough; riders and team members are constantly searching for more.

The riders love it. 'The North West 200 is a unique circuit in a unique location, and it's got all the party carnival atmosphere going on,' says six-time winner John McGuinness. 'I enjoy the whole thing. I like the anticipation of going there too. It's the first big road race of the year, so I like driving over and getting there and seeing all the friendly faces. Everybody's chuffed to bits to see you, whereas you get to the British Superbike paddock sometimes and it feels like you owe them something. There's a whole different atmosphere at the North West. Some people say it's a boring circuit, but how can you say that slipstreaming each other at 190mph is boring?'

Triple North West winner Steve Plater agrees that the event has an atmosphere and appeal all of its own. 'My first road race was at the North West 200 in 1995,' he says. 'I went to watch it in 1993, the year before I started racing, and saw Carl Fogarty do the double and break the lap record on the Ducati, and I was really keen on the event and decided I'd like a ride round myself, so in 1995 I took my Supersport 600 bike over. I crashed out but still thought it was an awesome event with a cracking atmosphere. It was a very different atmosphere to short circuit racing in the UK –

a bit more relaxed and without as much pressure to win. When you're riding there with a manufacturer-backed team then you're there to win, but it's still a bit more relaxed because you're there for a whole week and can settle in.'

While the atmosphere might be more relaxed than at a British championship meeting, the schedule most certainly is not. Until 2012, all the races at the North West were crammed into a single Saturday (with practice taking part during the preceding week). Racing now takes place on the Thursday and the Saturday, but a rider may still find himself taking part in Superbike, Superstock, Supersport and Supertwin races all in a single day.

Now retired, former road racer Cameron Donald loved the event but found it hard going. 'There's so much hype surrounding the North West because it's the start of the year and it's all new teams and new bikes and everyone's wondering who's going to be up front that season,' he says. 'There's always 12 or 15 names in the hat as to who's going to win, but it usually comes down to the same few names at the front popping their heads up every year. It's hard, though. I just tried to slow the whole day down and take it one race at a time. That's the only way I could get through it, because five races in a day is verging on too much.'

The North West takes place in May, just a week or two (depending on how the calendar falls) before the Isle of Man TT, giving riders, teams and fans the first opportunity to see who's got the pace for the upcoming season.

First held in 1929, it occasionally attracts riders who would never dream of doing the TT but perceive the North West to be a safer option. The course is quite wide, there are many straights, and the corners are, in general, not as treacherous as some at the TT. With the course being 8.97 miles long – as opposed to the 37.73 miles that make up the TT course – it's also much easier to learn, which is why riders like former 500cc Grand Prix winner Simon Crafar has competed there, as has former 250cc and 500cc Grand Prix rider Jeremy McWilliams, former multiple 500cc Grand Prix podium finisher Niall Mackenzie and former World Endurance champion Terry Rymer.

That's not to say the Triangle doesn't hold any terrors – two corners in particular were feared and enjoyed in almost equal measure before one of them was neutered. 'Mather's Cross and Station Corner are the two big bad-boy corners at the North West,' according to Steve Plater, and Conor Cummins agrees. 'Station Corner and Mather's Cross are the two most notorious at the North West,' he says. 'Station is pretty much flat out on a Superbike these days, and you're absolutely screaming through there, throttle-to-the-stop on a 600.'

Michael Rutter – a 14-time winner at the North West – says Station Corner is the best corner in road racing. 'You can't quite do it flat out on a Superbike, but you get very, very close,' he says. 'The only concession is that you lift your head and shoulders up out of the screen a little to act as an air brake and just slow you down a fraction. Then it's all tucked in again and as fast as you can go. It must be about 175mph through that corner and there's only one proper line through it, so you have to get it right if you want to carry speed on to the next two miles of straight. When I became the first man to crack over 200mph on the roads a few years ago it was because I got good drive out of Station and carried it on to the next section where I was timed. Touch wood, I've not had any hairy moments at Station, but every time I go through it, I take a deep breath.'

When asked when he was last genuinely scared, Rutter didn't take long to think of an answer. 'You mean near-death scared?' he asks back. 'I'd say at the North West 200. When you're going down the straight at almost 200mph with slicks on and it starts raining and the thing's going sideways . . . You're always scaring yourself when you're racing. Normally, when you're winning it's dead easy – it's when you're trying that it's scary.'

Not everyone is a fan of the chicanes on the course. For racer-turned-television-star Guy Martin, they've spoiled the nature of the course. 'I'm bored to the back teeth,' he said, somewhat controversially during the 2015 event. 'Riding around chicanes just bores me to the back teeth – I have no interest in it. This track used to be mega, but it's so boring now. The bike is so fast and handles so well that my granny could ride it down the straights, and then it's just down to first gear, around a chicane and back to sixth. Station Corner isn't even fun anymore because the bike is so good that I can go around it flat out. I'll always give a hundred per cent on the bike, and I want to do well, but there's more interesting things to be doing!'

Among the big-name short circuit riders to have tackled the North West 200 is Carl Fogarty. Although he had raced on many roads circuits before becoming a four-time World Superbike champion and a household name, the one race that Fogarty had never won was the North West. In 1993, even though he was competing in World Superbikes that year, Fogarty was determined to win a race at the Triangle, so he arranged to have a Moto Cinelli Ducati 888 taken over to Northern Ireland for one final attempt. Fogarty calculated that he had led the North West on no fewer than seven occasions, but his bike had always broken down. 'I was so desperate for a win that if someone had said "Eat some dogshit for luck" I'd have done it,' he admitted.

Fogarty had been trying to win a race at the North West since 1988. He missed the 1989 event because he was racing in Japan, but returned in '90, '91 and '92, though all to no avail – despite setting pole position on several occasions and clearly being the fastest man out there, a win continued to elude him. 'It was bizarre, because the Honda RC30 was probably the most reliable bike ever built,' Fogarty says. 'It was usually bulletproof, but I had so much trouble with it in 1991 and '92 and it was really frustrating.'

Never short of confidence, Fogarty firmly believed he was by far the fastest man around the Triangle in his era. 'No disrespect to the other guys who were racing at the North West back then, but I was in a different class to everyone because I was a short circuit guy who did the roads as well, so it should have been easy for me to win,' he says. 'Joey Dunlop, Robert Dunlop, Phillip McCallen . . . they were all good riders but, really, I was so much quicker round that circuit than they were. But that's not enough sometimes on a circuit as fast as that – and remember there weren't as many chicanes back then. I qualified on pole in 1990, which was my first proper go at it, but I told my mechanics I couldn't win the race the next day because no matter how fast I was through the corners and on the brakes into the chicanes I just got blown away by Robert Dunlop's Norton on the straights [the rotary engine JPS Nortons were notoriously fast and many felt they had an unfair advantage due to the nature of their engines]. That bike was ridiculously fast. The distance I was making up on the brakes and through the chicanes was incredible, but it wasn't enough. Joey Dunlop's manager, Davy Wood, told me he'd never seen anybody ride through Juniper Hill chicane like that before. He said everybody was holding their breath every time I came through. So, I knew I was the fastest guy there, but the RC30 was just not capable of winning the race.'

The following two years were no better. 'For some reason my bike kept cutting out in 1991 and '92,' Fogarty explains. 'It was spluttering and misfiring down the long straights, then it would sort itself out again. The other guys knew I was having issues, and it became a bit of a standing joke. They loved it, because they knew how wound-up I got. I was shouting my mouth off about it all the time, about how I hadn't won a race yet. We changed the carbs and all sorts, but nothing helped. It was really bizarre to have fuel-starvation problems over two separate years.'

Despite having never won a race there, Fogarty was a huge fan of the North West, and that made him even more desperate to take a victory. 'I loved racing in Ireland – I loved the people, I loved the North West circuit and the organisers always looked after us so well,' he says. 'I had just been really unlucky not to win any races in 1991 and '92, so it was just a box I had to tick: I *had* to get a win.'

Family pride was at stake too. Fogarty's father George

had come very close to winning a North West but never quite managed it – his second place in the 1978 500cc race was the closest he ever came to a win. 'I've always had this thing about winning certain races and ticking certain boxes, and it annoyed me that the North West 200 box hadn't been ticked off,' Fogarty explains. 'I was the fastest guy around there, so if I had never won a race, then by the end of my career that would have really hurt me.'

In 1993 Fogarty was a factory Ducati rider in the World Superbike Championship, and he knew his team boss (former 500cc Grand Prix and World Superbike star Raymond Roche) would not be happy about his star rider racing at a roads event, so Fogarty simply didn't tell him. 'I rode for Hoss Elm and Moto Cinelli and didn't tell Raymond,' he says. 'He went fucking mental when he found out afterwards! I said, "But, Raymond, I won the race," but he was like, "I don't care, you shouldn't be doing these fucking stupid road-race things – they're dangerous!"'

Fogarty didn't just win the opening Superbike race of the day, he won the main feature North West 200 race and shattered the lap record too. 'I loved the course,' he says. 'Felt good on it, felt confident. It's a bit of a short circuit, really – and even more so nowadays with all the chicanes – and I was probably the best short circuit guy in the country at the time. Well, I *was*, no question. I cleared off and won both races easily, which I felt I could have done in previous years if I hadn't suffered so many problems. They were boring races, to be honest. I was so far in front of Robert [Dunlop], Joey [Dunlop], and Phillip]McCallen] that I never even saw them.'

With that, Carl Fogarty turned his back on road racing and went on to win four World Superbike championships. He had proved his point.

As impressive as Fogarty's domination was, and as proud as he was to finally win at the North West, no race around the Triangle can compare to the 250cc race in 2008. It remains one of the most emotional motorcycle races of all time, and one of the most incredible displays of courage ever witnessed on two wheels. It also beggars belief.

By 2008, Robert Dunlop was the most successful North West 200 rider in history, with 15 wins to his name. Often overshadowed by his elder brother Joey, Robert always had the upper hand around the North West – a circuit that Joey was never overfond of but which Robert loved.

During practice for the 2008 event, Robert's Honda TSR 250 seized at the super-fast corner of Mather's Cross and threw him over the handlebars at 160mph. The bike had been heavily modified to account for the injuries Dunlop had sustained at the Isle of Man TT in 1994. One modification was to the front brake lever, which was repositioned to where the clutch lever would normally be (i.e. on the left handlebar). When a motorcycle seizes at speed, the only way to avoid catastrophe is to pull in the clutch lever and coast to a halt. With the seizure happening so fast, Dunlop reverted to instinct to save the situation and reached for the clutch, except it wasn't the clutch, it was the front brake.

His son William Dunlop was following him and would bear witness to every terrifying moment as the tragedy unfolded. 'I saw smoke coming out of the back of my dad's bike,' he later explained. 'I tried to pass him to warn him, but he was too quick for me.'

Robert Dunlop was 47 years old at the time, and semi-crippled; his body so badly mangled from the '94 TT crash (when the rear wheel of his bike shattered following the jump at Ballaugh Bridge and he was thrown into a wall at 140mph), and yet he was still too fast for his son to catch him. Try as he did, William Dunlop simply wasn't fast enough to prevent the tragedy that played out.

After being thrown from his bike, Robert was struck by another machine and, seconds later, his eldest son Michael Dunlop came upon the scene. Now the most successful TT rider in history, Michael had only been racing for a few years at the time and his father had guided him every step of the way: he was his hero as well as his mentor. Michael Dunlop threw his bike aside and ran to his father, holding his hand as he awaited medical assistance. Robert Dunlop was still breathing at that point but would succumb to his massive chest trauma on the way to the Causeway Hospital in Coleraine. The North West 200 had lost its most successful rider, the racing world had lost a hero, and Michael and William Dunlop had lost their father and their best friend. What happened next is still difficult to believe.

Robert Dunlop died on Thursday 15th May. Two days later was North West 200 race day. As the riders wheeled their 250cc machines out onto the grid to begin their warm-up lap, spectators, teams, riders and organisers – not to mention the millions watching the racing online around the world – were shocked to the core to see both William and Michael among them.

The race organisers were horrified, knowing that the brothers were in no fit mental state to be racing motorcycles. They had already decided to deny them permission to race, but the pair had effectively sneaked onto the grid – the organisers feared a riot, should they attempt to forcefully remove them. Their hand had been forced, and there was nothing to do but let them go.

As chance would have it, William Dunlop suffered mechanical problems and had to pull out of the race, so at least one brother was safe. For now, at least. William later revealed that withdrawing from the event had never even been an option. 'Packing it in never entered my head – I was out in the next race,' he said. 'It didn't affect me too much as far as racing went. I know my dad would have done the same; he would have went on ahead and done his own thing. What will be will be – you can't change what's happened.'

The other brother wasn't safe. Michael Dunlop had never won an international road race at that point in his career, but on Saturday 17th May, 2008, nothing was going to stop him.

To enter a race on the same circuit that had claimed his father's life two days earlier takes a very special kind of courage. Michael would have to ride past the very spot of the fatal accident four times during the race. For most people it would be utterly unthinkable, and with so many people watching, the potential for further tragedy was on everyone's minds. The atmosphere was otherworldly. Many watched in stunned silence, those with a faith prayed, some wept, many kept their fingers crossed and looked on, grim-faced, jaws clenched tight as a young Michael Dunlop released his clutch lever, twisted the throttle and launched himself off the start line to begin the race of his life.

It turned out to be a battle between himself, Christian Elkin and road-racing legend John McGuinness, and the three battled closely throughout the four-lap race. But, inspired as he was and utterly determined to win the race for his fallen father, Michael Dunlop rode like a man possessed. Being beaten on that day simply wasn't an option. He looked wild on the bike, physically manhandling it and forcing it to do things it didn't want to do. He clipped kerbs, he spun the rear tyre, he retaliated immediately as soon as anyone passed him. He refused to take 'no' for an answer, and after four of the most nerve-wracking laps anyone had ever seen in road racing he beat Christian Elkin over the line by 0.08 seconds to take his first international road race win, and dedicated it to his dad.

Grown men cried all around the circuit, people looked at each other in disbelief, they shook their heads in quiet astonishment. Those at the start–finish line yelled, cheered and applauded as Dunlop pulled into parc fermé and collapsed off his bike in floods of tears, emotionally exhausted.

'I can remember small bits and pieces of that race but not much,' Michael says now, though he does remember how hard he was prepared to fight for a win to honour his father. 'I was prepared to take big risks to win that race, without a doubt,' he says. 'Anything I had to do I would have done it. I was going to win, no matter what it took. Valentino Rossi couldn't have beat me that day.'

Even Dunlop's rivals were in awe of the courage it must

have taken to do what he did. 'He was riding with his heart, and you have to give it to him for riding after what happened to his father,' Christian Elkin said. Hardened old warrior that he is, John McGuinness had never seen anything like the crowd support for Dunlop as the Irishman led on the final lap. 'All three of us were riding hard but it was fantastic for Michael to get the win, and he thoroughly deserved it. Seeing all those fans waving their programmes all the way around the circuit is something that will stay in my mind forever.'

But there were more practical reasons for continuing to race when most others would have turned their back on the sport that had so cruelly robbed them of a father. 'I knew no different,' Michael says. 'Racing was all I had. I wasn't great at school – I was a bit stupid. I only went to school about one day a month just to keep people happy, and I left when I was about 11 or 12. I was happier going to work with my dad as a steel erector.'

Two days after taking his first international road race win, Michael Dunlop – along with William and the rest of the family – buried his father in Garryduff church, just outside Ballymoney. Robert Dunlop was buried alongside his brother Joey, arguably the greatest road racer of all time. Joey had lost his life eight years previously in an obscure race in Estonia. William Dunlop would be killed at the Skerries 100 road race ten years later, leaving Michael Dunlop to race on alone. No family has sacrificed so much to road racing.

Robert Dunlop had crashed at Mather's Cross, the very same corner where his brother-in-law Mervyn Robinson had been killed 28 years previously. Robinson was married to Robert's sister Helen and had been one of the famous 'Armoy Armada'. The Armada included Robinson, Joey Dunlop, Jim Dunlop (Robert and Joey's brother) and Frank Kennedy and, in the glory days of Irish road racing in the 1970s, they raced against the 'Dromara Destroyers', which included Ray McCullough, Brian Reid, Trevor Steele and Ian McGregor. For three years, between 1977 and 1979, the battles between these two groups of riders were the highlight of the road-racing season. Each group had its supporters' club and road racing almost became a team sport rather than an individual pursuit.

Sadly, the great team rivalries came to an end in 1979 when Frank Kennedy was killed at the North West 200 on what became known as 'Black Saturday'. Three riders lost their lives as a result of crashes that day. Young Scottish rider Brian Hamilton was killed in the 350cc race, Frank Kennedy was seriously injured in the opening Superbike race and would die a few months later, and Tom Herron lost his life in the main North West 200 Superbike race.

Herron is still considered one of the greatest riders Ireland has ever produced. He was not just a brilliant pure road racer, he was also teammates with Barry Sheene in the Texaco Heron Suzuki 500cc Grand Prix world championship team. He had no need to be at the North West 200 – by that point, most Grand Prix riders no longer raced on dangerous road circuits – but felt he owed it to his home fans to make an appearance, despite his wrist still being in plaster from a crash at the Spanish Grand Prix. Herron's wife begged him not to race with such an injury, but he was not to be stopped. Close friend Hector Neill recalls that 'Tom was so determined to ride he had me cut the plaster cast from his hand with an angle grinder.'

Herron had been lucky to escape the carnage during the opening Superbike race when Kevin Stowe, Warren Willing and Frank Kennedy had crashed. Kennedy's bike had burst into a fireball and flew over Herron's head. Badly shaken by the horrific incident, Herron said, 'I went under Frank's bike, which was flying through the air. It was like riding into a wall of flame.'

Stowe and Willing would both recover, though neither could ever race again. Frank Kennedy clung to life in hospital for six months but ultimately succumbed to his head injuries and passed away on 16th November.

Undeterred by the horrors earlier in the day, Tom Herron went back out for the feature North West 200 race that closed off the day's programme. He would not see the chequered flag. On the last corner of the last lap, Herron lost control of his bike and struck a concrete post, sustaining serious injuries. He died in hospital two hours later.

That's why there's been a chicane at Juniper Hill ever since.

Steve Parrish had been battling wheel-to-wheel with Herron when the Irishman crashed. 'I was teammates with Tom that year and he was a great bloke – I got on well with him,' he says. 'We travelled to the North West together that year and teamed up when we were over there.'

Of the crash, Parrish says: 'I saw Tom's front wheel trying to pass me, then he just disappeared . . . and died. We were battling for third place, and he tried to ride round the outside of me at Juniper Hill – before there was a chicane there – but he didn't make it. People blamed his wrist, but I don't think that was a problem for him. I don't think it was a significant factor in his crash – he lost the front because he was on the wrong line at Juniper Hill, trying to get past me.'

Despite the tragedy of Tom Herron's death, Parrish continued racing at the North West, and always enjoyed the event. 'It was a spectacular circuit to ride back then, before the chicanes were added,' he says. 'I enjoyed the North West; it was so much easier to learn than the TT, and it didn't seem anything like as dangerous as the TT, either, although it probably was. But, because there were less corners, it didn't seem quite as dangerous and I really liked the mass-start element of it, because you knew exactly where you were in the race. There was always a great atmosphere, too, so I was always a big fan of the North West.'

Having been involved with the event since the 1970s (he's now a commentator for the BBC's online streaming coverage of the races), Parrish has witnessed the evolution of the course and the safety improvements that have been carried out over the years. 'It's considerably safer now,' he testifies. 'They've made lots of run-off areas wherever possible, they've put flat kerbs in at places, and there's Recticel air fencing on many parts of the course now too. The North West course is halfway towards being like a short circuit now. There's a lot of places where you could get away with crashing, whereas you wouldn't at the TT. That's why you see riders like Alastair Seeley doing the North West but not the TT.'

One year after Frank Kennedy's death, another Armoy

Armada rider, Mervyn Robinson, was killed at Mather's Cross. His death in 1980, alongside that of Frank Kennedy the previous year, meant the only remaining members of the Armada were Joey and Jim Dunlop – both brothers-in-law to Mervyn Robinson. Robinson's son Paul was there on the day. Five years old at the time, he would eventually grow up to enjoy a successful racing career of his own. In 2010 he would take his one and only win at the North West 200. He took the winner's laurels and placed them on his father's grave, exactly 30 years after he had been killed. Road racers never blame the sport; they know it's dangerous, they accept the risks, and it's almost unheard of for family members to turn their backs on the sport, however cruel it can be. This is what makes them road racers.

Although Mervyn Robinson had been killed at Mather's Cross, no action was taken following the tragedy to alter the corner itself. It remained a flat-out-in-top-gear corner until it claimed its most famous victim in 2008. Only after Robert Dunlop's demise was a chicane added.

That's why there's been a chicane at Mather's Cross ever since.

Thankfully, fatalities are now much rarer at the North West 200. The three chicanes and the new start–finish line design (riders now have to negotiate an extended dog-leg chicane instead of blasting straight past the pits as they did in the past) all help, as do modern air fencing and run-off areas where it's possible to have them. Roadside hazards which *can* be removed *are* removed, but there's only so much race organisers can do – racing 200mph motorbikes along everyday roads can never be completely safe, so many young Irish riders now look to the safer British Superbike Championship circuits rather than the roads to carve out their racing careers. Jonathan Rea is a good example – his father Johnny raced both the roads and the circuits in the 1980s but Jonathan never went near the roads. Instead, he focused on short circuits and became the most successful World Superbike rider in history, taking six world titles between 2015 and 2020.

Glenn Irwin seemed to be another such example. He was enjoying a successful career in various British championships until the lure of the North West 200 finally drew him in. His father Alan had been a successful road racer in the 1980s and 1990s but didn't want his son to follow in his tyre tracks. 'My dad never pushed me or my brothers into doing road racing, which I think was a good thing, because it's not a game you want to push your children into,' Irwin says. 'But the Ulster Grand Prix came about in 2014, and I decided to race a wee Supertwin as a bit of fun, just to have a bit of a play on. I finished fifth and dipped under the existing Supertwin lap record in the Dundrod 150 race [a support race, held on the same circuit ahead of the Ulster Grand Prix proper], first time out! I had an oil leak on Ulster Grand Prix race day so never got to race. Then Mervyn White [North West 200 race director] contacted me about doing the North West. My Gearlink Kawasaki British Supersport team was quite happy for me to go, so I did. I'd always kinda wanted to do it, but also thought I'd never do a road race, but after doing the Ulster on the Supertwin I was keen to do the North West on a Supersport bike.'

Because he had so much road-racing experience and

knew better than most just how dangerous it was, Alan Irwin wasn't keen on Glenn taking up the challenge of the roads. 'I was 24 when I made my road-racing debut at the Ulster, so your parents aren't actually in control of you at that age!' Glenn Irwin says. 'But I wouldn't say I was rebellious against my dad – in fact, I take his advice very seriously. He did what all racing dads probably would do. He said, "Well, I'll not be at any road races supporting you," but, once I had actually entered, he started driving me around the course, doing lap after lap after lap. He gave me all his guidance, knowing that would make me as safe and as fast as possible.'

Irwin's approach to road racing was a smart one – he waited until he had enough short circuit racing experience before even considering tackling a road race. 'I always think that if you're going to be a good road racer then being a very good short circuit racer will stand you in good stead,' he explains. 'The likes of Peter Hickman have proved that, and I've proved that; Dean Harrison is now doing more short circuit racing and it's all paying off for him too. I don't like to see people switching to the road racing side too young. I was 24 when I did my first road race – you can't do it at 18. It's a game that needs to be treated with an awful lot of respect. It's an incredible game, and something I very much enjoy, but you have to go about it with the right attitude and that's something that only comes with a little bit more maturity.'

Glenn Irwin made his debut at the North West 200 in 2017 and promptly won the feature Superbike race. He would ultimately win 11 consecutive Superbike races at the event, his domination a perfect example of how fast a top British Superbike racer can be if he sets his mind to road racing.

In 2022 Irwin went one step further and entered the ultimate road race – the Isle of Man TT. He became the fastest newcomer of all time with a lap at 129.85mph and enjoyed a safe week of racing, but then stepped away, saying he had to think about his family. A father of three, Irwin said: 'I found the anxiety side of things overwhelming. That side of things was just too much for me. Every morning you're thinking, *Will I be having dinner tonight?* It is difficult to switch off those thoughts and mindset.'

Glenn Irwin remains a top contender in the British Superbike Championship but will no longer race on the roads.

Despite all the hazards that surround the North West 200 course, riders often treat it like a short circuit, racing absolutely balls-to-the-walls. Five-time winner Ian Simpson admits he went all-in during the Supersport 600 race in 1998. 'That race has always stuck in my mind because me, Steve Plater, Michael Rutter and Bob Jackson were all riding so, so hard,' he says. 'About ten years later, I saw Steve being interviewed on TV after he'd won a Superbike race at the North West. They asked him if that had been his best race at the event, but Steve said, "No, my best race here was the 600 race with Ian Simpson, Michael Rutter and Bob Jackson in 1998, because we were riding so hard." I was amazed that he remembered that race as being one of his best too, even though I won it and he finished second.'

Simpson says the quartet simply couldn't have ridden any harder, even if they had been on a much safer short circuit.

'Honestly, if you'd have moved the North West course to a flat field where there were no walls or houses or lamp posts to crash into, and gravel traps as far as the eye can see, we wouldn't have ridden any harder than we did that day. We were all sliding our bikes everywhere, spinning the rear tyres, bouncing off the kerbs – it was insane. We were all just blanking out the fact that there were walls and houses and lamp posts; I honestly couldn't have ridden any quicker round Donington Park.'

When Steve Hislop made his debut at the North West in 1987, he was shocked to see how hard the riders attacked the everyday roads. 'I got a good lesson in road racing from Ian Newton and Gary Cowan [who was later paralysed in a racing accident at Daytona] during practice for the North West,' he said. 'I was right behind them on the run into the Ballysally roundabout, where there's a hard shoulder at the side of the road. I had only been going out as far as the white line and not using the shoulder at all, but those guys were using every inch of it, right into the gutter. They were riding the roads as if they were on a short circuit, and it taught me to up my pace and use every inch of the track from then on. It's no longer any good riding at 80 per cent on the roads if you want to win – you have to ride flat out.'

Glenn Irwin was blown away by the sustained high speeds when he made his debut in 2016. 'The first time I arrived at the North West I went out on the 600 and it was bone dry and that was absolutely mind-blowing,' he says. 'Going down to Coleraine at about 165mph was just unbelievable – it really is so hard to explain.'

Irwin found it difficult to judge his braking points when

slowing down from such enormous speeds. Every year he competed there he struggled on the first lap of practice. 'On your first lap you'll arrive at what you think is the braking zone and you'll sit up and brake and then you'll be straight back on the throttle because you're nowhere near!' he says. 'I find the North West course a very hard place to find braking zones. I was on and off the brakes coming into a lot of corners, trying to find the limit, but you're approaching corners so fast that it's really difficult to judge. You also have to add in the turbulence – sometimes you get a huge wobble and you're nearly out of control, so you can't brake properly. You can get turbulence from riders in front of you, but you also get it from the sheer speed and side winds. Alastair Seeley [the North West's most successful rider with 29 wins to his name] was telling me the turbulence is getting worse as the bikes get faster.

'Once you start to reach that 190–200mph mark the road plays a part, too, as it's not flat, it's crowned, and side winds can blow you all over the road,' Irwin continues. 'So, you often find you have to roll off slightly because you just can't keep it flat out.'

Irwin is a top British Superbike rider and multiple race winner, but the speeds at the North West 200 are far higher than those encountered in BSB and they take some adjusting to. 'The top speed you reach in BSB would be something just over 180mph on the back straight at Thruxton, so you're doing about 20mph more than that on a Superbike at the North West, and the road is about four or five times narrower than the track at Thruxton, so it feels even faster,' he explains. 'It's a totally surreal feeling.

Quite often in road racing I've been out there on my own, which is good because I trust myself. It's also good because it means you're leading the race! And when you're on your own you can hear every little noise the bike makes – you can hear it struggling to pull sixth gear because the straights are so long. Those first few laps are awesome – just a really incredible feeling.'

Despite being so successful at the event (Irwin won 11 consecutive Superbike races at the North West between 2017 and 2024, making him the most successful premier class rider in the event's history) and enjoying it so much, Glenn Irwin announced in 2024 that he would no longer compete there. With a young family to consider, the dangers suddenly seemed all too real, and he turned his back on road racing to concentrate on his British Superbike career.

It seemed that Irwin had finally woken up to the dangers of the event. The North West 200 has been running since 1929 and the first fatality was English rider Norman Wainwright, who was killed in 1939. Since then, a further 18 riders have lost their lives on the course, the most recent being another English rider, Malachi Mitchell-Thomas, in 2016. A hugely popular rider, Mitchell-Thomas was just 20 years old at the time of his death.

Simon Andrews was another high-profile rider to lose his life at the event. The 29-year-old Englishman was killed at the 2014 North West, but as is almost always the case, there was no bitterness or blame from his family. 'Road racing was in his blood and Simon preferred the roads to short circuits,' his father Stuart said after the tragedy. 'He was fully aware of the dangers involved but he loved the challenge that that offered. Simon always said, "Once you've been on the roads there's nothing else to compare with it."'

In 2011, Scottish rider Stuart Easton came perilously close to becoming another statistic at the North West 200 when the bike in front of him cut out at 140mph, leaving him with nowhere to go and no time to react. His story reveals the extreme lengths road racers are prepared to go through to return to racing, even from the very brink of death itself. It's a story of astonishing courage.

CHAPTER 3

DELTA 7

'I think if I'd had a gun I would have shot myself;
just put myself down.'
STUART EASTON

Stuart Easton is a diminutive rider, which helps with top speed on a super-fast circuit like the North West 200. At the 2010 event, he was the first rider to be clocked at 204mph. Despite having not raced at the North West since 2011, Easton can still talk his way through a lap in minute detail, and his description reveals just how many things riders have to cope with as they play their 200mph game of chess:

'Before a race starts, you're nothing but nerves, and I think that any rider who says otherwise is lying. If it means something to you and you want a good result then you're going to feel that tension no matter how much you pretend otherwise.

'As you're sat on the grid at the North West you need to be aware of tyre temperatures, because you're

on the coast and you're sitting on the grid with your tyre warmers off, so the tyres lose heat fast.

'As the flag drops and you head into the first corner, everyone is conscious of their tyres. The first two corners are quite fast, even from a standing start, then, once you're through Primrose, you're driving hard down towards York corner. That's a fast stretch, then York is a very tight hairpin before you're back on the gas up towards Mill Road roundabout. It's hard braking there and really tight through the roundabout. On the exit, you cut across the chevrons and rev hard, up through the gears and past the filling station, and you get into the seriously fast stuff from there, tucked in, driving as hard as you can, more than likely slipstreaming other riders as you come down the drop towards Station corner. When I was racing, you held a Supersport bike absolutely 100 per cent flat out through there, even on the first lap. It's known as one of the scariest corners in racing.

'In the early part of a race there are a lot of other riders very close to you and it gets a bit edgy, but the best form of defence is attack, so you have to be assertive and get stuck in. Basically, try to not think about it too much.

'When I was riding a Superbike, I would always just roll the throttle a little bit on the way into Station corner, just to get the weight on the front to settle it and get a good, fast corner speed and then a big drive out on the exit. That's so important because then you're flat out for miles.

'There's a crossroads after Station and you have to really grip the bike with your legs because your bike can easily wheelie or take off there due to the rise in the road. If your bike isn't handling right that's a worrying part of the course. After that you're flat out. This is the section where I was clocked at 204mph on the Swan Honda in 2010.

'There are always huge slipstreaming battles along this section of the course, and you have to be careful because you're travelling so fast, and, if you're slip-streaming someone and are really focused on them, and then the road kinks left or right, you could run out of road very easily. You have to be super-aware of where you are and where you're heading; it's so fast that your bike can jump five feet across the road with the slightest bump.

'You can enjoy those slipstreaming battles if you're riding alongside someone like John McGuinness because he's as safe as houses, but if you're riding alongside a bit of a desperado who's determined to scalp you it's not quite as enjoyable.

'The thrill of road racing comes from doing things that really should be illegal. Riding at over 200mph alongside a bunch of other bikes on public roads is something that a very small percentage of people ever get the chance to do. One year, after the North West, I drove my little hire car along the course towards the airport at 60mph, and that really knocked home to me what we riders had done the day before. That's when I thought how cool it was – 200mph-plus on an A road, *battling and dicing for the crowd and for yourself. It's a real sense of achievement.*

'After all the miles of slipstreaming, one of the hardest bits at the North West is judging your breaking into University corner. It's not like a short circuit where you have a fixed braking marker and you just pull on a full 12-bar of brake pressure. You're travelling at 200mph-plus on the run down to University and your braking point is different on every lap: you can't have a fixed braking point. You see other riders overshooting the corner while others brake too early, so they're on and off the brakes again trying to correct themselves. And you see riders almost hitting the backs of other bikes, so it can be a really dodgy part of the track, and it's different every lap.

'Once you're through University, you drive hard up the hill, being mindful of the rear tyre in case it steps out. It's a fast entry into the Ballysally roundabout, then you're cranked over to the left and aiming for a good exit for the fast stretch up towards Mather's Cross, where there's now a chicane. It's quite a bumpy stretch and, again, that's where an unstable bike gets found out. You're slipstreaming again, before braking heavily for the tight Mather's Cross chicane.

'A good exit is crucial here so that you get the drive up to the fast left before getting on the brakes for the Magherabuoy chicane. That's a hard chicane to judge because it's a really fast entry and you're always wondering how late you can brake.

'As the race goes on, and you're comfortable with

your tyre temperatures, you really start to bounce off the kerbs and the bike's moving about and the tyres are protesting, but that's all good "feel", so you really know what the bike's doing underneath you. At a place like Magherabuoy your back wheel will come up in the air under heavy braking.

'That also happens under braking for Metropole corner, which is the next heavy braking zone. It's a really, really fast downhill approach in top gear, but it's easier to find a braking point for Metropole than it is for University because it's a built-up area, so there are lots of reference points. It's one of the key passing places along with University and Juniper Hill chicane (which is yet to come). You see a lot of boys running wide at Metropole, but if you get it right the bike hooks in well for the next left. You have to be very careful on the exit as there's a sharp crown on the road, and you can easily lose the rear as it drops off the crown in the centre of the road.

'Back on the brakes into Church Corner. It's fairly fast through there, then you ride under the railway bridge and up towards Black Hill. You're back in among houses and buildings now, so you feel the speed a bit more, but I was never too stressed about that – I had raced at Macau [the former Portuguese colony stages a road race on a circuit lined with Armco and skyscrapers] and I liked things being close, because they offered lots of braking markers. When I raced on some big open European circuits there were so few reference points – the circuits were just all flat and

vague, with long, long hanging corners. I always found it hard to know how fast I could actually go on circuits like that. They're too open, so I liked being hemmed in by houses and stone walls.

'There's a fast right on the way up to Black Hill, and the tyres are protesting through there as the road falls away to the left, but you need to get the bike over to the right to line up for Black Hill, so you have to fight the bike through there to make it go where you want it to.

'Black Hill is a blind corner with a fast approach, and you change direction right at the top of it. That's a tough corner, especially during evening practice when the sun drops low in the sky. It can really blind you over there. That's where the experienced boys can really make up time by hitting the exact same marker on every lap.

'Once you're over Black Hill and have dropped down the other side you're onto a really nice, smooth stretch of road where you can almost relax and have a breather for a few seconds. You're all tucked in, catching breaths, and then there's the heavy braking zone for Juniper Hill chicane. It's another high-speed entry and, again, it's very difficult to judge. You're braking while the bike is leant over, so it's really easy to make a mistake.

'The chicanes have interrupted the flow of the North West circuit, but with 200mph bikes, we need them. But they do cause a lot of run-ons. The tighter corners and chicanes – like Metropole and Mather's

Cross – suit the short-circuit boys because they're used to much heavier braking. Having said that, all the top boys are on the money now with their braking into those tight corners, so it's maybe not as much of an advantage as it once was.

'You really need to watch out for the kerb on the left on the exit of Juniper Hill chicane. It's super easy to catch that kerb, and I've seen a couple of crashes there. If you run through the previous right a bit fast you can skim the kerb with the front wheel, but the rear wheel is a lot wider, so it can then catch the kerb and ping the rider off.

'Then you drive hard, with the tyres protesting, up towards the final corner. I never got that last corner right – not once. It's blind and you're hanging, hanging, hanging, and don't know when to pull it back to catch the apex. Again, it's one for the experienced North West boys.

'Then you've just got the right-hand kink that leads to the finish line and that's a lap of the North West 200. In a Superbike race, you have to do it all again for another five laps.'

On the Thursday evening practice session for the North West 200 in 2011, Easton didn't do six laps – he didn't even complete one. He only managed a few corners before suffering the biggest crash of his career. The battle for Stuart Easton's life had begun.

*

Riding for the MSS Colchester Kawasaki Team in the 2011 British Superbike Championship, Stuart Easton was lying in third place overall, just six points off the lead, as he set sail for the North West 200. His teammate was Gary Mason, who had decided to try the North West 200 for the first time that year. He was about to get the shock of his life.

'Me and Gary pushed our way to the front row for Superstock practice, alongside Michael Rutter and Martin Jessop on their Ducatis,' Easton explains. 'Everybody shot away really fast, but I started a bit more relaxed because it was only practice. The two Ducatis pulled away and Gary was in front of me with his newcomer's orange bib on. He was a good rider, and he was fast through the first few corners. I had no opportunity to pass him through York corner, but I got alongside him on the way up to the Mill Road roundabout. He braked late into Mill Road, but I thought, *No stress – it's only practice*, so I just filed in behind him and decided to slipstream him on the way down to Station corner.

'I tucked in behind him to catch his slipstream, up to second gear, third, fourth, getting up to high speed, around 140mph. I had just raised my toe to go for fifth gear when Gary's bike stopped dead in front of me. I just had time to think *Oh!* and instinctively pulled to the right to try to avoid him, but I clipped the back of Gary's bike and then things get a bit vague for me, memory-wise. I remember sliding down the road with bikes coming past me at racing speeds. It happened so fast that I was over the handlebars and sliding down the road before I knew what was happening.

It was like *Oh!*, then I leaned right, then *BANG!* It wasn't Gary's fault – his bike just cut out and there was nothing he could do.'

Like all motorcycle racers, Stuart Easton was no stranger to crashing, but there's a world of difference between sliding off into a gravel trap on a short circuit at slow speed and being thrown onto a public highway at 140mph with a full pack of riders behind you. 'I had loads of crashes during my racing career, but this one was different,' he says. 'I just kept sliding and sliding and sliding – it was like a bad dream. There must have been a big impact, but I don't really remember that bit; I just remember sliding down the road for an exceptionally long time. I eventually ground to a stop and a bike whizzed past me at full speed, just missing me. I couldn't feel my legs. I thought I was paralysed, and that was my biggest fear.'

The major trauma Easton suffered had been caused by the initial impact, as he explains. 'I think my broken femurs [Easton broke both his left and right femurs – the largest bones in the legs] and broken pelvis were from me slamming into the petrol tank and the handlebars as I was thrown from the bike. The impact was enough to smash Gary's back wheel and puncture it, but somehow he managed to stay on.'

Unable to stand up, Easton lay in the middle of the track waiting for help. 'I couldn't move my legs, and I couldn't get up,' he says. 'I could move my hands, and I remember lifting them up before my eyes and my gloves were like ribbons – just absolutely shredded. There was so much blood, and I could see my knucklebones, and I thought, *Holy cow, this has been a big one. This is the real deal.'*

Easton also suspects he must have taken a blow to the head when he hit the road, as even his senses were traumatised. 'I shouted for help, but I must have had some sort of concussion, because it sounded like someone else shouting *Help!* at me,' he says. 'It was weird; I almost felt outside of myself, like my voice was coming towards me. From what I'm told I was slipping in and out of consciousness by that point. I never felt any pain but I just couldn't move. I managed to get up onto my elbow but couldn't move anything from the chest down, and that's when I thought I was paralysed. It was scary.'

Delta 7 was first on the scene. While still lying in the road, Stuart Easton was attended by travelling doctor John Hinds, a true legend of the sport and nothing short of a guardian angel to the riders he cared for. His call sign was Delta 7.

Dr Hinds worked as a consultant anaesthetist and intensive care doctor at Craigavon Area Hospital in County Armagh but regularly gave up his weekends to volunteer as a bike-mounted travelling doctor, or 'flying doctor', at road races all over Ireland. He had saved countless riders' lives and was all but worshipped by them. Stuart Easton was about to find out why. 'I must have slipped away again, because it only felt like two minutes later that I was in hospital,' he says. 'John Hinds was great throughout. He immediately injected me with ketamine to stop the pain as I was lying in the road. I was taken to a hospital near the track at first and then moved to Royal Victoria Hospital in Belfast. In the first hospital, I only have a slight memory of seeing a couple of green dots at the foot of my bed. It turned out to be Chris Anderson and Phil Borley who had come to see me – they were wearing their green Kawasaki team clothing.'

As bad as things were for Easton, they were about to get even worse, and even more frightening. 'The next thing I remember was not being able to see at all,' he says. 'I could think, and I could process things quite well, but I was blind. Woolsey Coulter [former top Irish racer] somehow managed to get in to see me and he was talking to me. I couldn't speak and I couldn't see, but I could hear him and knew it was him. I think the drugs stopped me from panicking too much; I was worried, but not hysterical. They tried to bring me back from heavy sedation, but then I was in a lot of pain and started losing the plot a wee bit, so they put me back under again.'

Easton was so badly hurt that surgeons didn't dare operate for fear of losing him. 'They couldn't operate on me for ten days because I had a lot of internal bleeding and a ruptured bowel,' he says. 'Once they finally brought me out of deep sedation, that's when I was in big pain. I could see again by that point, and realised I had a colostomy bag attached to me and external fixators on my legs [metal frames that are screwed through the skin and into the bones to stabilise them and correct deformities after breaks] and an external fixator on my pelvis. By then I had never felt pain like it – it was absolutely unbearable. It was very touch and go at one point whether I would make it or not. As well as the ruptured bowel I had an infection and got blood poisoning, and there was a lot of internal bleeding from my pelvis. So, I had pain from all my broken bones, pain from my infection . . . it was big trauma.'

Some medical professionals don't look too kindly upon badly injured motorcycle racers, believing the wounds to be essentially self-inflicted, but road racing is a huge sport in Ireland and this played in Easton's favour. 'Over the next few days I became aware of the extent of my injuries once the consultants explained everything to me,' he says. 'Everyone was amazing in the Royal Victoria Hospital, and it felt like they were onside because they all love their road racing over there. I think if I'd have been in hospital back in Scotland, I would have been frowned upon.'

Now more conscious of what was going on, Easton was told the full extent of his injuries, and they were both extensive and horrific. 'As I said, I had a ruptured bowel, so they put a colostomy bag on me straight away as a life-saving measure,' he explains. 'My pelvis was broken in six places – just shattered. My sacrum and coccyx were shattered, and my anal wall had collapsed. Along with that, there was a lot of nerve damage: my right hand, my right butt cheek and the top of my right leg were numb, and still are a bit today. I remember them telling me they didn't know if the nerve damage would recover. That meant my future sexual function and my ability to go to the toilet were unknown at that point. That freaked me out a bit; I started to realise I might never be right again; I might be in big trouble. That was a real worry, but at that time I was just focusing on dealing with the pain – that was the overriding thing. There were a few grim days when my bowel infection kicked in; I had never felt as rotten to the core in all my life. Burning hot, sore, infected from the inside out, right from my core. That was the darkest point;

I think if I'd had a gun I would have shot myself; just put myself down.'

Despite his dire situation, once Easton was fully conscious and more stable his thoughts turned to racing again. 'Paul Bird [owner of the Paul Bird Motorsport Team that Easton had previously ridden for] came to visit me in Belfast and told me that if I was ever well enough to race again, and *wanted* to race again, he would always have a bike ready for me,' Easton says. 'I think he was just trying to boost me up a bit – give me a bit of a carrot to chase. Incredible as it seems, I *did* start thinking about racing again, as soon as I started making progress. There were times in the Royal Victoria Hospital when I thought that was me finished, and that I would never race again, but Paul got me thinking. I still don't know why I thought it was a good idea to get back on a bike, but I know I didn't want to be beaten by a crash that wasn't my fault. I didn't want to finish on that note at just 27 years old. I mean, if you're racing at that level you're not a scaredy cat, are you? So I was up for a comeback and proving to everybody that I could do it.'

This is what differentiates road racers from most other people: the sheer determination to recover from hideous, life-threatening injuries so that they can return, as soon as possible, to the very sport that caused those injuries. This desperation to get back on a motorcycle and race again proves just how much the riders get out of it, and how hard they find it to turn their backs on the sport. There is literally nothing, short of death itself, that will stop them.

Dr Hinds remained attentive and supportive throughout Easton's time in Royal Victoria Hospital. 'He came to visit me, and I was struggling; I was in a lot of pain at that point,' Easton admits. 'He told me ten days was a key time frame, and that if I could get through the first ten days then I would start to feel better. Then, in two weeks, I would notice another difference, then I was to give it another week and would feel better again. He kept telling me to dig in, dig in, dig in . . . I got through the first ten days and didn't feel any better, but I think John was just trying to motivate me and give me a target. He knew I was in a lot of pain.'

After having saved the lives of so many other riders, John Hinds was tragically killed at the Skerries road race outside Dublin in 2015. He had crashed his motorcycle while en route to attend to a fallen rider and suffered fatal injuries.

Hinds was just 35 years old at the time of his death. Yet, even in death, he continued to help others. He had long campaigned for Northern Ireland to have its own Air Ambulance Service but was constantly frustrated by the lack of funding to make it happen. It was an ambition he never lived to see realised, but eight months after his death, on 16th March, 2016, it was announced that funding would be made available to launch an Air Ambulance Service in Hinds' name. The helicopter's call sign would be the same as the one used by Hinds himself when he had worked as a flying doctor at road races. Two years after Hinds' tragic death, Delta 7 was operational and attended over 500 emergencies in its first year of operation. The road racers' guardian angel was still watching over them: Delta 7 was – and still is – responding to emergency calls.

Despite the close attentions of Dr Hinds, Stuart Easton now had a whole new level of trauma to deal with, and it was even more hideous than the pain. 'The morphine they gave me really didn't agree with me,' he says. 'I had some horrendous hallucinations; it was like I was living a constant nightmare. I kept hallucinating that I was a wing-walker on an aeroplane, and I kept getting thrown off it. I would land on the airfield and then be battered by gremlins. It was always really dark, bad stuff – never anything nice. I would hallucinate that I was sinking underneath turf and was suffocating or slipping down through the carpet into the ground and suffocating. Or I would be in a spinning room and all the furniture would get lifted up and would smash into me. These hallucinations became more and more frequent, and they got worse and worse. To me, they weren't hallucinations – they were absolutely real. I remember my hearing went supersonic too; the place seemed so noisy. Every beep, every machine, people talking . . . everything was hyper amplified.'

After two months of living hell and at least ten operations (Easton himself lost count and still isn't sure) he was moved to the Royal Infirmary of Edinburgh for a month and was then finally allowed back home to Hawick, a shadow of his former self. A very slight rider even in full health, Easton had lost a lot of weight during his ordeal and now weighed just 54kg (8.5 stone) as opposed to his normal race weight of 64kg (10 stone). As well as needing to gain weight, he also had to endure months of agonising physiotherapy in order to restore as much flexibility and movement to his limbs as possible. 'When I got back home, I started months and months of physiotherapy, getting my knees bending, getting my mobility back, starting to go on little walks to build my strength back up,' he says. 'There was a physiotherapist in Hawick called Stevie Marshall who used to give up his time to treat me for free every single day, just as a friend. So Stevie was a huge part of me getting back to racing. It would have cost a fortune to have a private physio with the amount of work that needed doing. There was a Portakabin at the garage where I worked and we would just clear the wee canteen table and I'd lie on that and Stevie would treat me.'

By January of 2012, just eight months after the crash that almost took his life, Stuart Easton was making preparations to get back on a racing motorcycle. He persuaded his consultants to remove his colostomy bag and then travelled to Almería in Spain for a three-day test in March. There would be no initial trial on a less powerful bike – Easton jumped straight onto a fearsome Superbike, right in at the deep end. Full send. Although he was mentally prepared to get back on a bike, results were not encouraging. 'My knee ballooned up on the first day and I couldn't bend it,' he says. 'My hip was in agony, too, so I realised I was in trouble. That test was a bit of a disappointment and a bit of a worry, and the first race was just weeks away.'

Easton made the grid for the first race of the 2012 British Superbike Championship and gained more strength and confidence with every race. By the third round at Oulton Park in May, almost exactly one year on from the accident that had so nearly killed him, Stuart Easton stood on the podium alongside Shane Byrne and Tommy Hill, both British Superbike champions. That he had withstood more pain than most people could even begin to imagine and fought his way back to the podium in the world's toughest domestic bike racing championship was a staggering accomplishment, but what he did the following year was even more impressive.

After finishing tenth overall in his comeback year on a Superbike, Easton switched to the British Supersport 600 Championship in 2013 and won ten races on his way to lifting the title. He had closed the circle. Well, almost. He still hadn't taken part in a road race, and nobody would have blamed him if he never did so again. But, despite his small stature, Stuart Easton was a fierce competitor and was not to be stopped. In 2014 he entered the Macau Grand Prix and once more found himself racing between Armco barriers and high-rise buildings on the 3.8-mile roads circuit in the Far East.

'I turned my experience into a positive and used it to drive me,' he says of his return to the roads. 'I was training well and was in pretty good shape. Sitting on the line at Macau, I was thinking, *Right, I set the lap record here and nobody has broken it* [to this day, nobody has] *and nobody has been through what I've been through*, so I was full of confidence and felt strong.'

Easton won the race by an astonishing 14 seconds; his demons vanquished.

*

In 2015 Stuart Easton was once more racing in the British Superbike Championship but suffered brake failure at Brands Hatch and crashed once again at 140mph, breaking both his lower legs. The following year he suffered an oil leak at Thruxton and was thrown from his machine at high speed yet again. He had signed to ride for Moto Rapido Ducati in 2017, but after pre-season testing realised his confidence had finally deserted him and that he could no longer continue. 'I called the team boss ahead of the first round at Assen and told him he'd be wasting his money taking me there,' Easton explains. 'So I handed over the reins and that was me done. Finished. Retired. I was ready to stop, and I've never missed it from that day to now.'

Easton now lives back in his native Hawick, where he runs an MOT garage and enjoys a much quieter – and much less painful – life with his wife Claire and their sons, Finlay and Ellis. By all accounts from those who know him, he has never been happier. He has found his peace.

CHAPTER 4

THE FASTEST ROAD RACE ON EARTH

'I quit. This course is too dangerous. It's crazy. A crazy track. A crazy place.'
VIRGINIO FERRARI

'We were nearly at the point of not going to the Ulster Grand Prix because it was so dangerous,' Tony Jefferies said, recalling the discussion he had with his son David. 'It's a mass start on a really tricky course, and that leads to a lot of dangerous situations that you don't get anywhere else. At the TT you're on your own, and the North West 200 is all fast, wide straights, but you get sucked into battles at the Ulster that take you off-line and leave you with nowhere to go but into a banking. I always hated the place, and maybe that rubbed off on David. It was like short circuit racing but with no run-off. It's the only circuit he'd come back from and say, "Bloody hell, that was dangerous," after a race, so we were very close to not going again.'

David Jefferies was one of the greatest road racers of all time and was not easily scared. So if a rider of that calibre says a road race is dangerous, it is. Following the natural contours of the landscape in the hills overlooking Belfast, the 7.4-mile Dundrod circuit played host to the Ulster Grand Prix, the event that has long been promoted as the fastest road race on earth. It still is, but only just. The race hasn't been run since 2019 due to finance and insurance issues, but that year Peter Hickman set a new outright lap record of 136.41mph. His current outright lap record at the Isle of Man TT, set in 2023, stands at 136.35mph.

Fast and dangerous, the Ulster is a favourite with many riders, double winner Ian Simpson among them. 'Dundrod is a hard track to learn, and it's so dangerous, but I loved it,' he says. 'I've always said the track layout would be the perfect model for a short circuit, although it's 7.4 miles long. But if you could have the exact same layout, without walls and trees and bankings to crash into, it would be the best circuit in the world. The layout of the track and the way the corners all flow into each other is just brilliant.'

Michael Dunlop agrees. 'The Ulster Grand Prix is big fast flat-out flowing bends,' he says. 'It's 190mph, left, right, left – so many corners, one after the other. And it's a real smooth circuit with lots of grip. I love it.'

Dundrod was also the favourite circuit of Dunlop's older brother, William. Tragically killed at the Skerries road race in 2018, William Dunlop loved the place. 'It's just a brilliant circuit – everything about it is brilliant,' he said before his untimely death. 'It's just so fast and flowing – it's phenomenal. I wouldn't say it's dangerous, it just depends on your riding style. A lot of these English boys ride the roads like short circuits now. Dundrod's got such a brilliant surface that it allows you to scratch round like that, but it doesn't mean it's any more dangerous than the other road circuits – it just means you've got more grip!'

Ryan Farquhar, who has a staggering 201 Irish national road race wins to his name, also lists Dundrod as his favourite circuit: 'It's fast, it's flowing and it's a real riders' circuit – I just love it. And if the weather's good, there's a real nice atmosphere at it.'

Manxman Conor Cummins is another fan. 'I really, really enjoy riding round the Dundrod circuit,' he says. 'It's such a scratchy circuit – it's like a pure roads version of a short circuit, and it's got all the balls-out corners rolled into one. That's the one road race where I can really use my short circuit scratching experience. It's a bit hairy in certain places but, if anything, the hairier a racetrack is, the more aware and careful it makes you as a rider. In the first Supersport race in 2009 there was ten of us going for the lead and you simply don't get that anywhere else. You have to be brave, but you have to use your head as well. It's a brilliant course.'

The Ulster Grand Prix was first held in 1922 on the 20.5-mile Clady circuit, just a stone's throw from today's Dundrod circuit. The Clady course was reduced to 16.5 miles in 1947, but the event was moved to Dundrod in 1953. Before his passing in 2017, John Surtees recalled racing on the Clady course in his first Ulster Grand Prix. 'I'd done a lot of short circuit racing, and then at the end of 1952 I wanted to sort of perhaps go on to a different, more international level,' he said. 'I'd been asked by Norton and

I had a Norton allocated to me, which came in time for the 1952 Ulster Grand Prix – the last race to be held on the old Clady circuit. It was my first world championship event and my first event off the mainland. I was a little fluky because of Les Graham and others retiring, so I finished sixth and got a world championship point, which hadn't been planned, and that ruled me out of the Manx Grand Prix.'

Ruled out of the Manx, as it was an event for amateurs, Surtees' result at the Ulster meant he progressed to the TT quicker than he'd planned. 'I had only the opportunity to go to the TT, so I went to the island,' he said. 'I was asked by Joe Ehrlich to ride a 125 EMC and I thought, *At least it will teach me the circuit a little more*, so I went along with my Norton, but when I got there, Syd Lawton – the works Norton rider – had had an accident, so Joe Craig turned round and said, "We want you to ride the works Norton in the TT." I didn't even know which way the circuit went!'

Surtees not only won seven world championships on two wheels, he also won the 1964 Formula 1 world championship, making him the only man ever to win premier world titles on both two and four wheels; a feat which will most likely never be matched.

*

Between 1949 and 1971 the Ulster Grand Prix was just that – a Grand Prix. It was one of the rounds of the Motorcycle Grand Prix world championships. Eventually being deemed too dangerous, it lost its status in 1972 but continued as one of the 'Big Three' road races, alongside the Isle of Man TT and the North West 200.

Although the North West 200 course is closer to Joey Dunlop's hometown of Ballymoney, he made Dundrod his own in the 1980s and 1990s, taking 24 wins and 44 podiums at the Ulster Grand Prix and a further 24 wins at the Dundrod 150 meeting, which was held on the same circuit. Dunlop was nigh-on unbeatable round the 7.4-mile course, but that didn't stop other riders from trying.

In 1983 the Ulster Grand Prix was part of the now-defunct TT Formula 1 world championship (for large capacity four-stroke Superbikes) which, that year, included rounds at the Isle of Man TT, Assen in Holland and Dundrod. Coming into the final race at Dundrod, Rob McElnea was lying second in the championship and needed to beat Dunlop on his favourite circuit – and in the wet, too. Dunlop excelled in wet conditions, McElnea was not so keen – on the roads, at least.

McElnea had won the Senior Classic TT just a few months earlier, so he certainly wasn't afraid of pure roads circuits, but he admits to throwing the towel in early at the 1983 Ulster Grand Prix despite being in serious contention for the world title. 'Joey won the F1 race at the TT and I finished second, then I won at Assen and Joey finished second, so we were equal on points going to the final round at Dundrod – Joey's home turf,' McElnea says. 'It was absolutely pissing down, and I got the holeshot [first rider off the line] but rolled off at the first corner and Joey came past me and took off at a suicidal pace. I was never really up for riding in the rain on the roads, and every time I came past that corner for the rest of the race there was a crowd of Irish fans giving me the wanker sign!'

McElnea finished the race in third place and lost out on the TTF1 world championship by just seven points.

As the championship grew throughout the 1980s it incorporated more rounds held on short circuits, and so it attracted more short circuit specialists. They could opt out of the TT and the Ulster Grand Prix and make up points at circuits like Assen, Donington and Hockenheim instead. Former 500cc Grand Prix winner Virginio Ferrari was one such rider. He had finished second to Kenny Roberts in the 1979 world championship, and in 1987, in the twilight of his career, he was in contention for the TTF1 world championship, so he decided to travel to Dundrod with the intention of picking up a few points. He soon changed his mind.

Ferrari, accustomed to super-smooth wide Grand Prix circuits with acres of gravel traps, couldn't believe his eyes when he completed a lap of Dundrod for the first time. It was a dangerous enough course at the best of times, but it must have looked truly lethal to a man more accustomed to riding on relatively safe Grand Prix circuits. He took part in the first practice session and posted a time that put him 35th fastest, but by the time the second session began Ferrari was on his way home. 'I quit,' he said. 'This course is too dangerous. I quit. It's crazy. A crazy track. A crazy place. A crazy race. I like to win the championship, but I like my life to go on as well. I go home.'

One practice session at the Ulster was enough to convince Ferrari that road racing was a suicidal occupation, and a world title was not worth dying for. He won it, nonetheless. Thanks to the ratio of road circuits compared to short circuits in the 1987 TTF1 world championship, the Italian took the title from Joey Dunlop by three points.

Ferrari was not unreasonable in declaring the Dundrod circuit dangerous. The year before his one and only visit saw the death of popular German rider Klaus Klein in hideous conditions. It was so wet that Skoal Bandit Suzuki rider Paul Iddon tried desperately to have the race called off. 'That race should never have been started,' he says. 'I actually pleaded with the clerk of the course not to start the race because it was so wet. Going down the Flying Kilo [a super-fast kink-then-straight after the start line] on the warm-up lap, my bike was going lock-to-lock, aquaplaning at 180mph. I got off my bike when we got back to the grid and said, "You cannot start this race. Someone's going to get killed," but the clerk of the course said he had a duty to his sponsors and that was that. I was following Klaus and had only just gone past him when the accident happened. He was the closest friend I lost in an F1 world championship race.'

Since 1955, when Julian Crossley lost his life, there have been 25 fatalities at Dundrod. It's a dangerous course, but for some that's the attraction: danger can feel good.

Davey Todd was very lucky to survive a massive crash at the Ulster GP in 2018, and the cause of the crash proved just how many dangers the riders face during a road race. 'I think it was a gust of wind,' he says. 'People like Conor Cummins and Davo Johnson messaged me afterwards to tell me the wind is always bad at the top of Deer's Leap, so you have to be careful. Being a bit fresh to it all, I simply hadn't realised that. I didn't feel like I was pushing too hard, but I just tipped in, and the bike wouldn't turn, and at

150mph you get no chance to correct anything. I remember aiming for the grass, then the next thing I knew I was waking up in hospital.'

Footage of the crash on YouTube makes for terrifying viewing, but Todd says there's even more frightening clips of it in existence. 'The TV footage of the crash looked pretty tame compared to the footage that some spectators sent me!' he says. 'I didn't find it difficult to watch though – in fact it was quite exciting. Mind you, I was pumped full of drugs at the time. It brought my dad to tears watching it, though.'

Given the high-speed nature of the crash, Todd was lucky not to be more seriously injured. 'I broke my heel and took a big chunk out of my arm, which probably led to the bladder and kidney infection,' he says. 'I had a bit of a gash to my knee and needed a few stitches, but I got away incredibly lightly, given how big a crash it was.'

It was a crash at the Ulster Grand Prix in 2015 that was the beginning of the end for Guy Martin's racing career. He was leading the Dundrod 150 Superbike race (held on the Thursday before Saturday's Ulster Grand Prix) when he lost control of his Tyco BMW at high speed on the run out of Ireland's corner. Martin was thrown into a field and barrel-rolled over and over, picking up more injuries with every crushing blow. He broke several vertebrae as well as his sternum and several ribs. 'I'm not saying it was the biggest crash I ever had,' Martin admits, 'but it's the one where I broke the most bones in one sitting!'

Although he made a brief comeback with Honda in 2017, Martin then retired again to concentrate on his television work. Since then, he has only competed in a few Irish national road races, riding a classic BSA Rocket 3.

Another household name, Carl Fogarty, credits the Ulster Grand Prix with launching the career that would ultimately see him win four World Superbike championships. 'I won the Ulster Grand Prix [Formula 1 race] in 1988, which shocked everybody, including myself,' he says. 'I think I qualified in about 21st place but came right up through the field and won, and then I had a chance of winning the TT Formula 1 world championship. That's where it all started for me, really. I was coming back from two years of injuries, having broken my leg badly in 1986 and then again in 1987. In 1988 I wasn't even meant to be racing, to be honest, but when I got on the Honda RC30 I realised I was comfortable for the first time in nearly two years after the leg injuries. I ended up going on to win the TTF1 championship when I wasn't even riding that hard, if I'm honest. I was too frightened of falling off because I couldn't afford to damage my leg again, so it was quite bizarre that I ended up winning that championship.'

Foggy would win the TTF1 world championship for three consecutive years in 1988, 1989 and 1990 before concentrating on World Superbikes and becoming the most famous rider in Britain.

Like every road race, the Ulster Grand Prix has had its share of emotional moments and victories that mean so much more than just a race win. Adam McLean's debut victory in 2018 was one such race.

The backstory was tragic. McLean was teammates with his friend James Cowton that year and the two headed across the Irish Sea in July to compete at the Southern 100 road races on the Isle of Man. The Billown Circuit is not for the faint of heart. For much of its 4.25-mile length it's hemmed in by drystone walls. It's also very narrow and very, very fast. It's not a place to crash at, and if you do, the consequences can be fatal. James Cowton would lose his life at the 2018 event.

'The Southern 100, Thursday 12th July, 2018, was a very, very dark day,' McLean recalls. 'For myself, for the team, and most of all for my teammate James Cowton's family. It was just a horrendous day. We had just lost William Dunlop at the Skerries on the previous Saturday too. As a road racer, you know these things can happen, but this time it was so close to home because it was within our own team and our own awning, so it was really personal. I didn't know if I was coming or going for a while.'

Adam McLean was only 22 years old at the time; it was a lot to take in, and he was very lucky to escape unscathed, physically, if not mentally. 'James crashed just in front of me, and I just managed to avoid his bike,' he says. 'I looked back when I got to Castletown corner and saw pure carnage – four bikes went down – so I dropped my bike and ran back to try to help James, because he was my friend as well as my teammate. I just wanted to go back and check he was okay and reassure him and comfort him and tell him the medics were on their way, but unfortunately I was too late – he was already gone. It wasn't a nice thing to witness.'

McLean struggled to process the tragedy and seriously considered walking away from the sport. 'I think every road racer, at some stage in their career, has to deal with something like that, but it hit me pretty hard and brought a lot of things home to me and I struggled, mentally, after that. I still do. When I got back from the Southern, my head was all over the place. I didn't know what the team wanted to do, I didn't know what I wanted to do . . . I spoke to Winston [McAdoo, team boss], and he said, "Look, let's just forget about racing for the rest of the year. We'll regroup over winter and go again next year." So that was the plan, but a couple of days before the Armoy road races I was still considering entering. I didn't want to miss Armoy, but I didn't want to do it either. It was a strange feeling. I remember wishing it was just another two or three weeks away, as I'd only had about three weeks to deal with what happened to James. Then, the day before Armoy, I said, "Frig it – we'll go." Winston gave me the Supersport 600 bike, and I threw it in my van with my Supertwin and just rode the two bikes under my own steam. This sport gets an awful hold of you. You think to yourself, *I've had enough*, but then you can't bring yourself to miss a meeting!'

McLean didn't manage to win a race at Armoy, but a few weeks later he took his debut international road-race win in the Ulster Grand Prix Supertwin race and dedicated it to his fallen friend. 'I didn't really get to enjoy the moment, or to soak up the emotions, because we had the 600 race straight afterwards,' McLean says. 'Chris Kinley from Manx Radio interviewed me after the Supertwin race and the first thing I said was, "That one was for James." Chris was good friends with James, so he was a bit emotional, too, so it was nice to do that for him.'

Outsiders looking in often wonder what drives riders

to take such massive risks racing on everyday roads. The answer is simple: it feels incredible. For privateer James McBride (a proud member of the 130mph club at Dundrod), there's a corner at Dundrod that sums up exactly why he was attracted to road racing. 'Ultimately, the sheer thrill of road racing is what keeps you doing it,' he says. 'I mean, going through Budore at the Ulster Grand Prix? *Oh my God!* It was like going off the end of the world if you got it right. Sixth gear, no braking . . . you just roll the throttle a tiny bit to make the bike turn in, then immediately crack it back open to get out the other side. Then, when the road dips away a bit, the front end rises as the rear end digs in, and the bike weaves and snakes like a king cobra rearing up! When you get through that and the front end lands again, you're just like "Fuck! Wow! That was *mental*!" You try to enjoy it and let it sink in, but you can't because you've got the next corner to deal with – down two gears and into a fast right. Get that wrong, and you're going through a hedge.'

Budore corner has since been named 'Lougher's' after Ian Lougher, and the man himself agrees with James McBride on the nature of the high-speed bend. 'Funnily enough, Budore corner at Dundrod has always been a favourite of mine, and they went and renamed it Lougher's!' he says. 'It's just a brilliant corner. It's so fast; a fifth- or sixth-gear approach, then back one gear into the corner, and then you're almost flat out straight away again on the exit.'

As crazy as road racers might appear to be, they're not; if they were, they wouldn't last a single lap of a race, according to McBride. 'There's a balance of exhilaration and sensibility,' he explains. 'None of it's sensible, but you certainly can't be insane to do this because you wouldn't make it round the first corner. Nobody who's mad or crazy could do this – you have to be supremely focused.'

So focused that it's usually only afterwards that the riders can download the experience and fully appreciate what they've just done. 'You're concentrating so hard while you're racing that you don't really have time to enjoy it, so it's only after the race that it really hits you,' McBride continues. 'When you ride up that muddy return road at the Ulster Grand Prix and put your bike on the paddock stand, and the bike looks like it's caked in cow shit from the wet roads, and you relive the race with someone like William Dunlop or Dan Kneen – two riders I raced with regularly at Dundrod – it's just a great feeling. If you've had a right ding-dong, you walk up to each other with big grins on your faces and just laugh and say, "How fucking good was that?" It's an amazing feeling.'

Aside from the sheer elation riders feel during – and after – such battles, McBride says it's the community feel of road racing that is such a draw. 'It's that camaraderie and family thing, and I learned very quickly that it's a lot more pronounced in road racing than in short circuit racing,' he says. 'There's no sentiment in short circuit racing; people wouldn't lend you a tyre warmer or a rear wheel nut – they want to see you fail so that they can beat you. In road racing, even your closest rivals want to see you enjoying yourself and would lend you anything you needed to make that happen. When people's lives are on the line, they don't even think about the petty stuff. It's not all about results – it's about personal achievement and having fun at the same time. It's not worth pushing for results on the roads if things aren't quite right. How many times have we heard John McGuinness say, "You can always come back next year"? He knows when to back off, and that's why he's able to go back to the TT, year on year, because he never takes stupid risks.'

McBride has now retired from racing and knows he'll never experience such extreme thrills again. 'I mean, you just can't replace that feeling,' he says, 'so all you can do is get used to living without it, and that's not easy.'

As strange as it may seem, many motorcycle racers are not keen on riding normal bikes on the roads; they feel safer riding at 180mph on closed roads than riding at 60mph in among everyday traffic. 'I've had 15 years to detox now,' McBride says of his retirement. 'I raced up until ten years ago, but it's been 15 years since I last did the TT. You can't beat it, nothing else betters it, so why try? I still ride road bikes, but I felt scared when I went back to riding them. I would feel fear when I was lining up on Glencrutchery Road to start a TT race, but that fear would raise adrenaline and focus my attention, knowing that the whole TT course was closed off and set out in front of me. On normal roads, you've only got half the width to play with, and you obviously can't go anywhere near as fast, and then you have to consider other road users, too, so there's no comparison. I still enjoy it, though.'

Two of the greatest races ever seen around the Dundrod circuit were between Joey Dunlop and David Jefferies in 1999. Surprisingly, for two seemingly similar characters (both were hugely modest, down-to-earth men), Dunlop and Jefferies didn't always see eye to eye. While each had respect for the other's speed, Dunlop felt the new generation of road riders, spearheaded by Jefferies, were riding the roads in a super-aggressive short circuit style and taking too many risks. While Dunlop was never a fan of fairing-bashing clashes, he was quite prepared to prove that he could win races in that manner if he had to, and that fact set up a mouth-watering scrap between the two greatest road racers in the world at that time. What's more, there were all sorts of other factors that ensured the contest would be evened out. For example, Dunlop had already notched up 23 wins at the Ulster Grand Prix (and 48 at Dundrod in total), so his knowledge of the circuit was second to none. Jefferies, on the other hand, had never been to Dundrod before and would have to learn the circuit during practice. This would clearly go in Dunlop's favour. The Irishman was, however, 21 years older than his Yorkshire rival, in a sport which is usually considered a young man's game. Dunlop was also on a 750cc machine (Honda RC45) while Jefferies enjoyed the luxury of the more powerful 1000cc Yamaha R1, but he still had a bad injury from a crash at Knockhill and would be riding with two pins in his wrist. It was a mouth-watering prospect to see who would gain the upper hand: the old-school Dunlop with his intimate track knowledge and legendary smooth riding style; or the new pretender – the aggressive, short circuit style Jefferies, who was young enough to be Dunlop's son.

Jefferies explained to *Road Racing Ireland* magazine how he had managed to learn the daunting and super-fast 7.4-mile course in preparation for this clash of titans.

'Iain Duffus showed me around the circuit in a car, but I went out in practice and tried to learn it by myself. It's tricky and fast and I'll not learn it in six laps. Plus, I'm taking it easy with my hand in mind as I don't want to hurt it.'

When asked which parts of the course were the trickiest, Jefferies' complete lack of circuit knowledge became all too apparent. 'The wriggly bit up the hill,' he replied. 'I don't know the names. And the bit from the hairpin. Come race day I might be alright, but I don't want to go home thinking I should have backed off and just learned it this year. I'll be happy to come back again after learning it this year and being fit.'

The opening Superbike race was sensational, with a slow-off-the-line Dunlop eventually recording his fastest-ever lap around the Dundrod circuit at 125.14mph to battle through to join the leading trio of Duffus, Jefferies and Ian Lougher. When Lougher later pulled out with gearbox problems, it became a three-way fight for the win. Dunlop passed Jefferies to take second spot, but Jefferies then responded by passing both his adversaries to take the lead. Elbow-to-elbow and fairing-to-fairing, the two V&M Yamahas mugged Dunlop all the way round the circuit, sending Joey's loyal local fans into a frenzy.

Jefferies set his fastest lap of the race on the final circuit and came round the final corner with both wheels drifting across the road to take an emphatic victory in his first visit to Dundrod. It meant he had won all three major road races that year (the North West 200, the TT and the Ulster Grand Prix) and had beaten the acknowledged master, Dunlop, at his own game, and on his own circuit. Dunlop said of the two Yamaha riders, 'I just couldn't live with their speed. Even when I did move into second, they came blasting past down the straight again.' His thinly disguised anger at the two younger riders' styles was revealed when he said: 'On the last lap I didn't dare take any chances because I didn't know what line they were going to take. I saw what you could call some "interesting moves" around Dundrod.'

Unperturbed, a jubilant Jefferies openly admitted to having the time of his life, drifting and sliding his Yamaha R1 with complete mastery. 'It was great fun,' he beamed. 'I dived in a few times to get ahead of Duffus and pushed hard on the penultimate lap. On the last lap I had the machine weaving everywhere, and round the last corner I was just showing off.'

It was round one to Jefferies, but Dunlop approached him in the paddock afterwards to have a quiet word. It has not been recorded what was actually said, but it appears that Dunlop was warning his younger rival of the dangers of the Dundrod course and telling him to calm his riding down before someone got hurt. David's father, Tony Jefferies, downplayed the conversation. 'They didn't really have strong words,' he said. 'Dave was having to push really hard because he was on Pirelli tyres and he couldn't get the drive out of the slow corners. Joey was pulling away out of those on his Michelins, so DJ had to ride really hard to catch him up again. It was really frustrating for Dave because he knew he could go as fast as Joey, but his tyres were spinning up and he kept losing time. So, to stay with Joey he had to pull a few moves that were pretty close. Joey was pretty philosophical about it. He was like, "Well, that's what you've got to do sometimes, I suppose." He'd had days when he'd had to do the same.'

Jefferies V&M team boss Jack Valentine says he heard lots of partisan Irish fans branding his rider 'a complete nutter' because of his riding style, but he offers an alternative explanation. 'There were a lot of Irish fans coming over and saying, "Aye, yer man's crazy." We used to get that a lot, because nobody on the road-racing scene had seen a bike with proper horsepower before [the Yamaha R1 proved to be a game changer when it was released in 1998], and even at the TT, David was coming out of corners leaving big black lines, just power-spinning the tyres, and it was the same at the Ulster. They had never seen it, they said he was just crazy. I had a few of the regular Irish teams and team owners saying, "Your fuckin' man's crazy – slow him down," and all that. Again, it was just his handling of the bike.'

Nevertheless, some observers recall Dunlop being in an extremely rare furious mood after that race and seeming more determined than ever to beat Jefferies in the second encounter, no matter how hard he had to ride to do it.

Jefferies himself hinted at the frosty relationship between the two in an interview for www.ttwebsite.com in 2001, saying, 'If you totalled up all the times I've spoken to Joey and said "Hello" it would come to about four minutes. He was a very shy sort of guy, and I think he looked at me as the young new idiot. Even his friends who knew him well, he was quiet around, so someone who turned up and started doing what I did – he wasn't going to be my best friend. He wasn't that sort of person. I respected him as a rider, of course.'

Whatever the state of their relationship following race one, Jefferies may actually have done Dunlop a favour by getting his back up. There was no more dangerous opponent than Joey Dunlop when he felt he had a point to prove, and it was clear from his steely gaze as he took to the line in race two that he was intent on teaching the two young upstarts – Jefferies and Duffus – a lesson.

The Supersport 600 race – held in between the two Superbike events – had gone some way to backing up Dunlop's claims that Duffus and Jefferies were closer to the edge than they should have been. As Jefferies dived up the inside of his teammate to take the lead at the fast Wheeler's corner, he clashed fairings with Duffus and the Scotsman crashed out, his V&M machine careering into a road traffic sign while Duffus himself tumbled to a halt unscathed. And the carnage didn't stop there. As Jason Griffiths swerved to avoid the fallen Duffus, Adrian Archibald had no choice but to run into the back of the Welshman and he too went down in a heap.

The incident caused the race to be red-flagged, and the results were taken from the last time all riders had crossed the start–finish line meaning that Duffus, although laid out on the grass, was declared the winner. In any case, the accident did nothing to deter Duffus or Jefferies from resuming battle in the second Superbike race and Dunlop refused to back off either, leading to one of the greatest battles ever seen around Dundrod.

Clerk of the course Billy Nutt spoke to Jack Valentine before the race to ask him to remind his riders that the Ulster Grand Prix was in fact a road race, as opposed to an elbow-bashing no-holds-barred sprint around a relatively safe short circuit. It would appear neither rider took the slightest bit of notice.

Dunlop fluffed the start but was soon hunting down the yellow and red V&M bikes at the front of the field. When he eventually took the lead, the partisan crowd went wild to see the diminutive grey-haired Dunlop taking the fight to the two wild young guns. After biding his time in third place, Jefferies made his move past Duffus and set about attacking Dunlop, but even he admitted he scared himself, such was the pace the old master was setting. 'I ran wide and almost hit a telegraph pole at Budore and gave myself a big fright,' he said.

With a monumental effort, Jefferies finally caught Dunlop on the penultimate lap but had to set a new outright lap record of 126.85mph to do so – and this on his first visit to the track. But Dunlop was having none of it and responded by lapping Dundrod quicker than he had ever done before (126.80mph) to just edge the win from Jefferies, who showed how much he had enjoyed the race by pulling a monster wheelie out of the final corner. 'I was trying and was going to pass him into Wheeler's on the last lap,' Jefferies told *Road Racing Ireland* magazine, 'but just as I was going to, I realised I was too fast and shut it off. Then at the hairpin I had too much power to give it a handful coming out of the corner.'

Whatever their differences, Jefferies paid tribute to Dunlop after the race and openly admitted he simply could not find a way to beat him in such form. 'Joey is an unbelievable rider,' he said. 'Going into fast blind corners he knows when to hold it flat out and when to open her up at other corners. I just couldn't do that. He managed to make me look a bit stupid, really. My bike was a hell of a lot quicker than his, but he absolutely rode the wheels off it, you know? Just outclassed me.'

Fittingly, it was a draw between Jefferies and Dunlop, with each rider taking a Superbike win apiece. The older man from another era of bike racing had shown he still had the mettle to mix it with, and beat, the very best of the young road-racing hotshots. Dunlop's incredible win had even more poignancy when it turned out to be his last ever meeting at Dundrod. He couldn't have made a finer exit or handed the torch to a more worthy challenger.

Sadly, after those two epic battles came tragedy. In the final race of the day at that 1999 Ulster Grand Prix, popular Coleraine rider Owen McNally crashed and sustained injuries that would prove to be fatal. The 30-year-old died in the Royal Victoria Hospital in Belfast, leaving behind a wife, a son and a daughter.

There were calls for the Ulster Grand Prix to be boycotted in 2000 following a series of road-racing deaths. Joey Dunlop lost his life in an obscure race in Tallinn, Estonia, in July that year, and Gary Dynes and Andy McClean both lost their lives at the Monaghan road races just a week before the Ulster was due to take place. The mayor of Joey Dunlop's hometown of Ballymoney was among those calling for the race to be abandoned, but race organiser Billy Nutt defended the sport, saying, 'Ulster motorcycling is a large family and everyone feels one another's hurt. Of course, we are saddened by the events of Sunday – we have lost two well-respected competitors. But it would be their wish that the show would go on. That's the way it has always been.'

The Ulster Grand Prix isn't for every rider. Although he regularly raced at the TT, Oliver's Mount and the North West 200, Steve Parrish only raced at Dundrod on one occasion, but it proved to be an eventful trip. 'I only did the Ulster once, either in 1977 or 1979 – I can't remember,' he says. 'I had a factory bike, and Kiwi racer Stu Avant came with me. We teamed up together to keep the costs down and went over in my van. We had left my caravan behind because the organisers had sorted a hotel out for us, which didn't usually happen. Anyway, we got to the hotel on the Thursday night and I showed the receptionist my reservation, but in a really strong Belfast accent she said, "Your room's gone. Your room's gone." I was about to start arguing with her for letting the room out to someone else, but she took us down the corridor and showed us where our room had been. *Had been.* It was nothing but a pile of rubble. The whole wing had gone – it had been blown up, along with about 15 other rooms! Stu and I pissed ourselves laughing, and we had to find a Mrs Miggins-type boarding house instead.'

The drama was by no means over, however. 'When the racing started, Stu had a massive crash on his Yamaha TZ750 at Deer's Leap, and I was convinced he was dead,' Parrish continues. 'When I came round there were wheels lying about and the petrol tank had come off – there were bits and pieces everywhere; the whole bike had disintegrated. When I got back to the pits, I started going through Stu's trouser pockets, looking for a phone number for his mum, because I thought that was the end of him and I had to inform her. Then he came walking back into the paddock, as right as rain, and thought I was going through his pockets trying to rob him!'

It wasn't the only time Parrish was reminded of the Troubles in Northern Ireland. 'Another time, when I was at the North West 200, I threw a banger out of my window at [fellow racer] Barry Woodland and everybody around him hit the floor immediately, thinking it was a bomb! That didn't go down too well.'

The Irish Troubles were so bad in 1972 that the Ulster Grand Prix was cancelled over fear of a bombing. Although the Good Friday Agreement was firmly in place by 2001, and peace had largely been restored, double Ulster Grand Prix winner Ian Simpson still wasn't taking any chances. 'A guy approached me in the paddock at the Ulster Grand Prix in 2001, saying he had this bike that he thought might be my old Yamaha OW01 race bike,' he explains. 'He showed me a picture, and I knew that it was mine because it had unique brackets on it that my dad had made. I asked him if he would sell it to me and he agreed, but I told him I didn't have my cheque book with me so couldn't pay him the £2,000 there and then. He said he trusted me to post him a cheque, so we went to his house and I put the bike in my van to take home. I thanked him for his trust and promised him that I would send the cheque as soon as I got home, and, in his strong Northern Irish accent, he said, "I know you will, or I'll have you shot." He was kind of laughing when he said it, but I wasn't taking any chances in that part of the world – that cheque was in the post about three minutes after I got home!'

It wasn't the fact that his hotel room was bombed, or that he was convinced that his friend was dead that kept Steve Parrish away from the Ulster after his initial visit – it was the nature of the course itself. 'I didn't go back to the Ulster because I just didn't gel with the circuit,' he says. 'I felt it was more like the TT than the North West, so I left it at that. Which races you did back then depended on what you were offered money-wise. If somebody offered you loads of money, then you would race, which I don't suppose is the right attitude, but that's the way it was.'

A two-time winner of the Ulster Grand Prix, John McGuinness is a massive fan of the event and sums it up better than most. 'The strongest point of the Ulster is probably the circuit,' he says. 'It's such high speed with big, fast corners. It's a shame that the Ulster doesn't get the credit it deserves, because the racing's probably as good as anywhere else in the world, if not better. It's just where the circuit is located – there's nowhere to go when you get there, so it doesn't seem to get the backing of the tourist board or whoever. If you could lift the whole circuit up and stick it on the coast somewhere, it'd be rocking. As it is, everybody tends to just come for the day then disappear again. But a good close race round the Ulster is as good a race as you'll ever see anywhere in the world.'

The Ulster Grand Prix has not taken place since 2019, and despite ongoing efforts there are no immediate plans to reinstate it. In 2020, the organisers of the event – the Dundrod and District Motorcycle Club – were issued with a winding-up order as they had reportedly run up debts of £300,000. The Covid-19 pandemic then further complicated matters and the race has not returned. There had been hopes of a return in 2022 to mark the event's centenary, but those hopes were eventually dashed, with organisers unable to raise the required funding.

'The whole history of the event goes way back,' says nine-time winner Ryan Farquhar. 'It's a massive blow for Irish racing. For the Ulster Grand Prix to possibly never go again would be a massive shame.'

In late 2025, it was announced that the Ulster Grand Prix will return in 2027.

CHAPTER 5

TT: TRIUMPH AND TRAGEDY

*'It was my first TT, and I would lose three close friends
within the space of a few days.'*
IAN SIMPSON

'The TT has a buzz that money can't buy. You're going as
hard as you can go on tiny roads around the Isle of Man,
and if you make one mistake, you're coming back in a box.
Skydiving, short circuit racing, mountain biking, moto-cross
– I've tried a lot of things in my time, but nothing comes
near to the TT buzz.'

Guy Martin's statement makes it clear why riders race at
the most famous road race of them all – the Isle of Man TT.
The sheer thrill of it is like nothing else on earth, but there
can be a terrible price to pay for those thrills when things go
wrong. Almost everyone who has been involved with the TT
for long enough has a love–hate relationship with the event.
Love, because there are few things on earth more spectacular

and triumphant when all is going well; hate because there are few sporting events on earth where so many tragedies play out. Anyone involved with the TT for long enough will experience both the terrific highs and the catastrophic lows.

As TT winner turned rider liaison officer Richard 'Milky' Quayle once pointed out, 'If Roger Federer misses a shot, he loses a point – if I miss an apex, I lose my life.' Yet Quayle, like every other TT racer, was prepared to take whatever risks were required in order to experience the ultimate high that the sport provides. 'It's like sex,' he told the *New York Times* in 2017, 'we all love it, but the best bit's the orgasm, isn't it? And you can't have that all the time, can you? But here, when you're riding around here, you're getting that orgasm all the time.'

First held in 1907, the TT (which stands for Tourist Trophy – the original purpose of the race being to test touring bikes) is the pinnacle of pure road racing. Run over a 37.73-mile course that takes in humpback bridges, tram lines, jumps and even a partial climb up a mountain, the TT is as extreme as road racing gets. Speeds of over 206mph have been recorded and, despite all the hairpins and slower corners, the top riders post *average* lap times of over 135mph.

From 1949 until 1977 the TT counted as the British round of the Motorcycle Grand Prix world championships, during which time it played host to some of the all-time greats, including Geoff Duke, John Surtees, Mike Hailwood, Phil Read and Giacomo Agostini, before it was deemed to be too dangerous for a world championship course. Since it lost its status in 1977, the TT has become more of a specialised event and has made stars out of the likes of Joey Dunlop, Phillip McCallen, Steve Hislop, John McGuinness and Michael Dunlop.

Although an accurate figure does not exist (as riders can be injured at the TT but die several months later), it's safe to say that the course – used both for the TT and the Manx Grand Prix – has claimed over 265 lives. The TT is extreme sport at its most extreme, and there have been calls for it to be banned almost since it began.

Tony Jefferies won three TT races before being paralysed from the chest down following a crash at the relatively safe Mallory Park short circuit in England in 1973. His son David was killed at the TT in 2003. Before he passed away in 2021, Tony Jefferies offered a measured opinion of the risks of racing at the TT and the way in which riders must deal with them. 'The TT is a dangerous place, and it has to be treated with respect, there is no doubt about that, but riders have a choice – they don't have to go there,' he said. 'The riders that do go there go there know full well what the risks are. Various arguments are put forwards about the number of miles to complete, and this, that and the other, but I don't think that really makes a lot of difference; the fact is that you do have the choice, and if you ride in a sensible manner – but still obviously try and be competitive – the risks are minimised. What *is* a problem – and let's face it, it can happen anywhere – is machine failure. That's what riders fear the most, and there are certain parts of the circuit where that can happen and it is obviously very, very dangerous, so I don't know how anybody really overcomes that – I think they just tend to ignore it. I think that TT riders certainly have a mentality, maybe like people in the trenches in the First World War: whatever happens, it's not going to be them. But they're climbing out of the trenches, one way or another, and that's probably a philosophy that a rider has to adopt. So, really, it's up to the individual, and we can't knock anyone for saying it's dangerous, because it is.'

James McBride knows exactly how dangerous it is. Very, very few people survive high speed crashes at the TT and live to tell the tale: McBride is one of the lucky few. In 2008 he crashed at the fearsome Gorse Lea corner, a 160mph blind right-hand bend, completely surrounded by trees on both sides of the road. McBride believes he is the only man to have survived a crash there. 'A few people have crashed at Gorse Lea, but I think I'm the only one to get away with it,' he says. 'I remember Irish rider Derek Brien being killed there in 2011. Mark Parrett told me he was a few hundred yards behind Derek on the road, and when he got to the corner his vision was obscured by thousands of leaves fluttering everywhere. He slowed down, and as he went through the corner, the front forks from Derek's bike came down out of the trees and just missed his right handlebar.'

It was during practice for the 2008 TT that McBride had the biggest crash of his life. 'I had posted a time earlier in the week that put me in the top five fastest times in the Superstock class, so it was looking like being a good race week. I was on a good lap, but then I got to Gorse Lea and it all went blank.'

Mercifully, McBride has no memory of the crash at all. Yet, while that helped him to deal with the immediate trauma it has proven to be frustrating in figuring out precisely what went wrong. 'It wasn't until two years later that I was able to piece together what had happened,' he says. 'For those two years, the last thing I remembered was leaving the pits before the crash. Even when I rode round the course the year after my crash, it didn't bring anything back – I couldn't remember any of it. That messed with my head a bit for two years, as it's very strange to have that gap in your memory. But I've since learned that quite often when your body suffers a major trauma your brain blocks it out and kind of goes back a chapter. So I had to rely on eyewitnesses to find out what happened, but no two eyewitness accounts are the same – everybody remembers things differently.'

John McGuinness set off behind McBride during the practice session, but such was McBride's pace, McGuinness wasn't close enough to see what went wrong. 'John didn't know what had happened,' McBride says. 'He had followed me out of the pits on his Superbike – he was the last to be allowed out onto the course for the session – but he said he couldn't catch me. He told me that when he passed the crash site at Gorse Lea he knew it was me and thought, *Well, that's another one gone,* and was later pleased as punch to hear that I'd survived it. He wasn't close enough to see what actually happened, though.'

It was only much later that McBride began to get some sort of idea of what had occurred. 'Two years later I was testing in Portimão and Dan Stewart told me he knew what had happened,' he explains. 'He said it was down to the front tyre I was using, and explained it had a bad characteristic, in that, if you got off the throttle in fast corners – thereby putting some weight on the front tyre – the tyre got out of shape. Keith Amor said the same, and so did Gary Johnson and some other riders who had been using the same tyres at the TT that year. Every time they went through Gorse Lea, they noticed it. As soon as Dan told me that, I remembered having that sensation too. It only happened at high speed when the front tyre had some weight on it. Keith Amor told me he had saved a front tyre slide on his knee as he was going through Gorse Lea and thought, *Oh no – I'm going to do a McBride here.* I've still got that tyre in my attic at home.'

McBride escaped with relatively light injuries given the nature of the corner where he crashed and the speed at which he was travelling. Charles Salt had lost his life at Gorse Lea in 1957, as had Kiwi rider Stuart Murdoch in 1999 and the aforementioned Derek Brien in 2011. It is not a forgiving corner, and McBride knows how lucky he is. 'The only memory I have from immediately after the crash is seeing helicopter blades as I was being lifted into the medical helicopter,' he says. 'The next memory I have is of waking up in Noble's Hospital the next day and seeing my shredded leathers lying in a corner. I was like, "What happened?" I was in intensive care for three days. My injuries were pretty light, all things considered. No bottom-end injuries: I was fine from the waist down, but I had a punctured lung, four broken ribs and three broken vertebrae, and I had a compound fracture in my lower humerus and had shattered the head of my humerus. I've had a shoulder replacement now, so I've got titanium running through me.'

To this day, McBride is grateful that he can't recall the crash, but he's still puzzled about some of the details. 'I suppose it's a good thing that I can't remember the crash, because I really don't want to know in graphic detail,' he says. 'What we don't know is what shattered my arm. I thought I might have hit a kerb with it, but the marshals said I didn't. It wasn't from hitting a wall, either, so was it the bike? The marshals said I got tangled up with the bike, but I slid down the middle of the road, so I don't know how that could have happened. It turns out I jumped off the bike mid-corner because I knew it was out of control. Again, I didn't know this until someone showed me a sequence of photos of the whole crash unfolding. So I've had to piece it all together bit by bit over the years because, like I said, I have no memory of it actually happening.'

Perhaps because he had no memory of the incident McBride was able to get back on a bike in no time, ready to race again. The crash happened in late May and he was racing again in August. 'I didn't consider quitting racing for an instant,' he says. 'On the contrary, I was determined to come back stronger. It took me a while to be stronger, though. I wasn't as fast at the TT in 2009, but when I went to the Southern 100 in July, it was like *Bam!* and I was back. I was fully fit again and faster than I had been before.'

In 2010 James McBride won the TT Privateers Championship then walked away from the event. 'I was never going to do any better than that, unless a really good team offered me a ride,' he says, 'so I thought it was a good time to stop.'

The TT is the ultimate road race challenge. At 37.73 miles,

the course is the longest of them all, and a six-lap race is a punishing 226-mile test of endurance that challenges even the very best of riders. Winning a TT is the ultimate dream of every road racer, and they're prepared to take enormous risks to achieve that dream.

Bill Simpson won the Production TT in 1976, and his son Ian badly wanted to win one too. He made his debut at the event in 1989, and it was a debut that would have put most other people off the event for life. 'Little did I know what lay ahead over the fortnight,' Simpson says. 'It would turn out to be the worst meeting of my entire career. It was my first TT, and I would lose three close friends within the space of a few days. And I was only 19 years old at the time.'

Simpson was riding for Mick Grant's Durex Suzuki team, with Phil 'Mez' Mellor and James Whitham as his teammates. He had been racing on short circuits for four years and had also competed in the Manx Grand Prix for two years ahead of making his TT debut, but he had not – at that point – lost any close friends to racing. That was all about to change.

'The nightmare began when Phil Hogg was killed during practice week,' Simpson says. 'I'd had so many great races with Phil and we'd become good pals. We were at about the same level riding-wise, so every time we were both in the same race we'd be battling it out between us. Phil was a good rider and would have gone on to win TT races, I'm sure of it, if he'd only had the chance. Sadly, he never got it. He was killed on the Friday of practice week on the approach to Ballagarey when his bike seized and threw him into a wall. Phil's death hit me hard. He was the first rider that I knew really well who got killed. Sadly, I didn't have to wait very long until it happened again.'

Only five days, as it transpired. 'I started the Production 1300 TT at number 21, while my teammate Phil Mellor set off ahead of me at number 10,' Simpson explains. 'When I came round Doran's Bend on the second lap I saw that someone had crashed. I knew it was my teammate because the bits of bike were still recognisable, but I had no idea how badly hurt Mez might be. I tried not to look too closely, but the TT is so fast and the wreckage was strewn so widely that I feared the worst.'

Simpson carried on. 'I rode through the wreckage that was scattered all over the track because there was no red flag out to tell riders to stop,' he says. 'Twisted forks and snapped pieces of chassis, smashed bodywork, wiring, the fuel tank . . . it was horrendous. I already hated riding that big Suzuki round the TT course and my mind was now distracted, thinking, *Jesus, if Mez crashes out with all his experience and skills what hope have I got?* I remember thinking, *I don't like this. I really don't like this*, but I rode on.'

A few miles later, Simpson came upon another scene of carnage. 'I got round to Quarry Bends and it was absolute chaos,' he says. 'Three riders had crashed and there was wreckage all over the road. It looked like the aftermath of a plane crash – the track was absolutely covered in debris and Steve Henshaw was lying in the middle of the road in among it all. I could see that he was dead – there was no question in my mind. I had seen the wreckage of Phil Mellor's bike a few miles back at Doran's Bend but I hadn't seen Phil himself, so I still had at least some hope for him. But it was clear Steve had gone.'

Simpson's other teammate, James Whitham, had also crashed at the same corner. He too had witnessed the aftermath of Mellor's crash and was distracted by what he saw. His mind wasn't focused, and he smashed into the banking at Quarry Bends. 'It was sheer carnage,' Simpson recalls. 'You don't even want to know what it looked like. Mike Seward had gone down too: he suffered critical injuries but later recovered. There were no flags out but I saw Brian Morrison pulled over by the side of the road, so I stopped too. I asked Brian what the hell we could do to help. I've always looked to Brian to know what to do in situations, but there really wasn't anything we *could* do.'

Mercifully, Whitham was unhurt and was soon back on his feet, but with three bikes down, Quarry Bends looked like a bomb site. 'By the time I arrived on the scene there was just wreckage everywhere,' Simpson says. 'Stones and boulders and lumps of metal and plastic and wiring looms and bodies lying in the road . . . It was absolutely horrendous, and I'm still not sure that anyone knows exactly what happened that day.'

The race continued. Only Simpson and Brian Morrison pulled out. 'Brian was on an uncompetitive bike anyway and my GSX-R1100 was horrendous to ride round the TT course, so we just called it quits,' Simpson says. 'Dave Leach and Nick Jefferies and the other top boys were still riding flat out, and they negotiated the wreckage as best they could and carried on racing. I'd have done the same myself had my bike not been so bad.'

As Durex Suzuki team boss, Mick Grant was left to pick up the pieces following the death of his rider, Phil Mellor. 'There is a mechanism within the TT which is actually very good to cope with that sort of thing – unfortunately it's been very well rehearsed,' he says. 'From a team manager's point of view, suddenly I got a message that Mez had crashed and then, about ten minutes later, I got a message that James had crashed. You don't know how serious it is at that stage. As it happened, poor old Mez just made a riding mistake and, unfortunately, he paid for it. I think he was just diving up the inside of somebody and lost it. In my opinion, James fell off because he'd seen Mez's accident and I think he lost concentration.'

Phil Mellor and Steve Henshaw were two of the most popular riders in the UK at that time. Both lost their lives that day. 'It was terrible to lose Steve,' Simpson says. 'I'd known him for years and he'd been round to our house loads of times to visit my dad, who was really good friends with him, so it really was a personal loss. Same with Phil Mellor; I mean, he was my teammate, so we had spent so much time together and had become good friends as a result. I didn't find out he'd been killed until I got back to the paddock, and that was another devastating blow. With Phil Hogg having also been killed during practice week it meant that in the space of a few days I had lost three close pals. That tragic day became known as Black Wednesday at the TT. I was only 19 at the time so it was a lot to deal with, and I obviously had to question if I wanted to keep on doing what I was doing.'

Despite the horrors he had witnessed and the friends he

had lost, Simpon decided to continue racing, although he vowed not to return to the TT. It was a vow he would break. 'I knew I still loved motorbikes, and I knew I still wanted to race, but I decided not to go back to the TT,' he says. 'James Whitham made the same decision, and he never went back on it, but I found it much harder to keep my vow and would eventually return. But part of my love for the Isle of Man was definitely lost that day. It was a hell of a way to make my debut at the TT.'

As a means of self-defence, many road racers stay away from the funerals of other racers – it's the only way they can cope. 'It's a defence mechanism, and it's completely natural, even though it seems a bit callous,' Simpson says. 'Funerals are too harsh a reminder of the risks you're taking as a racer, and if you let that get into your head it can make things even more dangerous when you're on the bike. You need to be fully committed when you're racing or mistakes will happen, and going to funerals can affect that commitment. It's not out of disrespect that some riders avoid going to them, it's just self-preservation, but I went to all three of my friends' funerals in the aftermath of that TT.'

One week after the 1989 TT had ended under such a dark cloud, Ian Simpson was back out on a bike and racing again. Two months later he made his debut at the equally dangerous Ulster Grand Prix, saying, 'My vow to stop racing at the TT didn't extend to other road races, so I was still happy to race at the Ulster.'

Simpson would eventually win three TT races, including taking a Formula 1/Senior double for the Honda Britain team in 1998. His career was cut short in 2000 after he suffered hideous injuries at the relatively safe Brands Hatch circuit in England. He and James Whitham still go to the TT together every year as spectators.

Only a few of the top riders can ever hope to win a TT race in any given year, yet upwards of 60 riders usually take part in each race (these numbers used to be far higher but have been reduced for safety reasons in recent years). For those who have no hope of winning, they race for personal satisfaction – they have their own goals, whether it's a faster lap time than they achieved the previous year, a top-30 finish or just the achievement of making it to the finish line, which is no small achievement in itself given the demanding nature of the course and how punishing it is on machinery.

But for many of the top riders, the two weeks they spend on the Isle of Man represents their biggest pay packet of the year. As former TT racer Steve 'Stavros' Parrish points out, 'There's two sides to the TT: some riders genuinely want to race there, but at the same time it's where riders like Peter Hickman and Davey Todd make their wages for the year, so there's a financial incentive too.'

Parrish himself never went to the Isle of Man expecting to win but he did race there on and off between 1975 and 1986 despite the objections of his best friend Barry Sheene, who was a staunch critic of the event. 'I first did it in 1975, but I never really gelled with the TT course, to be honest,' Parrish says. 'And I was always getting earbashed by Barry not to go. "You're fucking mad, Stavros! Don't be such a twat!" But Barry had more money than I did and he had the ability to just say, "Fuck off – I'm not doing it." When I signed for Suzuki GB they wanted me to do the TT, so I did it in 1977 with Pat Hennen as my teammate. I could probably have said no but they were supplying all the bikes and parts, and I was getting paid to go, so I did.'

Not short of celebrity friends, Parrish was then talked out of going back to the TT the following year by former Beatle George Harrison. Harrison was Parrish's main sponsor for the 1978 season, and while he was happy enough for Parrish to ride at the North West 200 in 1978 (where he took two fourth places), he drew the line at the TT. 'George was of the same opinion as Barry Sheene about the TT,' Parrish says. 'He hated it, because he felt it was just too dangerous. But it was Sheeney who told George to tell me not to go there.'

Harrison's fears were not unjustified. At the 1978 TT, Parrish's Suzuki GB teammate from the previous year suffered a career-ending crash and very nearly lost his life. Pat Hennen was the first American rider to win a 500cc Grand Prix (Finland, 1976) and was battling Barry Sheene and Kenny Roberts for the 500cc Grand Prix world championship when he went to the TT in 1978. After becoming the first man to set a sub-20-minute lap of the course, he lost control of his Suzuki RG500 at Bishopscourt and suffered brain damage among other severe injuries. To this day, no one is entirely sure what happened as there were no eyewitnesses to the crash. Hennen was affected by the injuries he sustained right up until his passing in 2024.

As a regular in the Texaco Heron Suzuki garage at various Grands Prix, George Harrison would have known Hennen as well as Sheene and Parrish. He was devastated by Hennen's injuries and also by the loss of riders' lives at other race meetings in 1978, and withdrew his sponsorship of Parrish the following year. He had seen enough. 'At the end of the 1978 season I asked George if he might be able to sponsor me again the following year, but there had been about four or five riders killed that season and Pat Hennen had suffered life-changing injuries at the TT,' Parrish explains. 'George had clearly been thinking a lot about this, and he said, "Stavros, if you go and kill yourself with my money, I'd never be able to forgive myself." So he didn't want to be involved again in case something went wrong.'

Ironically, Hennen's exit from racing meant Parrish got his seat at the Texaco Heron Suzuki team and found himself back at the TT in 1979, but he was never prepared to push hard enough to challenge for wins. He went for the money and the fun of riding the circuit but wasn't prepared to risk everything to stand on the top step of the podium. Perhaps Sheene's constant badgering had paid off after all. 'I treated the TT with the utmost respect, most probably because I didn't want to die!' Parrish admits. 'So I wasn't one of those people who were hell-bent on winning a TT, but I wanted to go there and I'd usually finish about sixth or seventh. I probably never learned the course well enough to be able to use that extra yard out nearer the kerbs everywhere.'

The Isle of Man TT is by far the most famous road race of them all. It's known all over the world, even by those who have no interest in motorcycles or motorcycle racing, mostly because it is such an extreme event that seems at odds with every other sporting event on the planet. Football players do not die at Wembley if they miss a penalty, golfers don't die at Turnberry if they miss a putt, and cricketers are not fatally wounded should they be bowled out. The TT is more akin to gladiatorial combat – a vicious dance on the edge of existence, and in a world of ever-increasing anti-risk legislation it has never been more popular. It's a last bastion for the daring, a repository of the brave, and it offers thrills for both spectators and riders like no other sporting event on earth. It's real, and so are the consequences when things go wrong. But for every tragedy that plays out at the event there are a hundred triumphs, and perhaps none more emotional than that achieved by the Chrysalis team in the year 2000.

CHAPTER 6

A QUANTUM OF SOLACE

'I wanted to show people that you can still do incredible things after such a tragedy; that you can step up and do something good out of something so awful.'
NEIL MORRIS

There have been so many extreme highs and lows since the TT was first held over one hundred years ago, but few stories encapsulate both the triumphs and tragedies of motorcycle racing more powerfully and emotionally than that of the Morris family.

Dave Morris had won the Singles TT (for four-stroke single-cylinder machines up to 750cc) in 1997, 1998 and 1999, riding thoroughbred bikes he had built himself. A hugely gifted engineer, Morris's hand-built Chrysalis BMWs were as reliable as they were fast, and while other bikes regularly broke down around him at the TT, Morris's machines were almost bulletproof. He came to dominate the single-cylinder class, not only at the TT but also in the British championships together with his Chrysalis racing team.

'My dad was an accomplished engineer [he had worked at British Aerospace] as well as a very good rider, so the Singles class brought his two greatest strengths together as the technical rules were quite loose, so he had a lot of freedom in building his bikes,' says Dave's youngest son, Neil Morris. 'He was mechanically sympathetic and that helped, too, because the Singles TT was often a race of attrition – many of the bikes were fast but fragile.'

In September of 1999, Dave Morris wrapped up his second British Supermono Championship (another name for the Singles class) by winning the first leg of the day at Croft, so the second race should have been a more relaxed affair with no pressure and no drama. It wasn't. While out on his own, leading the race as the newly crowned British champion, Morris lost control of his Chrysalis BMW and was killed in the resultant crash. 'He won the first race, and with it the championship, then crashed in the second leg, and that was that,' Neil Morris says bluntly. 'Me and my brother Lee were usually at every race with my mum and dad but had got to an age where we had other responsibilities, so we weren't there for his final race.'

Ignorant of what had happened, and at a time when not everyone had a mobile phone, Neil only learned of his father's death when his girlfriend's mobile rang with the tragic news. 'I can remember sobbing by the door of my dad's garage the day I found out he had died,' he says. 'Because we weren't at the race we only had the recollections of other people about what happened – if we dared to ask, that is. My mum saw what happened, though, and I think that experience served to increase her difficulties with it. My dad had been leading the race; it was just a freak accident, with no one else involved.'

Heartbroken and shocked to her very core, Neil's mother Alison – who was team boss for the Chrysalis outfit, and every bit as committed to racing as her husband – died soon after.

'I think it's a bit of a given that my dad's death contributed to my mum dying six days later,' Neil says. 'She had developed a blood clot while flying back from Daytona four years earlier and was receiving treatment for that, so the coroner determined that was the cause of death, but my brother and I saw how hard she took our dad's death. They'd been together since they were teens and were absolute soulmates, so it's hard not to think that our dad's death contributed to our mum's death. Dad's funeral was planned by the time Mum passed away, so we had to rearrange things to ensure there was a joint funeral. Some arrived on the day still unaware Mum had passed. It was tough.'

Neil and Lee Morris – just 22 and 26 respectively at the time – had lost both of their parents inside a week. Emotionally destroyed and utterly bereft, the two brothers were desperate to do something to honour their parents – a tribute that would really mean something. 'My brother and I decided we wanted to defend our dad's title at the TT,' Neil says. 'It was hard enough losing Dad, and then Mum, but we both found it hard to think of someone else winning the Singles TT because our dad wasn't there to defend his title. We started making a list of possible riders and John McGuinness and Jason Griffiths were the top two. My brother and I were inundated with calls from people offering their condolences at that time, and one of them was Bob McMillan from Honda. He offered us whatever help we needed, so we asked if he could secure the services of John and Jason to ride for us at the TT, and he did [both riders were already contracted to teams for the other races at the TT, so special permission had to be sought to allow them to ride for the Morris brothers in the Singles race]. Both of them rode for free, too, because it was all about my mum and dad.'

Dave Morris had finished building his bike for the 2000 TT just a few months before his death, so that bike was used as part of the effort, and the brothers sourced out the building of a chassis for a second bike to long-time partners Harris Performance. They had a healthy supply of engines and spare parts, including Morris's handmade barrels, made from solid billet aluminium. 'It took Dad 400 hours to make each barrel, and he made four of them,' Neil says. 'If you wanted to talk to my dad, you'd do best to get down to the garage! He was always in there. Those barrels are works of art, though.' The boys would use their inheritance money to fund the project. 'The ACU paid out about £20,000 in insurance money, so we used that as our budget,' Neil explains.

The brothers decided to enter the bikes as AMDMs rather than BMWs. Although they used BMW F650 Funduro engines, the bikes had been built from scratch, so Neil and Lee were free to call them whatever they liked. They decided on using their parents' initials: Alison Morris and Dave Morris: AMDM.

Jason Griffiths and John McGuinness knew how

important the race was, and everything it stood for. They put their hearts and souls into riding the AMDMs throughout TT practice week. 'Jason was faster than John in practice, but come race day, John did what John does and attacked the course flat out while the other riders took time to get up to speed,' Neil says. 'That was John's trademark tactic – to break the other riders in the first half-lap.'

The race was held over four laps, meaning there would be a pit stop to refuel after the second lap – for most riders, anyway. John Barton's Ducati Supermono had two fuel tanks (perfectly legal within the loose regulations for the class) and did not need to stop. John McGuinness held a 50-second lead as he coasted into the pits at the end of lap two, and while his stop was slick and smooth (the team had practised endlessly to ensure it was), his bike failed to start once he was fuelled up. Neil Morris and chief mechanic Dave Bromfield pushed McGuinness all the way down pit lane before the bike fired into life. With Jason Griffiths having overtaken McGuinness with a quicker pit stop, McGuinness had to now give chase to his teammate as well as having to deal with John Barton, who had gained a significant time advantage by not needing to stop for fuel.

Because of their starting order on the road, and because McGuinness missed a gear coming out of Governor's Dip (the last corner on the course), the two teammates crossed the line together to start the final lap, providing photographers and TV camera crews with the hero shots they needed. Until he later learned about the missed gear change, Neil Morris thought his two riders had adjusted their speeds in order to cross the line together. They hadn't

– it had been a genuine mistake on McGuinness's part but it certainly looked like the planets were aligning and that the dream might just come true. Morris couldn't believe what he was seeing. 'They crossed the line side by side, which remains my favourite memory of that race to this day,' he says.

The last lap of the four-lap race was unbelievably tense, as McGuinness led with Griffiths in second place. A perfect one–two was on the cards in a race that meant everything to the Morris brothers. *Everything.* If only the bikes, built under such pain and duress, would hold together for one final lap of the most demanding racecourse in the world.

It's a tradition at the TT that a light appears on the scoreboard at the grandstand for each rider as they pass Signpost Corner, three miles from the end of the 37.73-mile lap. The idea is to alert teams that their rider is approaching so they can prepare themselves for a pit stop, should one be required. On the last lap of the race, John McGuinness's light failed to come on. This usually means the rider has broken down, or worse – crashed out of the race. The Morris brothers had no way of knowing what had become of McGuinness. The seconds ticked by with an agonising slowness, everything hanging in the balance. 'It was a bit of a nervous moment, especially with the commentary team stirring up the drama of it all, but you could hear those booming single-cylinder bikes from miles off, so we soon heard John, then finally saw him coming into view,' Neil says.

The light on the scoreboard had simply been faulty, and while it failed to illuminate, John McGuinness came into view as he crested the gentle rise that brings riders onto the start–finish straight. Closer and closer, faster and faster, McGuinness buried under the bodywork of the immaculate little single-cylinder bike, the throttle pinned to the stop, one of the greatest riders in TT history calling on all his years of experience, calling on everything he had, to deliver a win that he knew would make TT history, would capture the hearts of millions, and would stand as an eternal memorial to Dave and Alison Morris. Not least, he was fully aware, it would bring joy to the hearts of Neil and Lee Morris after they had endured nine months of unimaginable grief.

John McGuinness thundered over the finish line to rapturous applause and a standing ovation from those in the grandstand and hung his head in relief. He had done it, he had made the dream come true. But there was more to come. Just 48 seconds later, Welshman Jason Griffiths crossed the line in second place to give the Chrysalis team a perfect one–two. It was straight out of a Rocky movie, except it was real. It had actually happened.

The entire paddock erupted – even rival teams were caught up in the emotion of the occasion and were as thrilled for the Morris brothers as they would have been for a win by their own riders. Everyone knew the story; everyone knew what the boys had been through; it was not lost on anyone. Grown men were crying all around the circuit as they heard the news on the radio coverage of the event. Others shook their heads in disbelief at the courage of the Morris brothers and at the sheer beauty and poignancy of the victory. At the Isle of Man TT, every race win is important, but some are more important than others, and this ranked among the greatest – and certainly most meaningful – of all time.

Neil Morris was in an absolute daze. 'It was an incredible feeling when John crossed the finish line to win the race, with Jason in second place: a perfect one–two,' he says. 'Just amazing. We had some very close friends in that team who had been with us for years and we were all hugging each other. It was like a cheesy Hollywood movie. The whole paddock was rooting for us; people were crying . . . it was just incredible.'

As McGuinness pulled into the winners' enclosure he was elated at what he had managed to achieve for two friends who he knew had been through a living hell for the last nine months, and who would be affected by the loss of their parents for the rest of their lives. He had, at least, offered them some temporary relief and let some joy back into their lives, however briefly. He could not have given any more.

McGuinness revealed that the pit-stop drama had been his fault and that he'd forgotten to switch the ignition back on. But that aside, it had been a perfect race for him. 'Brilliant – the bike never missed a beat,' he said. 'Absolutely awesome. Just me cocking up the pit stop! It was the only drama in the race, though. The two boys asked me over the winter if I'd ride the bike and everyone [in his Honda team] agreed that I could. They provided me with the winning machine; the best thing I could do was bring it home.'

The McGuinness tradition of wearing knee sliders with the saltire flag of Scotland on them (despite being from Lancashire) began in that race. 'I'm not the most prepared person in the world and just before the Singles race I looked down and thought, *Fuck me! I've not got any knee sliders on!* I ran across to [Scottish rider] Jim Moodie's truck and asked him if he had any, and he laughed and gave me his ones with the Scottish flag on. I thought, *You cheeky bastard!,* but I won the race and have worn them ever since for good luck.'

It had been an emotional ride for McGuinness, as well as everyone else involved. 'As I came around on the last lap the emotion started building up,' he said. 'To be riding this bike in the memory of Dave and Alison meant a lot to me. I'm not sure I will ever feel so pleased to win a TT, having been asked to help in such a way.'

It was only when he went down to meet McGuinness and Griffiths that the enormity of the Chrysalis team's achievement finally struck home for Neil. 'We went down to the winners' enclosure and the world was spinning and everything was just a blur,' he says. 'I couldn't really focus on anything or anyone. And then I just started crying. Then my brother grabbed hold of me and hugged me, and that was the picture that made the newspapers.'

One of Jason Griffiths's crew, Tony Beaumont, witnessed the effect the perfect one–two had on the Morris brothers after so many months of heartache and desolation. 'I remember when McGuinness was spraying the champagne on the podium,' he said. 'Lee and Neil stood underneath, catching the spray. They looked genuinely happy. It was so great to witness that after all they had been through.'

For the Morris brothers, the result was infinitely better than any therapy or counselling, and the relief at having achieved what they had set out to do in their parents' honour was immense. 'When I broke down in the winners' enclosure, I think it was the relief, the hard work and the pain just washing out of me,' Neil says. 'Mission accomplished.'

The nine-month project helped bring the Morris brothers closer than ever. 'My brother and me were very different people and, while we never fought or fell out or anything like that, we had been going our separate ways in life until our mum and dad died,' Neil explains. 'Then the whole effort to run our dad's bikes in that race brought us much closer together. The emotion of that day – and in the weeks that followed with all the press attention – was quite hard to deal with.'

Neil Morris believes his parents would have been very proud of what he, his brother, the riders and the whole Chrysalis team achieved at the 2000 TT. 'I hope our mum and dad would have been extremely proud of what we achieved in their names,' he says. 'Racing made us a very close-knit family – it was the bond and the glue that stuck us all together. We never worried about the danger aspect of it, we just wanted to help our dad do the best job he could. It wasn't just about the result we achieved in 2000 – I think our mum and dad would have been very proud of the way we went about it; how professionally the team was turned out, how we worked through everything calmly, how we practised pit stops, how we promoted our effort at the time, and how we've done so since. So, yes, I think they would have been proud of the whole job.'

In the wake of losing both of their parents so suddenly, the TT project had provided a distraction for the Morris brothers; a focus, a motivation and a reason for carrying on. The very sport that had caused the initial tragedy also provided a therapy that money couldn't buy. 'That whole project played a massive part in the healing process,' Neil admits. 'It remains something that I'm extremely proud of to this day. I'm so glad we did what we did. I won't speak for my brother but, for me, there were two main reasons why I did it: first and foremost was as a tribute to our mum and dad, but I also wanted to show people that you can still do incredible things after such a tragedy; that you can step up and do something good out of something so awful.'

After their astonishing achievement, the Chrysalis team members had 'one hell of a night' in Douglas, the capital of the Isle of Man, to celebrate. The two brothers' accommodation for the fortnight was around five miles away, but they decided to walk back together. 'We'd had a fair bit to drink, and we were coming down from the high,' Neil remembers. 'We had an ill-advised burger and then we walked for ages. We didn't talk much. I'm not sure we needed to. There was a sense of closure that night; of contentment; of a job well done. I don't think we were ever closer, before or since.'

After the success at the 2000 TT, the Chrysalis team kept on racing for another few years. They scored success in the British and European Superstock championships, but the money eventually ran out, forcing Neil and Lee Morris to step away from racing. It proved to be incredibly tough for the brothers to deal with life without it. Even now, more than 20 years after withdrawing from the sport, Neil Morris struggles. 'It continues to be a gap in my life that I can't fill, and the former team members feel the same,' he says. 'Racing was a way of life for us – the paddock was our social life. My parents never went on holidays – they spent all their money on racing. My dad didn't drink much, either – racing was his whole life. It was all I had known since I was a kid, too; me and my brother were taken to race meetings every weekend when we were at school. It was our life, it was what we did and it's impossible to fill that gap. When you've been so involved in racing for so long it's hard to function without it.'

Unimaginable grief and a soaring triumph had strengthened the bond between Neil and Lee Morris, and their victorious defence of their father's title at the TT in 2000 had provided at least a small measure of closure: a quantum of solace. But then, 12 years later, in another hideously cruel twist of fate, tragedy struck again.

'My brother Lee died in 2012 at the age of 39,' Neil says. 'He had moved to Thailand and was settling into a new life with his partner and a baby daughter who was just about to turn one year old. I think he was finally managing to find a way to plug the massive gap left when we stopped racing. It looked like his life was starting to make sense again, but then he contracted pneumonia and passed away.'

Some 25 years after losing his parents and 13 years after losing his brother, Neil Morris understandably still struggles with his emotions and still seeks ways to come to terms with his family tragedy. 'To this day, my tastes are massively schizophrenic: I either watch comedies or tragedies on television,' he says. 'Comedies are cathartic and give me a distraction from the dark holes in the annals of my mind. The tragedies – whether movies or documentaries – remind me that other people have been through worse shit than what I've been through.'

The achievement that Neil Morris was such a huge part of remains one of the greatest in TT history. The event was cancelled in 2001 due to the foot-and-mouth outbreak in the UK, and when it returned in 2002 the Singles class had been dropped from the programme. It means that John McGuinness's victory in honour of Dave and Alison Morris will stand forever as the last Singles TT win.

'The memories of our 2000 TT will live long until I run out of marbles upstairs,' Neil says. 'A small recompense for our loss. As Lee said back in the day, "After Mum and Dad died, I heard people say they'd rather die than lose both parents. You think about it, and weigh it up, and think to yourself, *No, I'd give both arms to get them back, but I had 26 years of love and life with them, and for me that's worth 70 years with anyone else.*'

Neil Morris now runs the Honda motorcycle dealership in Blackpool and is happily married to his wife Caroline. They have two sons, James and Alex, both of whom, since infancy, have proudly sat on and played on the motorcycle which sits on the landing, halfway up the stairs of their house. It's the motorcycle that their grandfather built, that their grandma knew so well, and that their dad and uncle prepared for John McGuinness to ride to one of the most emotional and meaningful TT wins of all time.

CHAPTER 7

DON'T LOOK BACK IN ANGER

'I just started screaming – I knew straight away.'
LOUISE JEFFERIES

When he arrived on the Isle of Man for the 2003 TT, David Jefferies was the event's biggest star, and by far the fastest road racer on the planet. The cancellation of the 2001 TT due to the foot-and-mouth disease epidemic notwithstanding, Jefferies had taken three triples at the TT in 1999, 2000 and 2002 to give him a total of nine wins in just three events. He was the TT's apex predator and the first man to lap the course at an average speed of 125mph (then later 126mph and 127mph), yet his down-to-earth, laid-back attitude and his friendliness with the fans also made him one of the most popular TT racers of all time. But on the Thursday of practice week for the 2003 event he lost control of his TAS Suzuki at the fearsomely fast Crosby Corner. He was travelling at around 180mph.

Jefferies' close friend John McGuinness set off ten seconds after him on that fateful Thursday-night practice. 'At the start of the session we were just acting daft and wrestling each other to get out on the grid a bit earlier so we would get a clear track,' he says. 'David, obviously being bigger, wrestled me out of the way and went ten seconds in front of me. I think I set off with Martin Finnegan and everything was just normal; normal practice and flat out up towards Ballagarey, around Ballagarey, down the hill towards Crosby, and I then I saw a stationary yellow flag. I thought it was a bit odd and then I saw a waved yellow flag, but not like mega-waved. Out of the corner of my eye I saw a lass and she had turned her coat inside out. It had a red lining (an unofficial version of a red flag that would denote that a session has been stopped), and I could see the fear on her face, so I just eased it right off and came up to the corner at Crosby. I could see the black line where a rider had lost control of his bike and gone into the wall. I've never seen anything like it – it must have lifted a ton of stone and mortar out of the wall and pulled all that onto the road.'

Jefferies' TAS Suzuki teammate Adrian Archibald had set off before Jefferies, so McGuinness didn't know which of the two had crashed at that point. 'I didn't know who it was, I just slowed down, and it was really bizarre,' he says. 'There was a visor on the road and a seat unit which was totally untouched. It was unbelievable. The seat was like brand-new, with a big number 1 on it, and I knew then that it was David, and that there was no way he could have survived that. I just stopped in the road. My Ducati was still running, and I was like, *"Fuckin' hell"* – I was shocked.'

The scene that greeted McGuinness was one of utter chaos and destruction. 'There was no way through,' he says. 'You couldn't get through because the bike had hit a telegraph pole and brought it down. All the wires were stretched across the road, so I was stopped. I was still shocked, and I put my bike against the wall and switched it off. I could then hear other riders approaching. A few had stopped but Jim Moodie obviously wasn't going to. That was horrific: I thought Jim was going to be decapitated. I was stood there, and he came round the corner and frightened me to death, bouncing over rocks and stones and all these bits of bodywork, and he went through it all and snapped the telegraph cables with his neck and chest.'

But amid the carnage, McGuinness testifies that David Jefferies was at peace. 'You hear all these stories about how David's boot fell off and all this shit, but it really is a load of shite,' he says. 'Dave were, like . . . as if someone had laid him on the road perfectly still; his legs and arms neatly alongside him. He was gone, but there was no way he was suffering. He was just finished. It was peaceful really, you know? It was weird. The noises and smells through it all, it was really strange. You know if you knock a wall down you have that smell? That dusty smell, and fibreglass and oil smells? Weird. It was the most horrible experience I've ever had in my life.'

*

David Jefferies was from a racing family. His grandfather Allan had raced at the TT, his uncle Nick had won the Formula 1 TT in 1993, and his father Tony was a three-time winner in the early 1970s before a crash at Mallory Park in 1973 left him paralysed from the chest down and confined to a wheelchair.

Despite the whole Jefferies family being fully aware of the risks of racing – and road racing in particular – they were all supportive of 'DJ' when he decided to do the TT for the first time in 1996. David Jefferies had raced in British Superbikes, World Superbikes and 500cc Grands Prix, so he had vast amounts of experience to call on when he first took to the 37.73-mile TT course, and because of this, his family was not unduly concerned about him racing at the event.

'We were all pretty cool with it,' says David's younger sister, Louise. 'We had always said it was his decision, whether he wanted to do it or not. I remember when Mark Farmer got killed at the TT in 1994 and David was quite close to Mark and he said, "That's it – I'm never going to race there." But he had a really good North West 200 in 1996 and he decided he liked racing on the roads, so he was going to have a go at the TT. As a family, we all said, "Well, if that's what you want to do, we'll support you all the way." But we also told him that if he went there and didn't like it he should park the bike up and we would all go home.'

He did like it, immensely, and by 1999 David Jefferies was the TT's biggest star and fastest rider but was still riding well within himself, according to Louise. 'I was never nervous watching David at the TT,' she says. 'He always rode pretty much within his limits; he was always fairly sensible about it. No one put any pressure on him to do it, so we didn't worry about him. Obviously we were aware of

Left: Dave and Alison Morris.

© Courtesy of the Morris family collection

Below: David Jefferies taking sister Louise for a spin round the garden in 1982.

© Courtesy of the Jefferies family collection

Cookstown 100, 2018.

© Actions Plus Sports/Alamy

Ian Lougher, TT 2007.

© Ian Walton/Getty

John McGuinness, TT 2007.

© Ian Walton/Getty

Joey Dunlop, TT 1996. *© Michael Cooper/Getty*

Michael Dunlop before the TT 2016. *© Linden Adams/Getty*

Lee Johnston clips the kerb at the North West 200, 2018.

© Stephen Davison

Alastair Seeley, Michael Dunlop and Dean Harrison carving their way round Metropole, 2002, North West 200.

© Martyn Bond/Alamy

Steve Mercer during the final qualifying session for the 2009 Macau Grand Prix.

© Stephen Davison

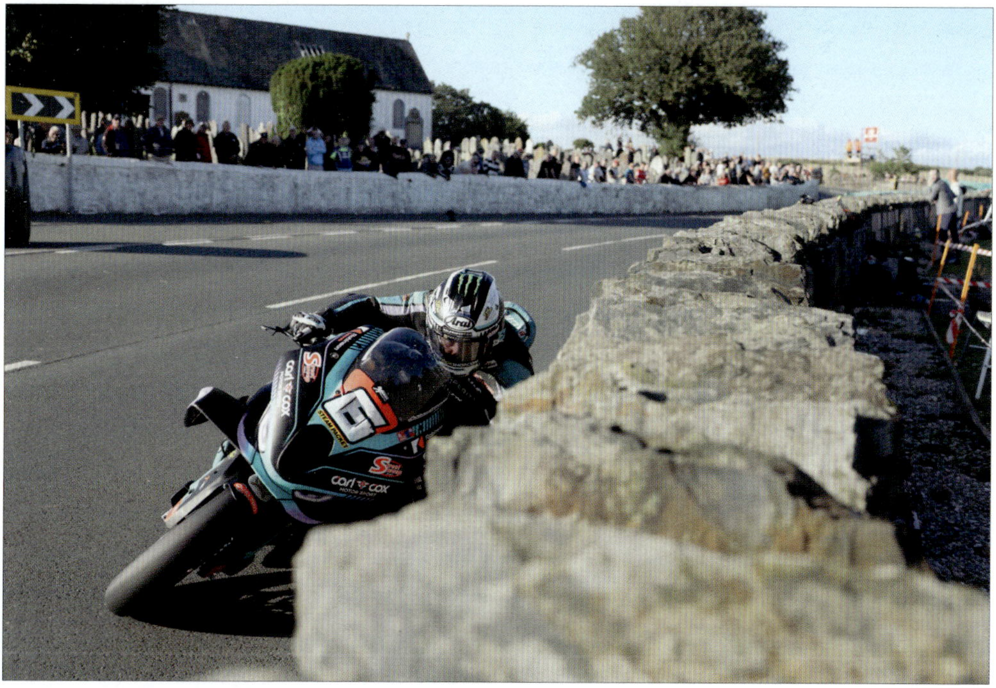

Michael Dunlop rounds Church Bends at the Southern 100, 2025.

© Courtesy of the Morris family collection

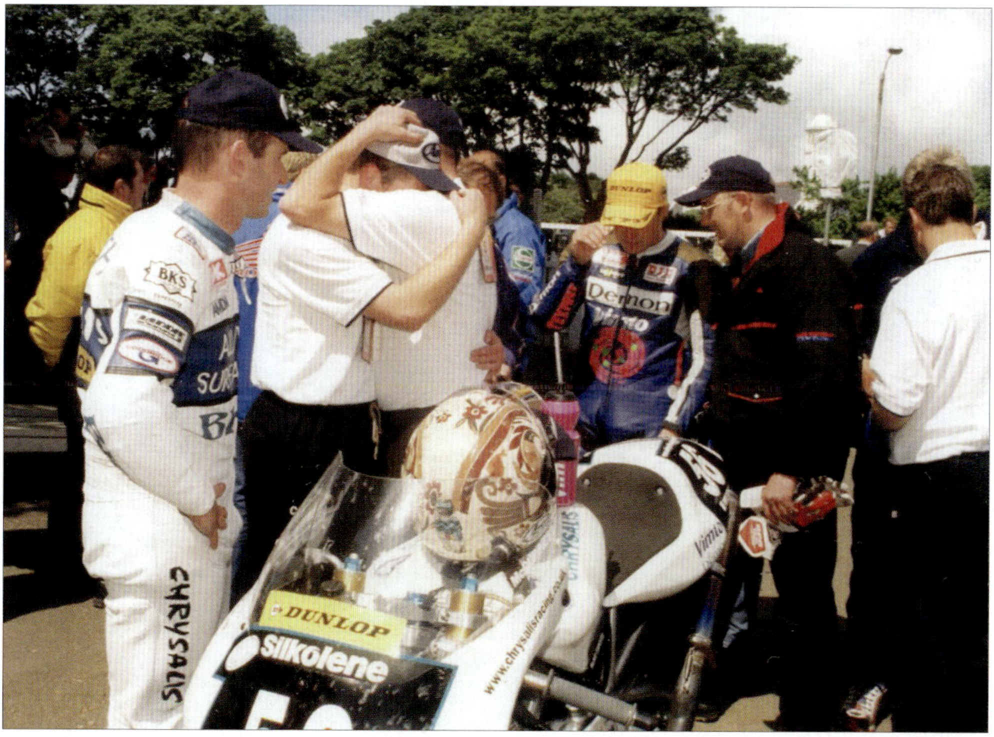

Neil and Lee Morris hug after their incredible achievement at the 2000 TT.

© Courtesy of the Morris family collection

Guy Martin suffered serious injuries when his bike exploded into flames at the 2010 Isle of Man TT. *© Sean Sayers*

John McGuiness leads David Johnson, Coner Cummins and Michael Dunlop over the mountain section, TT, 2016. *© Linden Adams/Getty*

Riders take the Melco hairpin at the start of the 57th Macau Motorcycle Grand Prix in Macau, 2025.

© Peter Parks/AFP/Getty

Guy Martin leads Paul Cranston at Tandragee 100, 2004.

© Radharc Images/Alamy

Joey Dunlop chasing down Shaun Harris, Isle of Man TT 1996.

© Michael Cooper/Allsport/Getty

Stuart Easton, 2014.

© Nigel French/PA Images/Alamy

Michael Sweeney,
Cookstown 100, 2022.

© Derek Wilson/Alamy

Steve Mercer with his
new Honda Fireblade.

*© Courtesy of the Mercer family
collection*

the risks, just as David was. He would have openly said to you, "If owt goes wrong, I'll come home in a box."'

While most TT racers admit that sitting astride their bikes on the starting grid is nothing short of terrifying, Jefferies could always be seen laughing and joking, apparently without a care in the world. It was part of what made him so popular. 'He was never nervous before a TT race,' Louise confirms. 'I remember Neil Hodgson [former World Superbike and British Superbike champion] always asking him how come he wasn't nervous – he couldn't get his head around it! But David was like, "Well, I'm just off to ride my bike." Once he started posting 125mph laps, and then 126mph and 127mph, everybody was wondering just how fast he could go, but he never let that get to him either.'

Jefferies was puzzled by the high regard he was held in. He saw himself as an ordinary bloke who rode motorbikes, nothing more, nothing less, so he sometimes struggled to accept the adulation that came his way. 'He never, ever changed, and never thought he was anything special at all,' Louise says. 'I remember when he had won at the TT in 2002, and Suzuki took us all out for a meal. I nipped off to go to the loo and I remember finding David leaning against a cigarette machine with a bit of a quivering lip. I asked what was up with him and he said, "I don't get it. There are people in there, like Colin Appleyard [former mechanic for David's grandfather Allan Jefferies, and later one of the most famous bike dealers and race sponsors in the UK], that I've looked up to all my life, and they're trying to say that I'm some sort of hero, but I'm not – I'm just some bloke that rides a bike." He never got it. He never knew how much he meant to people and never thought he was anything special. He used to say he was only ever confident when he had a bike between his legs.'

Born and raised in Shipley, West Yorkshire, David Jefferies was as grounded as they come, and completely lacking in ego, despite his TT superstar status. The fans loved him for it. 'David became so popular, and I think that's just because of who he was as a person,' Louise says. 'He was very straightforward and very down to earth, and as a family we made sure he stayed that way. I remember him once sulking and throwing his helmet on the floor on live television, and when my dad got back to the paddock he said, "Right, you best go and wash my car to bring yourself back down to earth. Who do you think you are, you little shit!" He was so talented, but he was also just DJ, doing what he wanted to do, and we supported him in that. Would he have been the same bloke if he'd been a postman? No, probably not.'

Despite the slight slip with the helmet temper tantrum, Jefferies took everything in his stride, even TT wins. There was no gushing emotion or adrenaline-fuelled bravado after a race, just a big smile and an understatement or two. 'He never got excited, even after taking a TT win,' Louise says. 'He'd take his helmet off and just say, "Yip, that was pretty good, that – I enjoyed that."'

On 29th May, 2003, Louise Jefferies was with her father Tony at a BMW conference in Savile Row, London. The family dealership (Allan Jefferies Motorcycles, which was run by Louise for many years after her dad retired) was up for a 'Dealer of the Year' award. The plan was to drive from London to Liverpool after the conference to catch a ferry to the Isle of Man to join David and his mum, Pauline, for TT race week. Yet there was an odd atmosphere, Louise remembers; something just didn't feel quite right. 'It was all a bit weird, because I had dreamed of David's funeral the week before, and just before my mum left to go to the Isle of Man with David for practice week, she said, "I don't think this is going to be good." There was just a bit of a weird feeling. I remember he broke down during practice for the Production race. We didn't know he had broken down at the time – we only knew that he hadn't come round to complete the lap – and when I saw my mum was calling me, I thought, *I don't want to answer that*. I mean, obviously I did, but all she said was, "He's okay", then put the phone down on me. She just wanted us to know he was okay.'

As the conference dragged on, Louise started looking at her watch, impatient to get going. 'I said to my dad, "Come on, come on – I want to get to Liverpool to catch the ferry," but Dad was like, "Shut up – I want to enjoy my free lunch."' A Yorkshireman through and through, Tony Jefferies enjoyed a free lunch more than most, and he was completely relaxed and looking forward to another TT. Then everything changed.

'My dad took a phone call, and I remember looking at him as he said, "I've got to go now, because I have to tell Loubie," and I just started screaming. I knew straight away. He said, "Shut up, you. Sit down. Be quiet. Don't behave like that in public."'

Tony Jefferies had lost many friends to racing, and he himself had had to mentally deal with being confined to a wheelchair at the age of 25. He was made of strong stuff, and was a good man in a crisis, even when that crisis involved his own son.

Time was now of the essence, so the drive to Liverpool and the lengthy ferry crossing was off the cards. Louise made the next move. 'I had to ring my best friend, Dawn Brown – who I used to work with as a travel agent – and I told her that David had been killed and that me and my dad needed a flight out of London, and we needed one *now!* I told her she couldn't tell anyone what had happened, because some of the family hadn't been informed yet. Dawn was great, and called back within half an hour saying she'd managed to get us a flight out of London City Airport. The plane had been held up for us, and people had been booted off it to make room for us.'

It was during the short flight that Tony Jefferies revealed what he was truly made of, how mentally strong he was, and how much he loved his daughter and wanted to protect her. 'My dad asked if I wanted a drink, but I didn't, because I just felt sick,' Louise says. 'You feel so sick and don't know what the hell to do with yourself – you can't comprehend what's going on. Anyway, he made me have a glass of wine and then said, "Right, you, I want you to promise me something; I want you to promise me you won't waste your life wanting to change something you cannot change, because it will make you bitter." It was the most profound sentence anyone had ever said to me in my life, and it still gets me to this day. I looked at my dad and thought, *You're 55. You were 25 when you got paralysed and could no longer walk, and now you've just lost your son and you're telling me that? I really do need to get a grip.* His experience had changed his outlook on life, but he was always, always an optimist, and he never ever moaned about what had happened to him.'

Jim Moodie was a family friend, and very close to David, but Tony and Louise still had no idea if he was alive or dead. 'When we were on the flight, we didn't know if Jim had survived the incident or not,' Louise says. 'When we got to Ronaldsway Airport on the Isle of Man, Becky McGuinness [wife of TT star John McGuinness] came to meet us, which I thought was incredibly brave of her. She told me straight away that Jim was okay – that he'd survived it – so that was a big relief.'

Then came the hardest part of all; the thing that no parent or sibling should ever have to go through. 'From the airport, we went to the house where my mum was staying, picked her up, then went to identify David's body,' Louise explains. 'That was fairly traumatic, as I'm sure you can imagine. There wasn't a mark on him, though; he was just laid there in his leathers, without a mark on him. Oddly, I remember checking his teeth, because he had just paid five grand to have them fixed, but they were alright. My dad couldn't get that close to him because of the wheelchair, so we got David's hand out from underneath the shroud and placed it in my dad's hand. We then all put our hands on David's hand and said the Lord's Prayer. I went to bits at that point and had to go outside. There's nothing more final than death, and there's absolutely nothing you can do about it.'

When tragedies occur in road racing, the riders, teams, fans and the entire road-racing community immediately rally like a protective herd around the bereaved. They are the only people who understand, the only people who don't judge, the only people who are capable of offering the comfort and support needed to help put heartbroken families back together again. The outpouring of grief over David Jefferies' loss was overwhelming. In 2004, upwards of 5,000 riders completed a tribute lap to him around his beloved Isle of Man TT course. It was led by Louise Jefferies (with her mum riding pillion) and David's great friend John McGuinness. The cavalcade of bikes was so great that it almost reached around the entire 37.73-miles of the course.

'The tribute lap and all the support we got from people helped massively,' Louise says. 'I've still got the massive wooden chest my mum had made that contains all the cards and letters and video clips that people sent to us. I mean, there were more than 5,000 people at his funeral. David would never have believed that. Never. Even Colin McRae came to the funeral, which touched my dad a lot.'

That support hasn't wavered over the years. 'I still get so much support,' Louise says. 'I still go to race meetings and I still meet up with the girls who helped me so much at that time: Louisa Duffus, Miriem Moodie, Becky McGuinness, Charlotte Pullen, Fay Pullen, Sarah Moore . . . We still have weekends away together. Those girls are like family to me now, and that will never, ever change.'

Like most families bereaved by road racing, the Jefferies never turned their backs on the sport or blamed it for David's death. They never became bitter. On the contrary, when David's teammates and team offered to pull out of the TT in the aftermath of David's death as a mark of respect it was his mum Pauline who insisted they carry on and try to win a race for her boy. 'She said, "Don't you dare pull out on our behalf – get on with it,"' Louise says. 'We all felt the same. Me and my dad left the Isle of Man before the racing started, because I don't think we could have faced it at the time. But on the night David died we all stayed at the Sefton Hotel on the Isle of Man and Jim and Miriem Moodie came down, as did John and Becky McGuinness, and we had some drinks in the bar. I remember Neil Hodgson phoned me from wherever he was racing in World Superbikes. He told me he didn't want to race after what had happened, but I said, "Don't you dare be so ridiculous. David wouldn't want you to do that – he'd want you to get on with it, so get on with it." It turned out to be the only round where the podium was filled with British riders, and they all wore black armbands for DJ. So, yes, people were amazing, and they still are, more than 20 years on. DJ is still held in very high regard, which absolutely astounds me, to be honest.'

Neil Hodgson did race on and won the World Superbike Championship that year, no doubt with thoughts of his old friend in mind as he crossed the line at Assen to secure the world title.

Pauline Jefferies sadly passed away in 2008, five years after her son's death, almost to the day. Tony Jefferies died in 2021 after a lengthy illness, but Louise Jefferies speaks for all the family when she says, 'You can't choose to support somebody in something, and be part of it, and take so much from it, and get so much enjoyment out of it, and agree with it, and then change your mind when it all goes wrong. That would be the most hypocritical thing in the world. Becky McGuinness called me to tell me we had lost Owen

Jenner and Craig Richardson at Oulton Park in 2025, and I remember thinking, *God, I love motorbikes, but I also bloody* hate *them at times.*'

Louise Jefferies has been back to the TT three times since she lost her brother: once for the tribute lap in 2004, once in 2008 just after losing her mother (Tony, Pauline and Louise had all planned to go together, so following Pauline's death, father and daughter honoured the engagement), and once in 2024, that time just for fun. 'I had a great time,' she says. 'It was really good, and everybody came up to have a chat. Phillip McCallen got me tickets for hospitality, Steve Plater came to say hello, as did Maria Costello . . . lots of riders. Everybody was just incredible, and to think I was just DJ's hang-on little sister!'

Louise has also taken some comfort in the safety improvements that have been made at the TT since her brother's death. 'One good thing that came out of David's accident was improved safety measures at the TT,' she says. 'There were all sorts of different versions of what actually happened in David's crash, and we thought long and hard about whether to pursue any kind of legal action. In the end we decided that if David had had children that would have been different because they would have needed compensation to live on. But we realised a court case could dominate the next ten years of our lives and it still wouldn't have changed anything. The one thing we did insist on was that marshalling standards and overall safety were improved, and they have improved dramatically since then. That was incredibly important to us because we don't want anybody else to go through what we went through.'

Sadly, others have, and will no doubt continue to do so, such is the nature of road racing. But there's no telling how many lives the improved safety measures brought in after David Jefferies' death have saved.

Louise's son Thomas is 16 and has now taken up riding enduro bikes. He has, by all accounts, taken to motorcycling like a natural, just like his Uncle David. The story of the great Jefferies racing dynasty may not be over yet.

The unapologetic lines on David Jefferies' gravestone read:

Those who risk nothing,
Do nothing,
Achieve nothing, become nothing

CHAPTER 8

THE MOUTH OF THE WOLF

*'When they told me he had a high spinal
injury, I threw up.'*
CAROLINE MERCER

For Steve Mercer, road racing was love at first sight. He had been racing on short circuits since 2003, but when his MSS Kawasaki teammate Stuart Easton suggested a trip over to the Isle of Man to watch the Manx Grand Prix in 2008, Mercer was blown away by what he saw. 'I stood at the bottom of Bray Hill, and as soon as the first bikes came past it just blew my mind, and I thought, *My God – this is where it's at!* and I knew I had to do it.'

The following year, Mercer took part in his first TT and became hopelessly addicted. 'It's really hard to explain what it feels like to ride a bike flat out around the TT course,' he says. 'It gave me a sense of freedom – just pure freedom. When I was lined up on the grid for the first time, I had a voice in my head, saying, *What are you doing? What are you doing?*, but another voice would say, *Shut up –*

this is what I want to do. But, as soon as I got the tap on the shoulder [from the start line official, meaning it was time to go], it was almost as if I was completely at peace; everything went quiet, and it was just me and the bike, trying to hit every braking marker and every apex for the whole race, so in a strange way there was something quite peaceful about it. There was no time to worry about anything else, you had to just concentrate fully on riding the circuit, and that gave me a sense of pure freedom that I've never been able to find in any other way.'

After so many years of racing on short circuits, the sustained high speeds of the TT took some getting used to. On parts of the course, riders hold their bikes flat out in top gear for *minutes* on end. For Mercer, it was a thrill like no other. 'The sense of speed is much greater than you'd ever experience on a short circuit,' he says. 'The first night of practice used to always blow my mind, and I would wonder how the hell I was ever going to ride round at that pace for two weeks. But the more laps I did, the more I would get acclimatised to the speed, so although I was getting the sensation of speed, and was aware of how fast I was going, things started slowing down for me mentally, and I could process much more. When you watch a TT race from the side of the road it looks absolutely ridiculous, but when you're actually on the bike and your mind is up to speed you really can start processing stuff a lot easier, and you sort of forget about just how fast you're going – you're just joining the dots and enjoying the ride.'

Over the ensuing years, Mercer would take two eighth and two tenth places at the TT, a fourth at the Classic

TT, and a win at the Spring Cup at Oliver's Mount in Scarborough in 2012. He also raced at the North West 200, and finished in the top ten at the Ulster Grand Prix, the Macau Grand Prix, the Armoy road races and the Southern 100. He was a dyed-in-the-wool road racer, but in 2017 all that changed.

'I rode for RC Express Racing at the TT in 2017,' Mercer says. 'It was a real shame, but things didn't work out as I just couldn't get the bike to work for my riding style. I crashed at the 11th Milestone – I hit the wall but skimmed off it and went skidding down the middle of the road. The next evening, Dutch rider Jochem van den Hoek had the same crash at the same place, but he hit the wall and got killed. When I went back to the corner and looked at the road surface I could see that the black lines left by Jochem's bike were only about a foot away from the black lines my bike had left, and I thought, *Maybe it's time to not do this anymore.*

'I kept riding through the rest of the 2017 TT, even though I was knocked about and had broken some ribs in an earlier crash on my enduro bike – which I didn't discover until I was X-rayed in hospital – but it was a difficult fortnight, and I decided to pack it in. Maybe I should have waited for a few months to see how I felt, but I announced soon after the TT that I was quitting road racing. I was done.'

Road racing, however, is a notoriously difficult sport to walk away from – riders become so addicted to the thrill that it's as hard to quit as a heroin habit. 'Road racing *is* an addiction, it's a drug, and come January of 2018

I regretted what I had said because I wanted to race at the TT again,' Mercer says of his about-turn. 'I had kept in contact with Jonny Twelvetrees from Honda racing. In 2016 I had ridden for the official Honda Superstock Team – Jackson Racing – in the World Endurance Championship, with John McGuinness and Conor Cummins as teammates, and I also rode Hondas for Jackson Racing at the TT. So I spoke to Jonny, and he explained that Honda had built a Superstock bike for Ian Hutchinson for the 2018 TT but he wasn't sure if Ian would be fit enough to ride, so I said I would ride the bike if Ian couldn't. As it turned out, Hutchy was able to ride at the TT, so Honda supplied a bike for me to ride under the Jackson Racing umbrella. Unfortunately, things didn't turn out as we'd hoped.'

It was a sliding-doors moment. Had Mercer stuck to his decision to walk away from road racing, then what happened next may never have happened at all. 'That decision does haunt me a little bit,' he admits. 'It was a decision that changed my life forever. But doing the TT is such an addiction, I just couldn't say no.'

There's an Italian expression *'In bocca al lupo'* which is used to wish someone good luck when they attempt something difficult, challenging or dangerous. It's similar to the English expression 'break a leg'. Directly translated, *'In bocca al lupo'* means 'Into the mouth of the wolf'. When Steve Mercer had his head-on collision with an official car on the TT course, he entered the mouth of the wolf. Surviving such a savage encounter was by no means a given, and the fight for his life began immediately.

Following the collision, Mercer was taken by helicopter

to Noble's Hospital on the Isle of Man, but despite the extensive experience of the surgeons and specialists there (the hospital had dealt with countless TT trauma injuries), Mercer's condition was too severe, and he had to be flown to Aintree University Hospital in Liverpool, a specialised centre for severe trauma cases.

Mercer's wife Caroline now has to take up the story, as her husband was unconscious at this time. 'They put Steve into an induced coma at Noble's Hospital that night and they told me that he had a high spinal injury and could only communicate by blinking. The authorities kept the Isle of Man airport open after its usual closing time and flew Steve to Liverpool that night. I then had a choice of whether to go with him or to stay with our kids on the Isle of Man. I stayed with the kids and then we all flew over at 5am the next day.'

Caroline Mercer was going to have to be every bit as strong as her husband if they were both going to get through what lay ahead. The news of her husband's injuries shocked her to the very core. 'When they told me he had a high spinal injury, I threw up,' she says. 'That was our worst nightmare, and it was the injury they were most concerned about at the time. When we got to Aintree, I was told that Steve had been very lucky and that he might make a full recovery, because they didn't appreciate the extent of his injuries at that point. Over the course of the next few days he could move his hands a little bit, but as the bruising on his brain started getting worse he literally couldn't do anything. Those first few days were really quite tricky, because Steve was completely locked inside his own body. I was told by one doctor that he was locked in, and could only blink, and that's all he would ever be able to do.'

The future looked desperately bleak for Mercer. And as the days passed, specialists began to realise the full extent of his injuries. 'After a few days they brought him out of the induced coma, and he was in a real mess,' Caroline Mercer says. 'He'd lost ten centimetres off his femur, so they needed to rebuild that. But, I mean, apart from the crash itself, all the stars aligned afterwards, because the pelvis surgeon was on call that night, so he put Steve's pelvis back together within a matter of hours. Lots of little coincidences like that happened during this period and it made a huge difference. Since initially being told that he would be permanently paralysed from the neck down, we were so grateful for every tiny improvement after that. It's like we hit rock bottom right at the beginning, so the only way was up. I remember at one point telling him that the surgeons couldn't do any more, so it was all down to him now – I told him that he had to fight.'

And fight he did. He may have been trapped inside his own body, but Steve Mercer's spirit was unbroken, his determination intact.

'When I came into the hospital the next day, he gave me the tiniest of a thumbs up, which was like the biggest thing in the world to me,' Caroline says. 'He could only just move his hand, but he managed to give me a thumbs up. At that point I thought, *This is fantastic! We can get him a wheelchair that he can control with a joystick, so at least he'll have some mobility.* Then, as the brainstem bruising started reducing, his arms started working a bit more, and with every little improvement we were just so grateful. We had faced the worst-case scenario in the early days and now things were gradually starting to improve. My mum was great in looking after the kids so that I could focus on being with Steve, so that really helped too.'

Even at the lowest point, when he could do nothing more than blink, Mercer was aware of everything that was going on around him, and some of what he heard was terrifying. 'I was conscious throughout, and it was quite bizarre, because at one point some of the doctors thought I was dead – they thought I was completely brain-dead. I could hear them talking, and I desperately wanted to tell them that I was conscious, and I could hear them talking, but I couldn't speak, and I couldn't see properly because I had hit my head so hard in the crash and had really bad double vision. I also couldn't – and still can't – control my body temperature due to the brain injury, so they had to put me in a water jacket and pump cold water around me to keep me cool. I couldn't move, either, but my brain was still functioning. I had a brain scan, and when the specialists looked at the data they couldn't believe that my brain was still working – I had bleeds and shearing all over the brain, so it was quite a miracle, really. So when Caroline told me the surgeons had basically given up on me and that it was down to me to fight now, I thought I had best pull my finger out.'

Mercer had still not been made fully aware of the extent of his injuries, and when he was finally told, they were so severe that he felt the specialists must be mistaken. 'There was one surgeon who told me something that made me really angry, because I didn't believe him,' Mercer says.

'He sat down next to me and told me that I was in quite bad shape but that I might recover. He then told me that he had put Conor Cummins back together after his massive TT crash in 2010. I don't like saying this, because I don't want to downplay Conor's injuries – we all know how bad they were – but this surgeon told me that my injuries made it look like Conor had only scratched himself. I looked at him and thought, *You have to be lying! You* have *to be lying!* I knew how badly Conor had been beaten up, and I thought I surely couldn't be as bad as that. But as time went on, and I learned the extent of my injuries, I realised how bad things were. It wasn't just my broken back and my shattered leg, I also had a brain injury and so many other complications.'

Conor Cummins had been very lucky to escape with his life and make a full return to racing following his massive crash on the Verandah at the 2010 TT. His injuries, as Mercer knew full well, were devastating. 'I broke my back in five places,' Cummins says. 'There were four stable fractures of the vertebrae and one unstable fracture, which they called a burst fracture, which meant it had completely come away. I also dislocated my leg and utterly destroyed my knee, including all the ligaments and tendons [Cummins now has donor tendons in his reconstructed knee]. I broke my upper arm in four places and suffered nerve palsy in it, too, so I lost the use of my left hand. And I fractured my pelvis, which is the biggest bone in the body, and my left shoulder blade. I also suffered bruising to my lungs. So it was my back, my leg, my arm, my pelvis, my shoulder blade and my lungs.'

And now Mercer was being told he had suffered even worse injuries. It seemed impossible that anyone could still be alive having undergone such drastic trauma. The full list of his injuries almost defies belief:

Broken larynx and paralysed vocal cord
Open-book pelvic fracture
Punctured lung
Broken ribs (Mercer doesn't even know how many)
Diffuse axonal injury midbrain – bruising of brainstem, causing temporary paralysis from the neck down, and shearing all over the brain
Damage to spine at C2/3, T4/5, T5–T8 and burst T11
Severe lumbosacral plexus lesion
Lumbosacral arachnoiditis
Left testicle died – starved of blood
Open fracture right femur, resulting in 10cm
    shortening of right leg
Compound fracture of right heel
Right ankle fracture
Multiple right and left knee injuries
Four broken teeth
Acute kidney injury

While teams of specialists did everything in their powers to save Mercer's life, his own inner battle was just as crucial – his positive mental attitude, his determination and his resolve to win through became everything. These are traits shared by all road racers, and no doubt helped him pull through even the darkest moments. While many others might have given up, Mercer resolved from the very outset that he wouldn't be one of them. What drove him through it all was his passion to get back on a bike again; to race again. 'I fought, right from the start, but I was really deluded; I thought I could be riding again by Christmas,' he says. 'I really didn't quite understand how injured I was, so in a way, that kept me going. But then Christmas came [seven months after the accident], and I still wasn't fixed, so I thought, *Well, I'll be okay in another few months*, but another few months came and went, and I wasn't. Gradually over the years I learned to accept that I wouldn't race again.'

And yet the lowest point was still to come. Having been treated in four different specialist hospitals in Liverpool over a five-month period, Mercer was then transferred to King's College Hospital in London and spent a further month there before realising it was not the place for him to heal, mentally at least. 'That's where I had my lowest point, and I actually discharged myself from King's,' he says. 'The nurses in Liverpool couldn't do enough for me – they were absolutely amazing – but when I arrived in London, they didn't know where to put me, so they put me in a major trauma ward and almost every person in that ward had either been shot or stabbed. Because I was still getting morphine and lots of strong painkillers, and was still a bit out of it, it made me really anxious, and I couldn't take it anymore, so I said to Caroline that I was going home.'

After all he had been through and knowing that he would be using a wheelchair for the rest of his life, Mercer was not given one; another sign of just how overwhelmed the capital is in terms of sheer numbers and budgets.

'We had to borrow a wheelchair from Caroline's nan because they wouldn't give me a wheelchair,' Mercer says. 'It seems they don't give you wheelchairs in London hospitals.' [In point of correction, wheelchairs *are* available, but they must be paid for or rented.] 'Anyway, like I said, I borrowed one and went home to Maidstone, but I didn't realise just how ill I still was, so looking back it was probably a bit naughty. Caroline had our two boys to look after and she had me to look after, and I couldn't even get out of bed. My weight was down to 8.3 stone (53kg), whereas I had been 11.8 stone (75kg) before the accident. There was nothing of me – I was completely malnourished. I couldn't even sit up in bed, so yeah, I was quite beaten up.'

Over the next few years, Mercer continued to make progress, though he still faces a battle every single day. 'The medication is a real pain, but I still have to take it because I have so much spinal damage and get loads of nerve pain. I don't want to take all those painkillers; I just want to be me, but, unfortunately, I can't be. If I don't take the medication then my life's going to be more difficult. All the injuries are still there – I still have to live with them all, and I'm still in constant pain. When I post things on social media I don't want to be negative, and I'm not looking for sympathy, so I try to stay positive; but, yes, I am always in pain. Always. Every day.'

There was another kind of pain to deal with in 2019. Daley Mathison had stopped to attend to Mercer after his crash. He had held his friend's mangled right leg, trying to stop the blood pumping out of the ruptured femoral artery. Mathison – a hugely popular rider in his own right – lost his life at the 2019 TT. His daughter Daisy, just three years old at the time of her father's fatal accident, has since written a book (*Hugsy Brightheart and the Missing Star*) with a view to helping other bereaved children to cope with their grief.

Steve Mercer has since settled his claim against the TT organisers out of court for an undisclosed sum.

Aside from the horrendous physical injuries Mercer suffered, not being able to race again has been another kind of torture for him: a mental torture. 'I've ridden motorbikes since I was a little boy, and when I look back to before the accident it's almost like I'm looking back on a different life. It seems like yesterday, but it also seems like forever ago. Anyone who rides a bike would be gutted if someone stopped them doing it – it's like taking a toy away from a kid!'

With years of legal wrangling finally behind him, Mercer began looking for closure of another sort. In the spring of 2025, he bought a Honda CBR1000RR Fireblade. Although he accepts that he can never race again, Mercer is hoping to at least ride again. 'Since the accident, I've always had this goal to get back on a bike,' he says. 'I want to prove to myself that I can do it, because so many people have said to me that I'd never ride a bike again. So I want to prove to myself, and to others, that if you want to do something badly enough, you can do it. For the last seven years, I've just wanted a bike. Obviously it had to be a Fireblade, because they were my favourite bikes, and it was the last bike I rode. I've converted it now, so it's ready to go, but now I need to wait for my broken foot to heal before I can get on it.'

Just days before being interviewed for this book, Mercer fell out of his wheelchair and broke his right foot. 'My right leg is my bad leg; it's paralysed,' he says. 'I can't feel it, which is why I fell out of the wheelchair. My left leg is about 25 per cent of what it used to be, pre-accident. Anyway, that was a pain in the arse because I'm trying to get back on a bike and that's set me back a bit. It's character building, though, I'll say that.'

Once his latest injury has healed, Mercer's plan is to try out the specially adapted Fireblade away from prying eyes before taking part in a public track day. 'The plan is to take it to somewhere like Bruntingthorpe Proving Ground first, because it's out of the way,' he says. 'I want to do that before I take it to Brands Hatch. There's going to be a bit of trial and error with getting on and off the bike and just sorting the controls out to my liking. Once I've ridden it for a day and have built up a bit of confidence, I'll do a track day. It's going to be a bit of a shock to the system when I crack that throttle open for the first time in seven years! I've always said that my story needs an ending. I want to write a book, but at the moment it doesn't have an ending. The book needs an ending, and that ending needs to see me back riding a bike again. It will also provide some form of closure for me.'

Despite almost losing his life to road racing, and despite the years of agony and struggle that followed his crash in 2018, and the battles he still has to face every day, Steve Mercer holds no bitterness or regret. 'I still love road racing, and I certainly don't blame it for what happened to me,' he says. 'What happened, happened. I still love the TT, and I will always love the TT, and all the other road races. I haven't been to one since the accident, mainly because I still want to be a racer, and I think that going there and seeing others doing it will be hard to take. But one day I will go back to a road race. One day.'

The jaws of the wolf were clearly not strong enough to hold Steve Mercer in their grasp.

CHAPTER 9

TT FORMULA 1

*'It was suicide. I remember beer bottles rolling across
the track in front of me at Vila Real.'*
PAUL IDDON

The Isle of Man TT is now firmly established as a stand-alone event, and it's by far the biggest road race in the world. But when it lost its world championship status following the 1976 event – because the course was deemed to be too dangerous – there were very real fears that it might just fade away, a relic of old-school racing, an anachronism with no place in the modern world.

To give the event a fighting chance of survival, motorcycle sport's governing body, the FIM (Fédération Internationale de Motocyclisme) granted the TT organisers three new world championships: TT Formula I, TT Formula 2 and TT Formula 3.

The Formula 1 class was for machines between 601cc and 1000cc, Formula 2 catered for bikes between 401 and 600cc, and the Formula 3 class was for 250cc to 400cc machines. As always, it was the biggest capacity F1 class that attracted all the attention.

Honda Britain boss Gerald Davison was one of the men who helped set up the championships. 'The new Formula classes grew out of the work I did on the FIM technical committee with Neville Goss [Davison was Honda's representative to the FIM, so worked closely with the governing body of global motorcycle sport], to create more racing opportunities for four-strokes,' he says.

Despite the world championship status, there would only be one race to decide each respective championship, and they would be held at the TT. Many thought the idea was ludicrous and, at first, there can be little doubt that it was, but the championship expanded over the following years to become a genuinely important one that the top manufacturers badly wanted to win.

By 1986 there were six rounds, and the grids were made up of a bizarre mixture of full factory hand-built exotica intermingled with an array of highly tuned and often experimental machinery entered by private teams. The championship was – initially at least – held mostly on public road circuits which were so dangerous that no other championship would go near them: the Isle of Man TT course, Dundrod in Northern Ireland, Vila Real in Portugal and Kouvola in Finland; some famous, some not so much. And with the exception of the TT – where riders raced individually against the clock – all the races were mass starts. That's around 40 Superbikes aiming between two rows of houses at full chat. The F1 world championship was as spectacular as it was deadly.

It was first held in 1977 as a fairly meaningless one-round championship comprising just a single race at the Isle of Man TT. Barry Symmons was involved with Honda Britain right from that first F1 race in 1977 and was team manager for the squad from 1978 onwards. Before he passed away in 2024, Symmons explained the logic of staging an F1 championship: 'It was the beginning of the move away from pure racing bikes towards production-orientated machines,' he said. 'One of the issues was cost, but the TT was also looking for something to replace the loss of its Grand Prix status, so staging an F1 world championship seemed a useful alternative. It was based on road circuits so that the TT could have something to hang a championship on.'

That first race – and hence the world title – was won by Phil Read. Always a controversial rider, Read's win in the inaugural F1 world championship race caused a commotion in the paddock, but this time it was his team boss Gerald Davison who bore the brunt of the flak. 'The weather was appalling, and in those days it had to be extreme for racing to be cancelled,' he says. 'Just over half distance, I had a message from Ramsay to say the roads there were awash with water, and I began to feel that the race could be cut. The Honda RCB was quite thirsty, and if I could cut the last fuel stop it could make all the difference, so I set off to find the ACU officials. Despite monsoon-like conditions, I eventually found them in a nice warm, dry tent, having tea and cakes. Bursting in like a drowned rat, I asked what was going on, and they calmly said they were cutting the last lap but had not yet made the announcement. I raced back to the pits just in time to wave Read through, and the time saved guaranteed the win. If we had taken on more fuel we would have come second.'

Davison's shrewd move naturally caused some controversy. 'I was accused – not for the first time – by all and sundry of cheating, but anyone could have bothered to find out what was happening. While I was grateful for the inaugural F1 win, it nevertheless left a bitter taste in my mouth that the ACU could be so cavalier with racing on the island in such treacherous conditions.'

While Read proudly added the title to the seven he had won in Grands Prix, few others viewed the championship in the same light. 'How can you take a world championship seriously when it's only one round?' asks Mick Grant, one of F1's biggest stars from the late 1970s up until his retirement in 1985. 'In my opinion, it wasn't a world championship in the early days. To sit there with a smug look on your face, thinking you were a world champion after one round – I think that would have been embarrassing.'

By the early 1980s the championship had grown to comprise three rounds – the TT, Assen in Holland (the first short circuit to be included) and the Ulster Grand Prix at Dundrod in Northern Ireland. Rob McElnea finished second to Joey Dunlop in the 1983 championship but still felt the series was lacking in rounds. 'It was a good series, but I don't think it should have been called a world championship with just three rounds,' he says. 'That was a bit of a joke. Each individual race was a great thing to be involved in, but I wasn't hanging out to be called a world champion after just three fucking races!'

As this feeling grew, more rounds were added and the

series peaked in 1986 when there were eight races in total. Unfortunately, some of them were horrendously dangerous and, by common consensus, one of the worst was Vila Real in Portugal. This was a street circuit in the strictest sense of the word, running as it did for 4.3 miles round the Portuguese town of the same name. 'It was suicide,' says Paul Iddon, former factory Suzuki rider and father of current British Superbike star Christian Iddon. 'They were typical Portuguese streets with tall buildings and people hanging out over their balconies to watch the race. I remember beer bottles rolling across the track in front of me at Vila Real. It wasn't done on purpose – the spectators just dropped them and they rolled onto the circuit. I remember following Andy McGladdery one year and his bike was spewing fuel over me because he'd overfilled it. At the same time, a beer bottle rolled in front of me, and I also had so much sweat streaming down my face and congealing round my mouth that I could have chewed it off my lips!'

Roger Marshall, another top contender in the series and an 11-time British champion, remembers having to negotiate the tram lines that ran across the Portuguese circuit. 'You had to keep the bike upright as you crossed the tram lines and then whack it straight onto its side for the following corner. You also had to cross an old rickety bridge over the river with a 100-foot drop on either side – it was quite a scary place to go to, much worse than the TT or the Ulster Grand Prix.'

As well as rickety bridges and rolling beer bottles, riders also had to contest with a less-than-perfect road surface. 'Vila Real was very fast, but the surface was always covered in sand,' Mick Grant says. 'It was a road circuit, and it was dangerous. I mean, people would have kittens nowadays if you suggested holding a race there, but at the time it was no big deal. But the most memorable thing about Vila Real was that the Mateus wine factory was right in the middle of it, so we all came home with crates of wine!'

Extreme heat was another major problem in Portugal, especially after a two-hour F1 race with only the briefest of stops to refuel. 'It was 108 degrees (42°C) one year,' Iddon recalls, 'and people were actually collapsing after the race. There were medical staff running around with stretchers and hosepipes to revive the riders.'

The little-heard-of Kouvola circuit in Finland was not much better. Carl Fogarty took his first world title by clinching the F1 crown in 1988, and in his autobiography, *Foggy*, he recalled the 1988 race at Kouvola: 'A fair crowd of around 15,000 turned up to watch us race around an industrial estate, where every corner was a right angle and you had to dodge the manhole covers in the middle of the road.'

Pergusa in Sicily was another dubious choice for a world championship event. It stank of rotten eggs due to the high levels of sulphur in the area, as the circuit went right round a bubbling volcanic lake. Conditions were dreadful and facilities minimal – there weren't even any showers, meaning riders had to rig up a hosepipe, drill holes in it, hang it up and shower naked in the street.

Barry Symmons admitted that the F1 venues were not always up to world championship standards. 'Occasionally the facilities provided by some of the organisers were a great deal less than one would have expected,' he said. 'On numerous occasions we came to loggerheads with the organisers over things like medical facilities, especially in Portugal.'

Love them or hate them, Roger Marshall says riders were forced to compete on such dangerous tracks if they wanted to progress their careers. 'If you wanted a factory ride you had to race on the scary F1 road circuits,' he says. 'The Japanese thought as much of winning the F1 world title as they did of winning Grands Prix, so if you wanted to get a factory ride in GPs you had to go to these scary road circuits and do the business. It was everything. Mr Michihiko Aika, who ran the Honda racing operation from Japan, said the TTF1 championship meant more to Honda than winning the 500cc Grand Prix world championship because it sold motorbikes – people could relate to the bikes as being more like road bikes rather than prototype two-stroke race bikes.'

Barry Symmons confirmed Marshall's claim. 'That championship was Honda's main aim – that was the only thing they were worried about,' he said. 'And it caused a bit of friction because we weren't allowed to use the TT Formula 1 bikes in the Senior TT or in anything other than TTF1 races in the UK [due to the unique F1 technical regulations]. We couldn't use them in the MCN Superbike Championship, for example. They were proper factory bikes. Honda's racing efforts are always paid for out of the R&D budget. Racing is part of the R&D procedure, so the TT Formula 1 world championship and the FIM Endurance World Championship were where Honda could develop their chassis technology. That's where innovations like the single-sided swingarm came from. Once World Superbike regulations came in in 1988 [which were much tighter and designed to keep the bikes as standard as possible], Honda had no reason to enter the World Superbike Championship.'

Roger Burnett was an occasional TTF1 rider before moving up to the 500cc Grand Prix world championship. Like Marshall, he knew that to get the best bikes he'd need to bite the bullet and race on dangerous F1 circuits, even though he wasn't keen initially. Fortunately for Burnett, he soon changed his mind and came to love the TT. 'Back in my day, if you didn't do the TT then you didn't get a factory ride,' he says. 'I didn't really want to do it, but if I hadn't done it then I'd have missed out on the most exhilarating, thrilling thing you can ever do in your life on a motorcycle. I'm not taking anything away from MotoGP, World Superbike or British Superbike riders, but in terms of what they experience compared to what you experience riding at the TT, they don't know what they're missing. I loved the thrill, and I think the danger just added to the thrill. And racers are all thrill seekers at the end of the day.'

Despite the dangers of the F1 circuits, Paul Iddon insists the riders attacked them with everything they had. 'Circuits like Dundrod and Vila Real, you scratched round just like you would on a short circuit,' he says. 'The TT was different – it was all about rhythm – but at the shorter road circuits you rode as hard as the bike could go. When you're racing, you don't really think of the dangers.'

During his years with the Honda Britain team, Marshall had the added pressure of having to 'do the business' if he wanted to secure competitive machinery for the following season. 'There was lots of pressure to win the F1 championship for Honda because whoever won the championship got next year's new bike, and the one who didn't win got last year's bike again,' he explains. 'And the new bike was always going to be better. Unfortunately, I was always runner-up to my teammate Joey Dunlop, so I never got Honda's new bike!'

It was the public-roads nature of the tracks involved that made F1 the most dangerous world championship ever staged. Houses, walls, bridges, tram lines, lamp posts and almost every other hazard imaginable faced the riders as they battled for supremacy. It led to a lot of lives being lost, so taking a trip down memory lane is not always a pleasant experience for former F1 riders, as Marshall explains: 'When I look back at some of the old pictures in my scrapbook there's only half of the grid left alive. It makes me realise that I'm very fortunate to have got to where I am these days.'

The 1984 season was one of the hardest-fought battles for the TT Formula 1 World Championship, and it was between the two Honda Britain teammates: Joey Dunlop and Roger Marshall. Dunlop won the opening round at the TT with Marshall second, meaning there were three points between them as they headed to Assen in the Netherlands, and that's where the needle began. 'They [Dunlop's crew] said I didn't stop the engine during the pit stop,' Marshall explains. 'The pit stops were so quick back then because we used dump cans [quick-filler systems], so you hardly had time to breathe – it was just *bang* and off you went again. I had a rapid stop, and the team pushed me off, but then it was claimed I didn't stop my engine, but I did: my engine was definitely stopped. That caused some aggro, though, and it left a bad taste. Joey never confronted me directly – it was his entourage who did that.'

Decades after the Dutch race, team boss Barry Symmons held his hands up and took the blame for the incident. 'I suppose I must take responsibility for that,' he said. 'I didn't remind Roger and his mechanics that they had to turn his engine off during his refuelling stop. It was my fault – which I didn't tell them! There was a bit of a row about it because it was against the rules. I don't know quite what happened in the end because we weren't pulled up in front of the stewards. Someone eventually shouted, "Turn your engine off", but the fuel stop was half over by then.'

Marshall – by that point a better short circuit rider than Joey, who was becoming more of a roads specialist – took the victory at Assen, with Dunlop in second place, meaning they were both even on 27 points apiece. Marshall then won again at Vila Real in Portugal to give him a three-point lead going into Dunlop's home round at Dundrod, where once again there was trouble. 'We had a coming together at the Ulster Grand Prix and there was all hell going on in the pits,' Marshall remembers. 'Looking back, that year, I was really up for it. We were both wanting it more than anything, and the Ulster Grand Prix was my favourite road race of all time – I just clicked there, and I loved it, and I could really push on there.'

So could Dunlop, however. He remains the most successful rider around the Dundrod course, so the stage was set for an epic confrontation between the two Honda

Britain teammates, who were also the biggest names in the series. The prize was a world championship. Dunlop had already won it twice and was the reigning champion, while Marshall had always had to play second fiddle. He was ready for a fight; he badly wanted a world title. Spectators are accustomed to physical contact between riders battling for a British title, a World Superbike title or a MotoGP world title, but all those championships are held on much safer and often purpose-built short circuits. Back in the 1980s, the same thing was happening on the unforgiving roads circuits, and never more so than in 1984.

'I took the Budore corner the best I had ever taken it,' Marshall says of that year's F1 race at Dundrod. 'It's a frightening right-hander, but if you get it right it gives you great drive up towards Windmill and Wheeler's corner. I took Budore perfectly and thought, *Fantastic!*, but then, as I tipped into Windmill, Joey came under me. Really, there was no room; I lifted my bike and skimmed the bank, and instead of driving out and getting down behind the screen, I had to change down the gearbox to get going again. To me, it was a bad move, which wasn't like Joey. That was the last lap. I did nearly catch him again but, obviously, I came second, and I was fuming. It was very rare that I lost it in racing, but I did that day. It all got a bit confrontational in the pits and Barry Symmons was trying to calm it all down. I was very irate, but I don't think Joey said much – which he never did anyway!'

Marshall accepted the move as a racing incident – he knew Dunlop was neither a dirty rider nor a man to cause a fuss, but he also knew how hard the diminutive Irishman was prepared to ride to win. 'Joey was one of the hardest men, one of the hardest riders ever on the roads, when he wanted to win, but he was fair too,' he acknowledges. 'The only time we ever had a word against each other was that particular day at the Ulster.'

One round to go, at Zolder in Belgium, and both Dunlop and Marshall were sitting on 54 points. Both had taken two wins, and both had taken two second places. It could not have been any tighter.

Zolder is a purpose-built 2.49-mile circuit, so it should have favoured Marshall. Nevertheless, he arrived at the circuit a week ahead of the event with his great friend and former mechanic Roger Burnett to settle in and make sure he knew every inch of the track before the race. It meant everything to him: he was desperate to win a world title, and there were Dunlop fans who (without any justification) believed that team boss Barry Symmons would rather Marshall take the title than Dunlop. Marshall was more media-friendly, more presentable, and more . . . well, English. 'Joey had a lot of fanatical supporters,' Marshall says. 'I mean, I had a lot of Irish supporters, too, because they liked to see me going over and taking Joey on. Not every Irishman was a Joey fan! They appreciated you going over there to race. But some of Joey's fans got it into their heads that Honda wanted me to win the title that year, not Joey. I have no idea where that came from.'

Among some of the 200-odd Irish fans who travelled to the event (not so easy – or cheap – back in 1984), paranoia was setting in. Writing in the bike racing annual *Motocourse* in 1984, Paul Fowler revealed that, 'One of them ushered me secretly behind a chip van. "We reckon they might do something to Joey's bike," he said. "Keep an eye on it and let me know if you see anything dodgy."'

Paranoia aside, the intra-team battle caught the media's attention, but Marshall and Dunlop were not natural enemies and buried any bad blood between them ahead of the final round of the season. 'The last race was in Belgium that year and it was all in the papers – all this supposed aggro between us,' Marshall says. 'But when we got to Zolder, I went up to Joey and I shook his hand and said, "Look, let's get on with it – may the best man win," and then we got back on track together.'

Who that best man was going to be was unclear during the first 12 laps, as the pair continually swapped places. Marshall spent slightly more time in the lead than Dunlop but on the 13th lap out of 36, his bike slowed, and Dunlop broke clear at the front. Marshall pitted, but as his mechanics could see nothing obviously wrong with his machine they sent him back out again. He never even made it to the end of pit lane before his bike blew its head gasket. It was over. The heartbroken Marshall spent the night in tears in Roger Burnett's caravan. It was the closest he ever came to winning a world championship.

Although the riders took the racing seriously, the Formula 1 paddock often seemed more like a boozy Club 18–30 holiday camp than a world championship enclosure. Paul Iddon remembers Joey Dunlop and his crew being at the centre of much of the mischief. 'You could never say no to a drink with Joey's entourage. They'd try and get you blitzed before the race to throw everything against you.

One time I was drinking with them but left at about 3am because I was absolutely paralytic. I got up with a thick head in the morning and Joey's gang were still sitting drinking crème de menthe because that was all that was left behind the bar. It was like a bomb had hit the place – all the curtains had been ripped down and the whole place was wrecked.'

As a factory Honda rider, Joey Dunlop could have travelled in relative luxury to F1 rounds, but as his team boss Barry Symmons revealed, that just wasn't Dunlop's style. 'When we were going to Vila Real, or somewhere else on the continent, Joey would take a few mates and they'd sleep in the van and go round and visit places of interest and make a trip out of it,' he says. 'I remember him reversing his van into a parking space at Hockenheim in Germany – the back doors were open, and an empty three-litre bottle of vodka rolled out, so it had obviously been a good trip. He was always there at the right time, though. We had no complaints at all about his professionalism. Things were slightly different in those days though.'

Dunlop found himself in trouble following the TTF1 round at Assen in 1986, as Iddon explains: 'The night after the race, Joey and about five or six others had been drinking and decided to take the Rothmans Honda car for a lap of the circuit. Joey rolled the car and it ended up on its roof in a ditch. His race trophy went flying around the car in the melee and my teammate Neil Robinson spent a night in hospital, Joey broke some ribs and Neil's mechanic broke his jaw in the crash. He had to drink through a straw for months after that and lost loads of weight. Somewhere in

Spain he had rice soup which kept locking his jaw up, which we all thought was quite funny.'

Roger Marshall remembers another impromptu Dunlop lap, this time in the middle of the night in Vila Real when the two were Honda Britain teammates. 'I was sharing a room with Joey, and we found some little bar in Vila Real,' Marshall recalls. 'We fell out of there about two in the morning and Joey wanted to do a couple of laps of the track in his car. We were leathered, all of us. Famed technician Chris Mayhew was in the back of the car while I was in the front with Joey. I remember Chris being sick as soon as he got out of the car and he lost his false teeth in the process. I managed to find them in among all his sick and handed them over. Anyway, as I said, I was sharing a twin room with Joey, and he went to sleep straight away after we got back. The next morning there was all this banging on the door. Outside our small hotel there were two petrol pumps and Joey had abandoned the car on a plinth between the pumps, preventing anyone from getting petrol. There was a big queue of cars waiting. I couldn't wake Joey up, so I found the keys and went to move the car. We'd left the doors of the car wide open, and Joey must have had a thousand fags in there, and the glove box had about a grand in cash in it – that's how Joey operated. Anyway, I managed to get the car off the plinth and went back to bed. Barry Symmons turned up that day and he was furious!'

Symmons said factory Suzuki rider Mick Grant was the instigator of the drunken laps, but that his cunning plan failed. 'The night before that race at Vila Real, Mick Grant thought he would be clever and bought Joey a big bottle of brandy. I suspect he was hoping to give Joey a hangover for race day. Anyway, Joey polished half of it off then decided he was going to do a lap of the track in *my* car – which I wasn't aware of at the time – with his mechanics, Chris Mayhew and Nick Goodison. Apparently he was driving with one hand on the gear lever while his other hand held the bottle of brandy and the steering wheel. As soon as they stopped, poor old Chris Mayhew put his head out of the window and was violently sick. But Joey didn't get a hangover, so Granty's master plan didn't work!'

As noted, the first ever TT Formula 1 world champion was Phil Read, who took the title by winning the only round at the Isle of Man TT in 1977. The following year saw Mike Hailwood's miraculous and victorious comeback to racing after an 11-year absence. Ron Haslam then took the title in 1979 before New Zealander Graeme Crosby won it for two consecutive years in 1980 and 1981. After that Joey Dunlop made the championship his own, winning five consecutive titles from 1982 to 1986. Italy's Virginio Ferrari – a former 500cc Grand Prix race winner – took the crown in 1987, while Carl Fogarty won the last three titles before the championship folded.

The relaxed nature of the F1 paddock was sometimes reflected in the less-than-rigid enforcement of racing rules and regulations at some of the foreign rounds. One rider – whose bike failed to get past scrutineering in Kouvola because it was too loud – simply bribed the scrutineer with a bottle of whisky and got his bike through. That same rider also admitted to taking a shortcut during qualifying at Kouvola to get himself further up the grid.

'It was a lot more laid-back and a lot more fun than world championship paddocks today,' Paul Iddon says. 'You didn't have all the corporate hospitality and stuff. You were still professional when you had to be, but our feet were much more firmly on the ground.'

The F1 championship was a favourite with privateers because of the healthy financial packages it offered, and for the chance to take on the factory-backed riders with their own home-brewed specials. Unlike today's production-based Superbike classes, the F1 series allowed almost unrestricted tuning and development. 'You could do almost anything you wanted with the chassis – it didn't have to resemble a road bike at all,' Barry Symmons explained. 'The first aluminum road bike chassis probably came out of F1, and the single-sided swinging arm on the Honda RC30 certainly did. The engine regulations were almost totally free, with the exception, I think, of the carburettors and the material in the crank cases.'

While major manufacturers like Honda and Suzuki created hand-built specials to contest the series, the rest of the field crafted their own machines. A competitive bike could be built for around £1,000 and the regulations allowed for almost anything. The carburettor sizes and the bore and stroke had to stay the same, but almost everything else on the bikes could be changed. It meant a decent engineer could build a bike relatively cheaply that could challenge the full factory machinery.

A factory Suzuki rider in the series, Rob McElnea still remembers the surprising array of private machinery he found himself up against. 'Suzuki and Honda were the main teams, but there were a lot of good privateer teams – it was a good grid,' he says. 'Some of the private kit was awesome. I remember Dave Hiscock turned up from New Zealand on a really trick monocoque Suzuki, which was a missile. There were Motech Kawasakis, too – there was all sorts. There were lots of well-funded decent teams running bikes they had built themselves. A lot of smart guys who aren't around anymore were building trick pieces of kit and getting one over on the factory teams. It was probably the last time when you could build your own bike, do your own development and get on the podium in a world championship race.'

F1 bikes may have seemed quite agricultural compared to the two-stroke 500cc Grand Prix bikes that Grant, Marshall and McElnea also rode, but they were still extremely fast. 'We used to call the F1 bikes "diesels" because that's what they felt like compared to the GP bikes, but they were great fun to ride, and fast as well,' Roger Marshall recalls. 'I remember Joey Dunlop and me were clocked doing 185mph at the Ulster GP in 1982. Those things were quick, bearing in mind the tyre and suspension technology in those days.'

Mick Grant verifies the importance of the championship to the big manufacturers. 'Honda and Suzuki took it very seriously,' he says. 'The bikes they ran in F1 were based on the world endurance racers – they were serious bits of kit, all hand-built. Bikes from the late 1970s got a bad reputation for having lots of power but inadequate chassis, but I think about 80 per cent of the poor handling was down to tyre technology. By the 1980s, the tyres were not a problem, and the chassis were good. The chassis on my Suzuki XR69 from 1982 was almost as sophisticated as any chassis now, as far as adjustment goes.'

F1 also provided early world championship experience for names that would later become legendary. Apart from giving Carl Fogarty his first world title, the championship also saw future 500cc Grand Prix world champion Kevin Schwantz finishing second to Joey Dunlop at Assen in 1986, and Mick Doohan (who won five 500cc titles between 1994 and 1998) taking a third place at Sugo in 1987, while GP star Kevin Magee won the race. The 1987 500cc Grand Prix world champion Wayne Gardner won his first race on European soil at the Vila Real F1 round in 1982, and another future GP star, Britain's Niall Mackenzie, won his one and only world championship race at the Donington Park F1 round in 1988.

By 1990 the F1 series had lost its world championship status and was downgraded to FIM Cup status, and the following year it was abandoned altogether. In contrast, the World Superbike Championship – which had first been held in 1988 – was going from strength to strength. So what went wrong for F1? Why did a series which was so popular with riders, manufacturers and the general public finally fold? Barry Symmons: 'I think one of the reasons why F1 died was because Maurizio Flammini did a much better job promoting the World Superbike Championship. He realised that people wanted to see big four-strokes going round, and that it wasn't the best PR to have riders racing around stone walls and sometimes crashing into them. He also realised that a lot more people would be interested in racing at places like Misano and Mugello rather than at the Isle of Man TT. If the F1 championship had moved onto short circuits it would probably still be going now, and probably with a lot more factory support.'

Mick Grant offers an alternative explanation. 'I think there are two reasons,' he says of F1's decline. 'First of all, the organisers couldn't make any money from road circuits, because they couldn't charge people to watch. And in racing, money is the be-all and end-all. The second reason is that some of the top riders wouldn't race on public roads. But I think the main reason is that they couldn't make any money out of it. The North West 200 is one of the best-attended spectator events in Europe. Imagine if you could charge 150,000 people £30 a head – I'd still be racing!'

The Formula 2 and Formula 3 world championships didn't attract as much attention as the headline class. Formula 3 only ran from 1977 to 1981, the champions being John Kidson, Bill Smith, Barry Smith (twice) and Ron Haslam (who would go on to become a 500cc Grand Prix rider).

The Formula 2 championship ran from 1977 until 1986 but there were only four winners. Alan Jackson won the first three titles, Charlie Williams took over in 1980, then Tony Rutter won four in a row before Brian Reid saw the class out with the last two titles in 1985 and 1986.

As relatively low-key as the F2 championship was, Tony Rutter's four championship wins between 1981 and 1984 on a 600cc Ducati Pantah Twin went a long way to saving Ducati as a manufacturer. As hard as it is to imagine now, the Italian marque was on its knees in the early 1980s and very close to collapse. Rutter's wins kept the Ducati name ticking over, encouraged the factory and helped in assuring its survival. 'They were just about finished at the time,' Rutter said before he passed away in 2020. 'They invited me to Macau to ride one of their works bikes – I think it was about 1984. I said, "Oh yes, please", but a week before we were due to leave, they phoned me up and said, "Tony, sorry, but we can't go to Macau – we're broke. We're bust." It was that bad.'

Ducati is now one of the world's leading motorcycle manufacturers with 14 World Superbike titles and four MotoGP titles to its name, and that might never have happened had it not been for Tony Rutter and the TT Formula 2 world championship. Not that he ever got any recognition for it. 'They paid me a few thousand quid – and that's all it was, no more,' Rutter said. 'But the people at Ducati now have probably never heard of me!'

Rutter had been looking set to win a fifth world title for Ducati until he suffered horrific injuries midway through the 1985 season. He was racing at Montjuïc Park, a particularly treacherous street circuit just outside Barcelona. 'It was quite bad, really,' he said with great understatement. 'I broke my neck in two places, I broke my leg, I broke my left hand quite badly. In fact, the doctors told me I would never be able to race again because of the hand injury, but it didn't bother me one little bit, so they were wrong about that one! There were one or two other injuries – like the nerves in my eyes were affected, so I struggle to look left. I can see straight ahead absolutely fine, but when I look to the left, I can't see a lot.'

Rutter would eventually return to racing but was never

quite the same again and decided to retire, even though he didn't want to. 'I would definitely have done another three or four years, no question,' he said. 'I loved racing and I still miss it so, so much. I was 42 or 43 when I had that big crash, so I could definitely have carried on for a few more years. I do feel like it was all taken away from me too early. I did try to come back at the TT, but it's hard to say why it didn't work out. I tried just as hard but wasn't getting anywhere [Rutter returned to the TT in 1987 and continued to race until 1991 but was a shadow of his former self. His last listed result was a 26th place in the 1990 Senior TT]. It was all a bit sad for me, really. After my crash I should have said "That's it" and just stopped, but I loved racing so much I carried on.'

After the demise of the TT Formula world championships, road races like the TT and the Ulster Grand Prix became standalone events, taking an edge off their importance and prestige. But for many it was the right thing to do. Barry Symmons certainly thought so. 'I don't really agree with racing on public roads for championship points,' he said. 'Riders should only race on the roads because they want to.'

Rob McElnea couldn't have cared less. 'I didn't think about the points situation, I just took every race as an individual race,' he says. 'There was no added pressure because of the points.'

John McGuinness, for one, would like to see today's classic road races strung together into a meaningful championship. 'Yeah, I'd like to see that happen,' he says. 'Why not? There's no chance anyone would be riding any harder just to chase points, because everyone's going as hard as they can as it is just for a race win. But maybe you shouldn't be encouraging people to race at circuits they don't want to race on just for points – especially if they're newcomers.'

Michael Dunlop, on the other hand, isn't overly enthused by the idea. 'I don't think it would make that much difference,' he says. 'It would still just be the same riders in it. Ach, I don't care if it's a championship race or a non-championship race, it's still a race. As long as I just get to go road racing, I'm happy.'

Somewhat bizarrely, Grand Prix riders in the 1970s often competed in road races on the Continent as a way of subsidising their meagre earnings. 'I did a few Dutch and Belgian road races,' Steve Parrish says. 'It sounds crazy now, but those were the kind of races that paid your wages. If you were in the top ten in Grands Prix, those road races would pay you good money to race. We used to actually *lose* money doing Grand Prix races. That's how bad the situation was back then – the organisers took all the money, so we had to race at other meetings to make a wage. So you did the Grands Prix for prestige but also to get better start money at those other races. It was almost like a ranking system, like you see in tennis and golf.'

The equivalent today would be Marc Márquez, Francesco Bagnaia and other top MotoGP riders lining up on road-race grids in between Grands Prix meetings to supplement their earnings!

In the absence of any kind of road-race championship following the demise of Formula 1, the Duke Road Race Rankings stepped in. Sponsored by Duke Video, the rankings awarded points to riders who contested various road races, and those points were added up at the end of each season, but since different riders raced at different events, the figures were fairly meaningless and the rankings were more a curiosity than anything else.

In 2010 the International Road Racing Championship (IRCC) was established and is now the only championship based on roads circuits. In the 15 years that it's been running, seven riders have lost their lives in the series. It takes in lesser-known circuits like Hengelo in the Netherlands, Frohburg in Germany, Chimay in Belgium, Hořice in the Czech Republic, Imatra in Finland and Schleiz in Germany, but funding is slight, media attention is minimal, and the championship lacks the big names associated with the TT and the North West 200. The days of full factory prototype motorcycles racing on the roads for a world championship are most likely gone forever.

CHAPTER 10

THE ORIENT

'I had to phone my wife to tell her that I couldn't come home yet because I was in prison in Macau for blowing up a brothel!'
STEVE PARRISH

'If you can imagine the Chinese authorities shutting off the streets of Hong Kong and allowing 190mph motorcycles to race full speed around them, you've got a pretty good idea of what Macau's like: in other words, it's fucking mental!'

So said road-racing legend Steve Hislop about the Macau Grand Prix. 'There is no run-off room whatsoever, as the whole track is lined with Armco, walls and high-rise apartment blocks,' he added. 'And because it's on the coast you could hit a wall and be thrown over into the sea at some corners. On one particular hairpin bend the braking area is a regularly used bus stop which is always covered in diesel and oil. All in all, there is absolutely no room for error at that place. Despite all this, riders still race flat out at Macau and just have to put thoughts of crashing from their minds, as it simply doesn't bear thinking about.'

Road races are not confined to Europe. The most famous non-European event is the Macau Grand Prix and, because it takes place in November after the main racing season is over, riders treat it as something of a holiday.

The first motorcycle race at Macau was held in 1967 on the same 3.8-mile Guia street circuit that is used today. It runs through the heart of the former Portuguese colony and almost every inch of the track is surrounded by Armco barriers on both sides, making it claustrophobic, difficult to learn and dangerous. Very dangerous.

But that doesn't stop riders from enjoying an end-of-season holiday in the Far East, and when motorcycle road racers are at play, trouble is never very far away. But of all the tales that make their way back to Europe after Macau, Steve Parrish's antics in 1981 take some beating.

Parrish enlisted the help of three others to pull a prank at a local brothel, as he knew some of the riders would inevitably be in there. The plan was simple: to set off a big barrel drum of fireworks and roll it into the foyer of the brothel. But as so often happens with Parrish, things got completely out of hand. 'I was with three people,' he explains. 'Howard Lees [a fellow racer] was one of them, and Paul Butler [who would later become MotoGP race director] was another. There was an Irish fella, too, but I had no idea who he was; he just heard what we were going to do and wanted in on it. I had a Mini Moke hire car, so I was designated as the getaway driver. Paul was going to light the blue touch paper because he smoked cigars, and Howard was going to roll the big barrel of fireworks into the brothel. That was the plan, but when the thing ignited it went off *so* much bigger and better than we ever imagined.'

What happened next was sheer chaos. 'You could buy these huge canisters of fireworks out there in Macau to celebrate Chinese New Year, so this thing was about half the size of a 45-gallon drum. It was enormous, and when Paul lit it, it just kept going off,' Parrish continues. 'The whole place filled with smoke, and the fireworks just kept going off for about five minutes solid. Where it all went very wrong was when we discovered that the chief of police's driver was sat at the bar, which meant the chief of police was probably in the building. There were people screaming and running around everywhere. Two famous riders came running out of their rooms, too, but we best not name them. There were half-naked people trying to get out, and prostitutes with their numbers on running about everywhere, and it was just pure pandemonium. If it happened today, everyone would think it was a terrorist attack.'

The sight was so spectacular that the protagonists couldn't help but watch, open-mouthed and transfixed as chaos reigned all around them. 'My getaway wasn't too good, because I wanted to watch what was going on,' Parrish admits. 'With hindsight, we should have driven away immediately, but we didn't, and the chief of police's driver saw exactly what had happened, and who did it, so he followed us back to the hotel. Within an hour or two, loads of police had turned up and we had to hand over our passports. Luckily, I gave them my dodgy old passport and not my proper one. The other three lads were all handcuffed, but I took off and used the fire escape to get away. I jumped in a taxi then got on a hydrofoil over to Hong Kong.'

Parrish's James Bond getaway didn't last for long. 'I got a phone call from Mike Trimby – who arranged for all the British riders to go to Macau – and he told me that, unless I went back, the police were going to impound everyone's bikes. So, I had to go back, and when I got on the hydrofoil, there was a huge "Wanted!" poster of me; it was like a Western – a "dead or alive" thing.'

Once he had turned himself in, Parrish and his co-conspirators were thrown into cells. 'We were all locked up for four days and were made to pay big fines and had to cover the costs of the damage. But the worst thing was that the police had impounded my Mini Moke hire car and the rental fees were just climbing and climbing. I ended up buying the car in the end, as it was cheaper than paying the rental fees while the police held it as evidence.'

The prank might have amused the riders in the paddock when they heard of it, but others were not so happy. 'I hadn't been married for very long, and I remember I had to phone my wife to tell her that I couldn't come home yet because I was in prison in Macau for blowing up a brothel! That didn't go down terribly well. It didn't go down well with Yamaha either. I was riding for them that year and they were *not* amused by the front-page headline in *Motor Cycle News* the following week! I got a call from senior management about that.'

While Parrish was guilty as charged, triple TT winner Ian Simpson was blamed for doing something he still swears he never did. 'I first raced at Macau in 1989 but didn't go back for another eight years because I wasn't welcome,' he says. 'Somebody did a big shite in the hotel swimming pool, and I got the blame! It *wasn't* me! I think it was James Whitham, but he's never owned up to it. I do know that it definitely wasn't me, but that the whole escapade – literally – caused a bit of a stink, and I wasn't welcome back to Macau until 1997.'

Given what he had seen in 1989, it didn't seem a great loss to Simpson. 'I got a bit put off the event very early doors,' he explains. 'Andy McGladdery had crashed and hurt himself quite badly in practice, and my Durex Suzuki team boss Mick Grant thought it would be a good idea to visit him in hospital. In the first practice session I had gone alright, finishing about ninth or tenth, but after seeing all the blood and snot in that hospital, I backed off. The place was horrendous; it looked more like a slaughterhouse than a hospital. After that, I qualified about 35th, because I *really* didn't want to end up in there.'

Simpson did like the circuit, however, despite the risks it posed. 'It was really dangerous, but it was good fun to ride, even though it's a very difficult track to learn,' he says. 'I'm usually very good at learning tracks, but at Macau all you see are the Armco barriers that hem the track in from all the skyscrapers and casinos. It's all blind, and you can't afford to make a mistake and run a bit wide, so it's very difficult to know how fast you can go.'

Glenn Irwin made his Macau debut in 2016 and loved the place immediately. 'As a circuit, Macau is phenomenal – you're *so* close to the barriers everywhere,' he says. 'It's a great buzz, and you get a great echo off the bike! It's a fascinating track and a fascinating trip – there's a great vibe about the place because we're all on the other side of the world doing something we love, and all within our little close-knit racing community. The first time I did Macau we also got a week in Thailand afterwards and it was one of the best trips of my life, being away with the boys that we race with and being able to switch off and have a few beers together. It's the end of the season, too, so you're not that worried about your fitness and can actually enjoy a beer.'

A top contender for the British Superbike title in recent years, Irwin explains how road circuits like Macau need to be ridden differently to short circuits. 'I don't push the front too hard in road races,' he admits. 'I try to focus on the exit and get the Superbike up onto the fat part of the tyre where there's more grip, so you can really get the power down. It's much easier to control things when the rear end moves, but not so easy when the front moves! We use qualifying tyres at Macau, so they allow you to push even harder on corner exit, but I never feel I'm at risk of losing the front end. You're riding the course hard, though – as hard as you can but as safely as you can. When I looked back on my qualifying lap this year [2018], I asked myself if I could have ridden it any harder and the answer was no. But then I wondered if all the barriers and Armco was removed, and there were a lot of run-off areas, could I have ridden it any harder? Probably. You've got to find the limit at Macau, because if you go over it you're going to get hurt.'

In 2017, after winning the Macau Grand Prix at just his second attempt, Glenn Irwin announced he wouldn't be going back. English rider Dan Hegarty was killed during that year's event and Irwin, having seen the wreckage, was deeply affected. Hegarty's helmet came off in the crash that saw him thrown into the notorious Macau Armco barriers at Fisherman's Bend. In July of 2018 Irwin announced that, 'Last year's incident is very, very fresh in my memory and I won't be returning to race there, certainly not.'

Road racing is self-policing; if a rider gets spooked, or if they have several scary moments, or witness a fatality as Glenn Irwin did, they are free to walk away. No team would ever force a rider to race on the roads if they didn't want to. Everyone involved knows the risks and respects any rider's decision to quit. They're the ones taking the risks, after all; the decision must rest with them.

It's too dangerous to run races in wet conditions at Macau, so when it rained at the 1989 event, race promoter Mike Trimby came up with a makeshift plan, as Steve Hislop explained: 'As it was raining, the organisers decided to wait and let us go out after the car race, if it had dried up. Mike Trimby, quite rightly, said there would be too much rubber and oil on the track after the car race, so that would also be too dangerous for the bikes. The solution, everyone hastily agreed, was to stage a race at a safe pace, but to make it look like we were actually challenging each other. Lots of passing on the straights, and anywhere else that seemed relatively safe, but no balls-out, real racing. After all, it wasn't a championship round or anything, and safety must come first. The alternative was to let down the spectators by not staging a race at all.'

Despite this gentleman's agreement, racers are racers,

and once they snap their visors down, often they can't help themselves – they have to race, it's what they do.

'Well, that was the plan anyway, but there's something about Irish riders which means they just can't seem to back off,' Hislop continued. 'They always have to beat each other, so they can say they're the best man back home. Robert Dunlop and Phillip McCallen had a history of not liking each other anyway, so I should have known that neither of them would settle for second place, even in a fake race.'

At first, everything went to plan, but it didn't last. 'For the first part of the race we all hammed it up for the spectators and TV cameras and no one was riding too fast, so it was actually quite good fun,' Hislop continued. 'Everyone was getting prize money based on their practice performance anyway, so there was no point in going fast to win cash, but about halfway through the race I noticed Robert Dunlop was starting to pick up the pace – and Phillip McCallen was going with him. I watched from a distant third place for a little while, not too bothered, then the racer in me came out and I thought, *Fuck this, if they're racing for real, so am I!*

'I pinned the throttle and immediately pulled away from the riders behind me. As I got up to real racing speeds I set the fastest lap of the race and closed down the gap to Robert and Phillip, but I'd left my charge too late and had to settle for third.'

Like every other racer who takes part in Macau, Steve Hislop treated it like a holiday, and when a group of motorcycle racers are on holiday together, hire cars get abused. David Jefferies' friend Dave Greenham remembers one particular night when Jefferies got a masterclass from Steve Hislop in a Mini Moke jeep on a lap of the Macau circuit. 'Steve was driving and it's fair to say he'd been drinking a bit,' says Greenham. 'DJ was in the passenger seat, Simon Beck, Lee Pullen and me were in the back, and a cameraman from Greenlight Television was sat on the parcel shelf facing backwards with his feet on the bumper. This was about 2:30am and Hizzy was giving us a running commentary and, to the best of his ability, trying to keep on the racing line while revving the tits off this thing in every single gear and trying to avoid parked cars and oncoming traffic. The tyres were absolutely screeching round every corner, and the cameraman was often thrown forwards into the front seat under braking. It was a fantastic experience – hideously funny – but it could have all gone so wrong.'

For David Jefferies, the holiday vibe continued out on track, as John McGuinness recalls. 'I remember at Macau we were going down towards Lisboa – probably 170mph – and we'd been looking across at each other and flicking each other the V-sign and waving at each other, and he was probably trying to hit my kill switch button, or whatever. You ride against some other guy and they're just so concentrating on what they're doing, but DJ would be pulling faces and giving you the Vs. We'd be on the front row of the grid at Macau, and he'd be going round winding everybody up, shaking their hands and laughing at them, telling everybody to relax and to enjoy it – pull some wheelies, do some skids. Everyone else was so focused but he was just so cool and collected. He was good to have around – he had a great aura on the grid.'

Hislop's protégé Stuart Easton would ultimately win four Macau Grands Prix, but he had no idea what he was letting himself in for when he made his debut in 2002. 'It was my first ever road race and I did it by pure accident,' he confesses. 'One of the lads in Paul Bird's Monstermob Ducati team [Easton won the British Supersport 600 title for the team in 2002] asked if I would like to do Macau, and I said, "What's that?" I had no idea what Macau was! He explained it was a race in China in November, and that it was a mega trip with a holiday in Thailand bolted on at the end. I loved the idea of racing in the off-season and John McGuinness and Ronnie Smith were going to be the other riders in the team, so it all sounded good. Someone managed to wangle me an entry – because I was only 18 I would be one of the youngest riders ever to enter the Macau Grand Prix, so the team had to convince organiser Mike Trimby that I was a competent and safe rider.'

While he now knew *where* the event was, Easton was still completely in the dark as regards to what *kind* of event it was. 'This was before YouTube existed, so I didn't even know it was a road race!' he says. 'I was standing in the pits with John McGuinness, and I said, "Where's the circuit, then?" and he pointed at this wee narrow road in front of us, lined with Armco barriers, and said, "That's it, right there." I thought, *That can't be the circuit – it's all Armco and high-rise buildings.* It's incredible, looking back, that I didn't even realise it was a road race! I was totally oblivious.'

Undeterred, Easton went about his work and discovered he had a natural flair for the roads. 'I got an entry and rode the Supersport bike alongside the Superbikes – it was a race within a race,' he explains. 'I went out and had a bit of fun on the bike and learned the circuit, and I ended up winning the Supersport race. I was 18th overall, but everything in front of me was a Superbike. The second placed Supersport rider was a young Australian called Cameron Donald, who went on to have a great career on the roads.'

Easton credits John McGuinness with helping him get up to speed so quickly. 'I got a huge tip from John to help me learn the course, and it was the best tip ever,' he says. 'The coast road is quite easy to learn, but up the topside of the circuit it's left–right–left–right–left–right, and that's the hard bit to learn. John told me to split it up into three sections – slow chicane, fast chicane, slow chicane. That's the gist of the top section, and everything just fell into place after that. It was a great bit of advice.'

As the newly crowned British Supersport champion that year, Easton was a top-level short circuit rider and found the layout suited his style. 'The layout of Macau is more like a short circuit, although it's surrounded by barriers and buildings, and there's zero room for error,' he says. 'The track has loads of rubber laid down by Formula 3 cars and World Touring Cars so it's really grippy and relatively smooth for a road race. It's always dry, too, as they don't run races in the rain at Macau. So the feel of the place was fine, despite the barriers and the buildings. I liked it because Steve Hislop was my hero and he had won at Macau in the past and everybody looked up to him. I was a cocky little 18-year-old, thinking, *I'm a real road racer now! This is great!* I had got my first taste of road racing and felt I wanted to do more. That's how I ended up doing the North West 200 a couple of years later in 2004.'

The first motorcycling fatality occurred at Macau in 1973 when Hong Kong rider Shea Lun Tsang lost his life at the event. Since then, another eight riders have been killed, including former 500cc Grand Prix rider and winner of the Bol d'Or and Le Mans 24 Hour races, Bruno Bonhuil (2005), and noted Portuguese rider Luís Carreira (2012).

The Macau Grand Prix is in rude health, nonetheless, and continues to attract full grids of riders from around the world, all willing to accept the dangers presented by this most fearsome street circuit – and all likely to return home with their own holiday racer tales.

CHAPTER 11

PARK LIFE

*'They wanted me to kill myself. One person said
it was a pity I didn't crash.'*
BARRY SHEENE

While the Isle of Man passed an Act that allowed for public roads to be closed for racing in 1904, and Northern Ireland followed suite in 1922, the UK government stood firm in its resolution not to allow any such dangerous activities on its roads. There was a loophole, though, and in 1946, race organisers exploited it.

Oliver's Mount in Scarborough is technically a parkland circuit rather than a street circuit or 'road race', but it's essentially the same thing. Little wider than a typical access road, the 2.41-mile circuit is surrounded by trees, sheer drops, bankings and hedges, making it every bit as challenging and hazardous as any other road race. It's known as England's only road-race circuit and it has attracted some big names over the years, but its heyday came in the 1970s with the famous battles between Mick Grant and Barry Sheene.

Mick Grant was a gritty, straight-talking Yorkshireman, racing on home turf in front of legions of local fans. Barry Sheene was the most famous and most popular rider in the world, and winner of the 500cc Grand Prix world championship in 1976 and 1977. But northern race fans didn't take to the Londoner with his champagne lifestyle, his Rolls-Royce, his helicopter, and his flamboyant and outspoken persona.

The races between these two contrasting characters at Oliver's Mount in the mid-to-late 1970s attracted more than 60,000 fans to the compact parkland venue. Nowhere was the anti-Sheene feeling demonstrated more openly than at Oliver's Mount, where more northern bikers resented 'southern softie' Sheene, perhaps more so than at any other track in the UK. He may have been the most popular rider in the sport, but Sheene was not without his detractors.

Sporting a moustache and speaking with a strong Huddersfield accent, Mick Grant was the complete antithesis to Sheene, and his fans loved him for it. There was nothing they liked to see more than one of their own beating the overpaid (in their minds at least) and overrated Londoner.

It has always been a matter of some conjecture as to why Barry Sheene raced on a circuit like Oliver's Mount, given his hatred of the Isle of Man TT course. At 2.41 miles long, the track is set on a hillside overlooking the Victorian seaside resort of Scarborough. It has absolutely no run-off areas and is lined with trees for almost its entire length. Worse still, the bottom section of the course – known as the rollercoaster section – is extremely undulating, with trees and bankings on one side and a near-sheer drop of several hundred feet on the other. It is not a place for the faint-hearted, yet Sheene continued to race at Scarborough until the end of his career in 1984: his victory in that year's season-ending Gold Cup would prove to be the last race win of his illustrious career.

Part of the reason may have been the fact that Oliver's Mount is, by a long way, shorter than the TT, and therefore Sheene knew it well enough to be able to avoid most of its dangers. The other motivating factor that Sheene did not hide was his friendship with circuit promoter Peter Hillaby; a friendship that ensured Barry's repeated return to the track to participate in demonstration laps long after his retirement.

Mick Grant explains the incentive to race at Scarborough and also reveals how he and Barry managed to keep the risks to a minimum. 'Scarborough always paid very well in appearance money, and although we never fixed or threw a race, we used to make a deal to put on a good show, then go for it three laps from the end,' he says. 'It just made sense on the more dangerous circuits to do that. The good thing about Barry was that he was very trustworthy, so if we did a deal, we did a deal.'

Sheene brought up the subject of racing at Scarborough in his regular column for *Motorcycle Racing* magazine in 1981, saying: 'I will ride where I want to ride, so I go to Scarborough, but I don't race at the TT. After 12 years as a regular there, I reckon I ought to know whether I like it or not.'

He may have enjoyed the track, but Sheene was surprised at the extremities of ill will that were shown towards him by some spectators. On one occasion when his bike broke down at Scarborough, spectators started booing and taunting him with obscenities from behind the fences. Sheene told the *Northern Daily Mail*: 'They wanted me to kill myself. One person said it was a pity I didn't crash.'

Verbal taunts are one thing, and unpleasant enough, but physical – and potentially lethal – abuse is another. At an Oliver's Mount meeting in 1977, some spectators started jabbing sticks through the picket fencing that lined much of the circuit as Sheene rode past, while others threw beer cans at him. Mick Grant was not proud of the fact and tried his best to calm things down, even going so far as to act as a bodyguard for his rival. 'At that time in Britain you were either a Sheene fan or a Grant fan,' he says. 'I remember one year when Barry won at Scarborough I actually went round in the car with him on his victory lap so that the spectators wouldn't throw things at him!'

Steve Parrish was a former teammate of Sheene's and was also his best friend. He says Sheene wasn't opposed to road racing as such, but that he just didn't like the TT. 'It's not true to say that Barry Sheene hated road racing – he did a lot of road races on the Continent, as well as enjoying Oliver's Mount,' Parrish says. 'I remember we often raced together at Sint-Joris in Belgium and at other road races in Holland and elsewhere. He just thought the TT was far too long and took too long to learn, and there was far more risk of sheep and dogs and cats running out in front of you. I think he just used his bonce properly and weighed up the odds. I mean, in 2025 Mark Parrett broke his arm at the TT when he hit a seagull! I know that could happen anywhere, but there's just lots of idiosyncrasies at the TT and he felt the risk factor was too high.'

Parrett's encounter with a seagull at 140mph changed his plans for retirement. The 2025 TT was supposed to be his last, as his intention was to record 100 starts at the event before calling it a day. The seagull put paid to those plans, so Parrett retrenched and decided to put in another year of work to achieve his goal. 'I want to end my TT career finishing my last race and then going out with the lads and celebrating,' he told *MCN*. 'It's a case of going back so that I can finish with the TT, rather than the TT finishing with me.'

Wildlife is yet another hazard that road racers must take into account, and it's not only seagulls they need to avoid, as James McBride discovered during his very first TT in 2003. 'That was the last year of early morning practice sessions [when riders would tear round the TT course at 5:30am to minimise disruption to normal road traffic], and a big bloody hare ran out onto the road in front of me on the run down to the 11th Milestone,' he says. 'It stopped in the middle of the road and just sat there, staring at me. It's 5:30am and I'm in fifth gear on a Suzuki GSX-R600, doing about 130mph on an open road heading straight for a hare. I was just like, "Fuck! Stay there! Stay there! Don't move!" I had no way of knowing which way it was going to bolt, and I couldn't alter my line at that speed anyway, so it was sheer chance that it stayed where it was and I rode past it.'

One of the most horrific animal encounters in road racing occurred at the TT in 1986 when a horse – frightened by a helicopter landing nearby to attend an injured rider – bolted onto the course and straight into the path of Irish rider Gene McDonnell. He was travelling at about 150mph at the time. Both he and the hapless animal were killed instantly, McDonnell's bike bursting into a fireball and smashing into some nearby parked cars.

Steve Parrish won the Scarborough Gold Cup in 1981 and is still a big fan of the seaside races. 'I always really enjoyed Oliver's Mount,' he says. 'I had some great times there, and great races, and managed to win the Gold Cup one year. I still enjoy the place; I mean, it's wild and mad, but there's something fascinating about it and it's great to see how close the spectators can get to the action. It's just a place I got along with really well, and when that happens you tend to go back again and again.'

It was the challenging nature of the circuit that attracted the great Geoff Duke way back in the 1950s. The five-time world champion and six-time TT winner loved the dangers Oliver's Mount presented. 'Modern circuits are almost totally safe, whereas even "safe" circuits in the 1950s were still lined with trees,' Duke said before his passing in 2015. 'But I still think those circuits were more fun to ride. People thought I was mad taking the big Gilera-4 to a narrow tree-lined circuit like Scarborough, but I loved the challenge of it. I beat John Surtees and set a new lap record which stood for about seven years when they changed the circuit quite a bit.'

As frightening as it is to ride round now, Steve Parrish used to race 500cc two-stroke Grand Prix bikes around Oliver's Mount – the most notoriously vicious race bikes ever built. The power band of a 500 was like an on–off switch, so riders had to have incredible throttle control in an age before electronic rider aids like anti-wheelie control. 'Yeah, it was hairy to ride a Grand Prix 500 around Oliver's

Mount,' Parrish admits. 'A lot depended on how long your clutch lasted, because you had to really slip it up the hill from Mere Hairpin. We had to replace clutches regularly at Scarborough. It was pretty wild over the jumps, too; that was quite exhilarating. It's very, very narrow. Even now I do some demo rides round Oliver's Mount and on the back straight towards the café, I'm always thinking, *Jesus! This is a bit fast!*

Being best pals with Barry Sheene meant Steve Parrish often turned up at Oliver's Mount in style – although not necessarily in the right place. Arriving by helicopter one year, the pair struggled to find their accommodation. 'We were trying to find the Wrea Head Hall hotel, but we couldn't find it, and the fuel gauge was going down,' he explains. 'So we aimed for a place that looked very much like a hotel. Barry was busy concentrating on landing, but I noticed that everyone sitting outside this supposed hotel was in a wheelchair. I told Barry I didn't think it was the right place, but he was insistent. So I got out of the helicopter and ran across the lawn like Anneka Rice, only to find out it was the Miners' Union retirement home, and they thought this was Arthur Scargill coming to visit them by helicopter!'

Oliver's Mount can also act as a stepping stone to the Isle of Man TT, as it did for privateer James McBride. 'My first road race was at Oliver's Mount in 2003,' he says. 'John McGuinness tipped me to go. He'd been watching me racing, and I'd beaten one of his mates in the New Era club championship, and John asked me if I fancied a go at the TT. Doing the TT had been in the back of my mind for a while, but while I'd been trying to win a club racing championship it stayed in the back of my mind. It was only when John suggested it in 2002 that I took the plunge and entered the TT in 2003.'

But not before he had done some homework at Oliver's Mount. 'John told me to get a meeting in at Scarborough before I tried the TT,' McBride says. 'He told me to be careful but that if I enjoyed Scarborough then I'd enjoy the TT. Oliver's Mount was scary, but I think it scared everyone around me more than it did me. The place does have a history and a bit of a reputation, though. My best result was a sixth place on my Suzuki GSX-R600, so it went okay. It was a real eye-opener, though, and you need to be properly focused to race around that place – the back straight feels about as narrow as a plank of wood at 140mph!' While he rode at the TT from 2003 until 2015, McBride never returned to Scarborough. Once was enough.

Like every road circuit, Oliver's Mount has seen more than its fair share of tragedies. One of the highest-profile riders to be killed at the track was John Hartle in 1968. A former factory rider for Norton and MV Agusta, Hartle had won five 500cc Grand Prix races and was considered one of the finest riders of his era before retiring in 1964. Unable to stay away, he returned to the sport in 1967 and won the inaugural Production 750 TT that same year.

A peculiarity of the Oliver's Mount circuit is that it has two pedestrian bridges over it, allowing spectators to cross from the inside of the track to the outside, or vice versa. The first of these is situated on the uphill stretch called Quarry Hill, just after the first corner on the circuit – Mere Hairpin. When the rider in front of him missed a gear, John Hartle collided with him and was thrown from his Metisse. He struck the metal support of the pedestrian bridge and was fatally injured.

Another high-profile rider who lost his life at Oliver's Mount was Neil Robinson. The young Irishman was superb on both road circuits and short circuits and was tipped for the very top: a future in the 500cc Grand Prix World Championship was all but assured, especially after Robinson had soundly beaten Joey Dunlop at Dundrod in the 1986 TT Formula 1 World Championship round in 1986. At just 24 years old, 'Smutty' had all the time in the world to get to the top, and as a Skoal Bandit Suzuki rider, he had one of the best rides in Britain at the time. He was hot property. Well-spoken, charming, hugely talented and with pin-up looks, Robinson had it all, but was never given the time to fully explore his talents.

Robinson had never raced at Oliver's Mount before, and after just six laps of practice he crashed on the same uphill stretch where John Hartle had been killed in 1968. Robinson hit the banking and was thrown back onto the track, where he was struck by another rider. He suffered severe head injuries and died in Hull Royal Infirmary that evening. At the time, he was the 13th rider to lose his life at Oliver's Mount.

Keith Huewen was caught up in Robinson's fatal crash and, two years later, was also involved in the crash that killed Kenny Irons at Cadwell Park. Neither horrific incident put him off racing. 'Not at all,' he says. 'Not even a little bit. That will sound weird to an outsider, but it was a racing accident [the Kenny Irons crash] that I had no control over.

I never gave any thought to the dangers. To such an extent that I used to think there was maybe something missing in racers' heads. I lost so many friends in racing but never thought about it at the time. I think about it a lot more now and it's scary. One death that did affect me was Neil Robinson at Scarborough in 1986. He was a close friend of my girlfriend at the time. He high-sided right in front of me and I actually rode underneath his bike and all the debris as it flew over me. He had looked over at me and pulled a silly face just a few corners before that and I still can't get that face out of my head.'

Niall Mackenzie was teammates and friends with Neil Robinson. Although known chiefly for his short circuit achievements (Mackenzie was a factory rider for Honda, Yamaha and Suzuki in the 500cc Grand Prix world championships and a triple British Superbike champion), he also contested the North West 200 in 1985 and, like all racers, lost a lot of friends during his career. Also, like all racers, he had to find ways to deal with such losses in order to protect himself. 'Every racing death is a shock, but I had this kind of safety valve system that must have developed subconsciously,' Mackenzie explains. 'When I was first told of a death I'd think, *Shit, no, no, no,* just like everyone else, but then after about five minutes I wouldn't think about it again. It's not that I didn't accept that it had happened, but I refused to let it bother me; or at least tried to. That sounds very cold, and I don't mean it to be, but every racer has to have a way of dealing with the dangers of the sport and their own mortality. If a really close friend or teammate had been killed, I might have stopped racing, but it's hard to say now what I would have done. Who can tell? It's strange and sounds heartless, perhaps even selfish, to others, but it's just a defence mechanism. After all, you don't stop driving a car when you hear that someone's been killed in a car crash, do you?'

Avoiding funerals was another part of the Mackenzie defence system. 'I didn't make a habit of going to funerals, either, and that's not out of disrespect, it's just all part of the same defence mechanism that allowed me to shut the dangers of what I did out of my mind as much as possible.'

Another rider to lose his life at Oliver's Mount was Bob Smith, who was killed there in 1983. His friend Gary Lingham feels that better riding gear might have led to a different outcome. Today's riders have far, far superior leathers, helmets, boots and gloves compared to riders in the early 1980s, and they also have very effective back and chest protectors. A great short circuit racer and occasional road racer back in the 1980s, Lingham shakes his head when he thinks back on how many friends he lost to the sport. 'Yeah, I lost a lot of friends,' he says. 'I was friends with John Newbold, I was friends with Dave Potter, Mark Salle, Kenny Irons . . . I was great friends with Bob Smith and used to stay round at his house. I watched Bob go down at Scarborough. At that time only a few of us wore back protectors and we had no knee sliders or any kind of padding at the elbows and shoulders of our leathers. Me and Bob had just got hold of two back protectors but our leathers obviously weren't made with space for them, so they were a bit tight and uncomfortable to wear. I opted to wear mine and Bob didn't. He went out and raced without it and crashed into a fence backwards and was killed. There was a slim possibility that had he been wearing the back protector it might have saved his life.'

As sad as they naturally are to lose good friends, road racers must learn to deal with it, and Gary Lingham was no exception. 'You just had to shut it out and get on with it,' he says. 'Racing's a business. I came round just as Mark Salle went down [Salle was killed at Brands Hatch in 1985], so I saw that happen, but you just have to put it out of your mind. I went to most of the funerals, and obviously they break your heart when you're there, but at the circuit you just have to get on with business. The show must go on.'

Steve Parrish raced on the roads in the 1970s and 1980s when the sport was even more dangerous than it is now: even short circuits saw far more fatalities. Losing friends was commonplace, but riders had to cope in whatever way they could. 'I lost lots and lots of friends,' Parrish admits. 'Some, I was pretty close to: Tom Herron, Mick Patrick, Mark Salle, John Newbold . . . Then there were about 15 or 20 other riders who were colleagues and who I raced against and knew but wasn't so close to. I lost some good pals from the Grand Prix world too: I was friends with Guido Paci, Michel Frutschi, Patrick Pons . . . it just goes on and on.'

The racing went on, too, despite the losses. 'I don't know how we carried on, and I've spoken with other riders about this, but somehow we did,' Parrish continues. 'Somehow, you manage to put those things away in a part of your brain where it doesn't affect you. You usually tell yourself that the rider in question was asking for it, or you make up some other silly excuse, like, "Oh, he was riding like a nutcase."

You had to; it's a bit like when you yourself crash and you make up an excuse for why it happened, and so we did that when riders were killed too.'

There was one particular aspect of losing a friend that greatly disturbed Parrish. 'The part that used to freak me out was driving out of the paddock on a Sunday evening and there would be a car or a caravan left there because there was no one to take it home,' he says. 'When my pal Mick Patrick was killed at Cadwell Park in 1977 I had to take his partner home, and it was just surreal. We stopped at a Happy Eater on the way. It was so weird – he was just gone, so you tell yourself that he must have been doing something crazy because, if you didn't, you couldn't carry on.'

Despite the fact that it was a road – or, more accurately, a parkland – circuit, Oliver's Mount hosted a round of the British championship in the 1980s. After Neil Robinson's death there were calls for this to be stopped, as chasing points on dangerous circuits could put too much pressure on riders. The final British championship round was held at Oliver's Mount in 1988 and, since then, only riders who want to race there do so. And many did: Carl Fogarty, Phillip McCallen, Ian Lougher and Guy Martin all enjoyed great success at the seaside circuit.

It was at Scarborough that Steve Hislop finally took his first race win after years of trying. 'That elusive first win came at Oliver's Mount seven years after I started racing,' he said in 2002. 'That sounds like an awful long time, but I only raced off and on up until 1986, and I certainly never took it seriously, so it's not as bad as it sounds. It's probably no coincidence that Oliver's Mount is more like a pure roads circuit than a purpose-built short circuit, and for that reason I always liked the place. It's very narrow, twisty and bumpy but that never bothered me, and I won that first race on a 350 Yamaha from Carl Fogarty, who came in second.'

For Hislop, racing at Scarborough was more like a holiday than anything else, and his recollection of those early years of his career proves just how grassroots road racing is, compared to MotoGP. 'That Scarborough win was brilliant as a few of my mates came down with me for the weekend,' he said. 'For us little Borders lads, Scarborough was a huge town, and we couldn't wait to get practice out of the way so we could go out and get drunk along the promenade. Our arrangements were pretty basic when we were at race meetings. We had a little stove and oven and managed to heat up Fray Bentos steak pies, usually with a tin of potatoes and some peas, and that was about as glamorous as it got. If we couldn't be bothered cooking, we'd just grab a burger and chips from a van.'

Facilities were as basic as they come. 'We used to shower at the circuits, and the toilet blocks back then weren't exactly luxurious, but it was the only way we could get a wash; and anyway, it was all part of the fun. If you've ever been camping with your mates you'll know what I mean. Sometimes roughing it is a much better laugh than staying in five-star hotels – not that we had the option back then.'

In the 1980s, boozing was just as important as racing for many of the competitors, Hislop included. 'As soon as practice was over at Scarborough, we got the steak-and-kidney pies down our necks, had a quick change of trousers, put on a clean shirt and headed off into town. It was real

Seven Brides for Seven Brothers sort of stuff, with all of us out on the pull. It was pure holiday-ville for us, being at a seaside town in the middle of summer, and a great way to spend a weekend when we'd just have been stuck back at home in Hawick if I hadn't been racing.'

Racing with a hangover back then was fairly common, too, so Hislop developed a way of getting past race scrutineers without being caught. 'Sometimes we'd get too carried away on the booze and I'd have to race with monumental hangovers, so I had to devise a little trick to get past the scrutineers when they wanted to check that my helmet fitted properly and was up to standard. Because they would have been able to smell the booze from the night before on my breath, I used to take a big gulp of air, put my helmet on, slap down the visor and stand nodding at them as they checked it over. I didn't dare breathe on them or I'd have been disqualified on the spot!'

In the 1990s, Yorkshire's own David Jefferies became a master of the Mount, winning the International Gold Cup there a record-equalling five times between 1992 and 2001. Jefferies made his debut at Scarborough in 1991. It was his first road race, and he was apprehensive enough about his first visit to a 'road' circuit that he carefully heeded the advice of his father, Tony, who had raced there back in the early 1970s. 'He still knew his way around,' said David at the time, 'and told me just when and where to put the power on, which is important in blind corners. He also pointed out the braking points, which were just the same as when he rode there 17 years ago.'

The bikes may have gotten much faster in the intervening

years, but brakes and tyres had also improved, and that levelled things out and meant that the braking points were still very much the same as they had been in the early 1970s.

Jefferies qualified on the front row for the Supersport 600 race and took pole position for the 400cc event in his first visit to Scarborough. He takes up the story of the races. 'The 600 race was a great battle; I took the lead through the Esses but lost it by braking too late for the last hairpin. Geoff Baldock got in front, and I never repassed him. He only beat me by a bike's length, and I suppose I should have won but I didn't, and anyway, second was a super result for me – my best yet at a national event. But better still was to follow in the 400cc race. After an indifferent start I took the lead from Andy Murphy on the first lap and led from then on to the end of the race. That was my first national win. I got a great cheer from the crowd and the team were jumping up and down on the motorhome roof so much I thought my mum would go through it!'

Some years later, when Jefferies invited a few friends along to watch the racing one year, they couldn't believe what they were seeing. 'We had never seen a road race, so David invited us along to watch at Oliver's Mount,' Adam Evans says. 'We were stood in the woods on the rollercoaster section down towards the finish line – it's called Jefferies' Jumps now – and he came flying along this little bloody narrow path at about 140mph on the back wheel, going over the jumps, and still managed to wave at us in the woods! We were like "Concentrate, you stupid bastard! Look where you're going!"'

Jefferies had one more little demonstration up his sleeve

to show his friends what road racing was all about, as Evans explains. 'My sister asked him what the plastic things on his knees were for [knee sliders], and if he used them. She didn't believe he would be touching the ground with his knee at those sort of speeds. So DJ got a marker pen and wrote "Kim" on one slider and her boyfriend's name "Dan" on the other. He came back after the race and handed them to her and there wasn't a name to be seen – the entire sliders were worn away!'

Sadly, two tragedies occurred in the late 2010s that would seriously affect the venue and see it lose the right to stage any racing at all. In 2016 a serving member of the Parachute Regiment, Billy Redmayne, suffered severe head injuries following a crash on the fastest part of the circuit. He was kept alive on a life-support machine, but his family were told the head trauma was so severe that Redmayne would never wake up. In a heartbreaking announcement on social media, Redmayne's partner of two years, Hannah Wright, wrote:

> *'We were told that the damage to his brain was too severe for him to ever wake up again. Even if we had waited for the swelling to go down, the damage was too bad. He also wasn't able to breathe for himself and was kept awake by machines. Myself and his family decided [that] rather than prolong the inevitable, we would turn off his life support machine and donate whatever organs we could. I am holding on to the fact that Billy died doing what he loved, and that was the way he always wanted it. Today was our*

anniversary; we had been together for two years. Today was also the day that I lay in Billy's arms whilst he took his last breath.'

In 2017 12 spectators suffered injuries at Oliver's Mount – some of them horrific – when racing bikes veered out of control and struck them. Four air ambulances and six road ambulances were required to deal with the tragedies (which were the result of two separate crashes) and racing was abandoned.

Oliver's Mount was then deemed to be too dangerous, and no races were held in 2018. It was only when a new company, Two Four Three Road Racing Association, took over the event and carried out safety upgrades costing £100,000 that races could be held again.

Husband and wife team Andy and Wendy Hayes now run the race meetings at Oliver's Mount, along with an experienced team of officials, and the events are going from strength to strength. England's only road-race meeting is safe. For now, at least.

*

The only other road race still held on the UK mainland is at Aberdare Park in South Wales. Like Oliver's Mount, it's technically a parkland circuit rather than a roads circuit, which is how it gets around the regulations. Although all legal and above board now, the first action Aberdare Park saw was illegally staged night-time races in 1949.

The Victorian-era park itself is supremely picturesque and, while the circuit is just 0.9 miles long, it's fast and notoriously difficult to master. There's only one race meeting a year, usually held in July, but it's a favourite with riders, and John Surtees – the only man to have won world titles on two wheels and four – credited the circuit with teaching him how to ride properly. 'Of all the races I did in my life, Aberdare Park was probably the one that had the most effect on me,' he said. 'For the first time I was no longer just a mechanic who rode a bike – the bike and I became one. We spoke to each other; we were exchanging messages through the seat of my pants. I realised that's what you need to get the best from a piece of machinery. It shaped the mould for the rest of my racing career.'

On 18th June, 1955, the BBC sent a live outside broadcast unit to Aberdare Park and made a little bit of history – it was the first motorcycle race to be shown live on television in Britain.

The circuit weaves between well-tended flower beds and there's a small boating lake in the middle, but, being a park, there are also lots of trees, as Neil Tuxworth found to his cost in 1986. Although he later became more famous as Honda Britain's team boss, Tuxworth was a fantastic racer in his own right until a high-speed encounter with a tree at Aberdare Park.

'I was dicing with Carl Fogarty on the last lap of a race at Aberdare Park when I lost control and hit a tree,' Tuxworth explains. 'It was 28th June, 1986. I broke my pelvis in seven places, my left leg was wrapped around my neck as the hip had popped out and was shattered, I also shattered my right femur, cut my stomach open, damaged my bladder, severed my urethra . . . I was very lucky to live. I was down to just four pints of blood at one stage. I think I was given 108 pints of blood before they could stop me bleeding. I was on life support for nine months, in hospital for two years, and couldn't walk for nearly three years. I got totally addicted to morphine – which is basically heroin – and it took me a year to get off that. I lost a lot of weight, too; I was 11-stone-ten when I crashed and six-stone-nine when I went home.'

Being supremely fit saved Tuxworth's life. 'I only survived because I was fit,' he insists. 'I was a long-distance runner back then and did a lot of marathons. All the doctors and surgeons said my fitness saved my life, that I should have been dead, but my body just kept fighting and fighting.'

Despite his horrendous ordeal, Tuxworth, like most road racers, couldn't stay away from the sport he loved so much and made a racing return after coming so close to losing his life. 'I was 34 at the time of the accident but I did race again, three years after it,' he says. 'I came back to the TT in 1989 and finished fourth in the Supersport 400 race. I was in a lot of pain, though, I have to admit. But I also went back to Aberdare Park, where I had my crash, and finished third in a Welsh championship race, and then I did the Ulster Grand Prix and finished fifth.'

Tuxworth hand-picked the final three meetings of his career. 'I did those three races for very specific reasons,' he says. 'I did the TT because it meant so much to me, I did Aberdare because it was a way of fighting back, and I did the Ulster because the Irish people had always been so good to me. I retired from racing on 14th August, 1989, and then on 21st August joined Honda as race-team manager.'

Neil Tuxworth went on to oversee more TT wins than any team boss in history. Working with the likes of Joey Dunlop, Steve Hislop, Carl Fogarty, Phillip McCallen and John McGuinness, he guided riders to 68 wins over a period of 27 years, his love of road racing unshaken after his near-death experience.

*

Scotland once had its own parkland road race too. Beveridge Park in Kirkcaldy hosted racing between 1948 and 1988. Like Aberdare Park, the circuit had a small boating lake in the middle and was lined by trees on both sides of the road all the way round its 1.37-mile length. The park itself dates back to 1892 and features formal gardens and play areas, which provided a picturesque yet incongruous backdrop to the sight and sounds of racing motorcycles.

Riders were not fooled by the quaint Victorian setting, however: Beveridge Park was a very dangerous place to race around, and if riders crashed, the chances were they'd hit a tree. Niall Mackenzie would go on to become a factory Grand Prix rider and a triple British Superbike champion, but early in his career the young Scotsman had to race at Beveridge Park as part of the Scottish championships. 'The championship was only held over three circuits because that's all Scotland had to offer,' he explains. 'We raced at Knockhill, East Fortune and Beveridge Park, and that place was a total nightmare. Donnie McLeod – my future teammate in the Silverstone Armstrong squad – said you can only sign the entry form for Beveridge Park once and then your hand won't do it again! [McLeod's hand, in fact, refrained from ever signing the entry form.] He wasn't far wrong. It's a left-handed circuit which runs through a couple of parks and it's pretty fast – certainly too fast for the state of the track and the amount of trees and obstacles round about it.'

While many Scottish riders have great memories of Beveridge Park, Mackenzie was never a fan. 'A lot of people got killed there and it just wasn't fit to race on,' he says. 'On one of the corners you had to stick your head through a hedge because that was the racing line! But the classic corner was the one that had the main road as the run-off area! If you overshot, you went onto the main road, round a roundabout and then back onto the track again; it was totally mad. I had always wanted to do that just for a laugh because I had seen lots of Sidecars doing it, but at the same time I was always after a decent result, so I never got round to doing it. Knowing me, I'd probably have got lost and gone right into town!'

It may have been dangerous, but some riders loved racing at Beveridge, including Ian Simpson, who took part in his first ever road race at the park in 1986. 'It was just a very narrow wee road that ran round a park, but it was a lovely place, all lined with trees and with a wee boating lake in the middle,' he says. 'And it was a great circuit to ride – a bit like Oliver's Mount at Scarborough. Beveridge was probably the hairiest road-racing circuit of them all, though; even more so than some of the smallest Irish races. There were trees all the way round and by the time I raced there in the mid-to-late 1980s the surface was all breaking up. I loved the layout of the track, though, and always enjoyed racing there, despite the dangers. The bikes eventually just got too fast for the circuit. In my last year I was racing a big Suzuki GSX-R1100, and Brian Morrison was on a Honda RC30 and bikes like those had just outgrown the circuit.'

That last year was 1988, after which Beveridge Park returned to its original Victorian purpose as a place for families to stroll, picnic and relax. Somewhat fittingly, Kirkcaldy's own Brian Morrison still holds the outright lap record (73.55mph) and took the final win at his local circuit before the racing stopped for good.

Beveridge Park hosted Scotland's first motorcycle race in 1948 – the Kirkcaldy Grand Prix – and played host to many famous riders over the years, from Jimmie Guthrie to Niall Mackenzie. Five riders lost their lives in the park over the four decades that it hosted racing: Jimmy Blair, Matt Redmond, Angus Callum, Davy Drummond and Brian McAnelly. A memorial now stands in their honour in the park.

*

In 2008 UK law underwent a change that would – in theory at least – allow local councils to close public roads for racing purposes. Almost immediately, two residents of the Isle of Wight – James Kaye and Paul Sandford – started making plans for an international road race to be held on a 12.4-mile stretch of public roads across the island. The event was to be called the Diamond Races, and the hope was to make a festival out of the event and to attract some 50,000 visitors to what would effectively be a southern version of the Isle of Man TT.

It was a serious attempt, and some hugely experienced

people spent a long time working on the project, including the current clerk of the course at the TT, Gary Thompson, former Honda Britain team boss Neil Tuxworth and Senior TT winner and British champion, Steve Plater. James Kaye himself was a former British Touring Car driver, so was well grounded in motorsport. The event also supposedly had the support of the local council.

It was estimated that the cost of running the event would be between £2 million and £5 million, as there's far more to running a road race than just closing the roads: the organisers stated that they would have to treat some 2,500 white lines, as well as treating 177 drain covers and removing 1,500 cat's eyes. Several telegraph poles would need to be removed, walls would need to be protected, and a host of roadside furniture would need to be removed and then replaced after racing. And that's just scratching the surface – running a road race is a complex and expensive business.

The first Diamond Races were due to take place in October of 2021 but were then postponed until April of 2022. In January of that year, however, organiser James Kaye announced the event was to be delayed again. 'Our Motor Race Order application was submitted on time to the Isle of Wight Council on 19th October, 2021, but has not yet been determined,' he said in a statement. 'We understand that there are some technical concerns, but this is out of our control and the clock has run down.'

Those technical concerns remain unsolved, and the initial excitement has faded, as have many people's hopes of seeing the races ever happen. Although the event's website (iwrr. co.uk) says dates are still to be confirmed, the site hasn't been updated since 2022 and it seems that, for now at least, the Isle of Wight road races have been shelved.

There had also been plans to stage a road race in Wales in 2018, but that too fell through, this time due to correct permissions not being secured and a change in the law which affected Welsh roads being closed for racing purposes. It seems that a new road-race event is now unlikely to happen, in Wales, the Isle of Wight or anywhere else in the UK. Unless an event is already well established, the British authorities seem determined to prevent motorcycles from racing around public roads at 200mph, much as they were determined to prevent much slower bikes racing on public roads way back in 1907.

CHAPTER 12

BETWEEN THE HEDGES

*'There are three religions in Northern Ireland –
motorcycle road racing, and the other two.'*
DAVY WOOD

'The only place you should race motorbikes is on a circuit. These courses should not be raced on at all. The sooner that they ban road racing, the better,' so said long-time road-racing sponsor P.J. O'Kane in 2005. Famous for having supported Robert Dunlop for many years, O'Kane was sponsoring Richard Britton in 2005 when the Irish rider was killed at the Ballybunion road races.

It was the inaugural running of the event and it would also prove to be the last time races were held there; the meeting was abandoned after Britton's death and was never resurrected. A winner at the North West 200 and a podium finisher at both the TT and the Ulster Grand Prix, Britton was one of Ireland's most popular racers and was a huge loss, not only to the sport but more keenly to his wife Maria and his five-year-old son Loris (named after former Grand

Prix star Loris Capirossi). Yet despite losing his father to the sport, Loris Britton took up road racing himself in 2016. Heaping tragedy upon tragedy, Maria Britton passed away suddenly and unexpectedly in June of 2024.

Although the Ballybunion races were never held again, road racing did return to Richard Britton's home county of Fermanagh in 2018 with the revival of the Enniskillen road races after a 66-year absence. There was a special tribute to Britton at the first running of the event in almost seven decades, with some of his bikes being ridden on parade laps and a race being named in his honour. Sadly, the meeting was only held twice before folding again. Like many organising clubs, the Enniskillen Club struggled with rising costs and lack of support. In November of 2019 the club released a statement which read:

> *'The cost of running a road race is high, and despite our best efforts to try and keep costs down, we have found that excessive cost and logistics of hiring safety equipment such as safety bales, rising medical costs etc., along with the fact that a trend of spectators choosing not to contribute by buying a programme or contributing towards the event means that not only Enniskillen, but the sport in general, is suffering, something clubs cannot sustain in the long run.'*

Road racing has always had its critics, and there have been calls for it to be banned almost since it first began, but those calls are usually from people outside of the sport who have little or no understanding of it: they simply disapprove of all dangerous activities. But for a long-time sponsor and supporter of the sport like P.J. O'Kane to make such a strong anti-road-racing statement was a very different matter, and his words carried much more weight.

The smaller Irish national road-race courses are notoriously dangerous. Many of them make the TT course look as wide, smooth and safe as a Grand Prix circuit, and while the very nature of those narrow, bumpy and fast courses adds to the spectacle for spectators, and the thrill for the riders, it also adds to the dangers.

Irish road racing is about as far removed from the glamorous and highly technical world of MotoGP as it's possible to get. Paddocks are usually muddy fields and race control buildings are often just Portakabins or old buses. Riders operate out of tents and from the backs of vans, and hospitality units are unheard of. But that's the attraction: everyone taking part in such grassroots racing events are genuine enthusiasts, meaning the camaraderie is second to none, and no one is doing it for money because there simply isn't any. The atmosphere at such events is unique too. Fans are not seated in grandstands, hundreds of metres away from the action, nor are they peering through chicken-wire safety fences – they're squeezed in between hedges, right on the very edge of the road, with a few tins of beer and a rucksack full of sandwiches to hand. For these people, road racing is *real* racing, and nothing else comes close. It's free to watch, too, which is another huge attraction in such straitened times (although if spectators don't contribute by buying a programme, more events will be forced to close down).

Those muddy paddocks can easily catch out the inexperienced, however, as Ian Simpson found out to his cost during his debut at the North West 200 in 1990. Although he would eventually win five races at the event, he fell foul of the muddy paddock first time around. 'I came out of the paddock on my Honda RC30, and my tyres were covered in mud because the paddock was just a muddy field for the most part,' he says. 'I got as far as the first corner and down I went. What a plonker! I really should have been aware of that.'

Illegal testing of race bikes on public roads is not unknown ahead of road-race meetings in Ireland, but with the sport being so popular in the country, blind eyes are often turned: bikes need to be tested, after all. At the 1999 North West 200, David Jefferies' V&M team only finished building his Yamaha YZF-R1 on the morning of the first practice session, and it was vital to ensure everything was in working order rather than wasting valuable time during practice, so the country lanes of County Antrim became an impromptu test track. 'DJ had to run the bike in on Irish country lanes,' remembers team boss Jack Valentine. 'It was pissing down with rain and David came back covered in cow shit, horse shit . . . everything. A brand-new bike, first time out, and it was covered with shit off those Irish lanes! But he said, "Yeah, yeah – it feels alright", so we headed to the North West paddock.'

Although the Isle of Man TT paddock is now every bit as glitzy as the British Superbike paddock, with VIP areas, champagne hospitality units and massive race trucks, it's an exception, simply because it's the biggest road race of them all and commands global attention. But many riders prefer the grassroots nature of the other road races. When he was still racing, Guy Martin was one of them. He has never approved of teams that spend more money on ever-more luxurious race transporters and hospitality units when it's the bikes themselves that really matter. It's part of the reason why he turned his back on the TT in 2017. 'I mean, it might be me and my mates turning up in our van and parking next to 40-ton team trucks, but we're not racing trucks, are we?' he said when still competing. 'We're racing bikes, so it doesn't matter how posh a team's truck is – that doesn't win races. The day we see the trucks lining up on the grid, then that's when you'd want to be in a bigger team. I'll chuck my motorbikes in the back of my work van, and I couldn't give a fuck. I've been getting grief from race organisers about needing to have the correct team uniform and needing to have a certain kind of truck, so I just switch my phone off. I'm a realist and I genuinely couldn't give a fuck about all that stuff. I don't earn my money from racing – I have my job for that. I go racing purely as a hobby and because I enjoy it. I like to win; of course I'd like to win a TT – that's what I want to do [despite taking 17 podiums at the event, a win always eluded Martin]. But, you know, fancy clothes and big trucks don't fuckin' win races: that's just a fact. I've got enough jobs; I don't need to go racing as a job. The day I stop enjoying it is the day I'll stop doing it. I certainly don't do it for the money. So if I've got some dickhead telling me I'm wearing the wrong uniform or I'm saying the wrong things, he can just fuck off.'

Taking part in an Irish road race for the first time can

come as something of a shock to riders from outside of Ireland, as Yorkshireman Nick Jefferies testifies. He had only ever raced at English short circuits when he first crossed the Irish Sea to ride in the Skerries just outside of Dublin in the early 1970s, so his debut was something of a wake-up call. 'It seems surreal now, but at the Skerries the race secretary invited us into his tent for drinks *before* the big race!' he says. 'I went in, and they were pulling pints for the riders. I refused a full pint, but I had a half of Guinness and then set off to race! That was typically Irish back then; I had so many piss-ups over there.'

The Skerries was unlike anything Jefferies had encountered before, and health-and-safety regulations clearly weren't high on the agenda in the 1970s. 'Road racing was very, very hairy in Ireland back then,' he says. 'The lack of practice time was ridiculous. You got to the Skerries circuit on Friday afternoon about 2pm, got settled into the paddock and went through scrutineering, and at 5pm we would all get a couple of laps of practice and then we went racing. We didn't have tents or awnings or anything – we just parked our bikes next to our vans and worked on them outside.'

In what was Jefferies' road-race debut, and in only his second year of racing (he was known as a very successful trials rider before taking to the track), he found himself lining up on the Skerries grid with the biggest names in Ireland. 'I was an absolute novice in my first ever road race, but there I was lining up on the grid with Sam McClements, Mervyn Robinson, Ray McCullough and Joe Dunlop; he was called "Joe" back then, never "Joey". There weren't a lot of straw bales or any other kind of protection around the track either.'

Jefferies found that the tactics of Irish racers could be a little more maverick too. 'I finished fourth in the last race behind McCullough, Robinson and Joey,' he says. 'Sam McClements was so angry at me for cutting him up on the last lap that he ran straight into the back of me after we crossed the finish line and knocked me off my bike!'

The Irish love their road racing, both in the north and south. It's almost like a religion; in fact, Joey Dunlop's former manager Davy Wood once said that, 'There are three religions in Northern Ireland – motorcycle road racing, and the other two.'

The Isle of Man TT may be the pinnacle of the annual road-racing calendar, but Ireland is the heartland of the sport. Since the 1920s there have been scores of race meetings on a huge array of pure roads circuits, many of which are no longer held. Over the years, popular meetings have included the Ulster Grand Prix, the Temple 100, the Carrowdore 100, the Tandragee 100, Fore Road Races, the Mid Antrim 150, the Killinchy 150, the Skerries 100, the Leinster 200, the Munster 100, Armoy, the Boyne 100, the Faugheen 50, Athea, Cork road races, the Enniskillen 100, Dundalk, Kells . . . the list is a long one. But while some of these meetings are still going strong, most have fallen by the wayside through lack of support and financial backing. Public liability insurance has also become a major problem in recent years.

When a rider makes the decision to enter a road race for the first time – as Adam McLean did in 2015 – it can sometimes be difficult convincing family members of that decision. 'My mum flipped her lid as soon as she got wind that I was going to do a road race!' he says. 'I think one of my mates accidentally let the cat out of the bag by mentioning that I was going to do the Cookstown 100, which is my local road race. I got round my mum by saying I just wanted to do that one race as it was my local race, and I wanted to do it to tick it off my bucket list. She said, "Right, okay, you can do this one, but that's it!" I finished fourth in the 125 race and fourth in the Junior Support race, then I tried to put an entry form in for the North West 200, but my mum found it, ripped it up and threw it in the bin, saying, "That's *not* happening!"'

Despite the protestations of his concerned mum, McLean wasn't to be deterred. 'Later in the year I managed to talk her into letting me do the Kells road race, because I said it was a really safe one with just three road-ends and a couple of straights,' he says. 'A few laps into the 125 race I was in the lead, and my mum went from being dead against me road racing to being my number-one fan! As I came past the start–finish straight, there was my mum hanging over the fence, yelling and cheering me on! I thought, *Eh? How does that work?* I ended up winning both the 125 and Junior Support races and was third or fourth in the main Supertwin race.'

Lee Johnston had trouble convincing his father about the wisdom of road racing. 'Ah, Jaysus,' he says, rolling his eyes but smiling at the memory of his much-missed late father. 'It started out that I was only going to do one, the North West,' he adds. 'Then I signed with JMF Millsport racing in 2012 and they wanted me to do the North West, the TT and the Ulster, so we [Johnston and his dad] agreed I could do three. Then I told my dad that if I did the Macau Grand Prix I would take him with me, so that made it four. In 2013 I had a go at Scarborough, because it's close to where I live near Hull, and I thought he wouldn't find out about it! But somebody wrote about it in the paper and Dad rang up the next day, going mad. So now we are up to five, but I think that's his limit!'

Johnston lost his father Everitt to cancer in 2016 and has since raised untold thousands for cancer charities through his F13K Cancer campaign.

TT legend Steve Hislop had a similar experience when he entered his first road race in 1983. The Manx Grand Prix is essentially an amateur version of the TT. Held on the same 37.73-mile course, it has often been viewed as a stepping stone to the TT proper, which is exactly how Hislop intended to use it, despite his brother Garry being killed while racing at Silloth (a former airfield circuit in Cumbria) the previous year. 'Many people have asked me why I didn't turn my back on bike racing when my brother was killed, and it's still a difficult question to answer,' Hislop said in 2002. 'I think I just had an in-built desire to achieve something in my life, and racing bikes seemed the only way I could do that. I certainly never blamed racing for Garry's death, as it was his choice to race, and I never hated the sport because of what it had taken away from me. Bikes have always been part of my life, and I continued to ride them after Garry died, just as I always had done.'

Most of Steve's family and friends were certain he would quit racing following the tragedy, but instead he entered a race on the most dangerous circuit of them all – the

37.73-mile Mountain course. It did not go down well. 'When I filled in the entry forms for the 350cc Newcomers' race and the 250cc Lightweight event at the Manx Grand Prix, the only person I told was [friend and mechanic] Wullie Simson, because I knew most people were against me racing after what had happened to my brother,' Hislop said. 'I felt a bit sneaky going behind people's backs and not telling my mum or anyone else about my plans, but that's the way it had to be. I really didn't want to upset anyone, but I knew I had to race. I even prepared my bikes in secret and just told anyone that asked that I was doing overtime at the garage.'

Hislop's guilty secret was soon exposed, however. 'It wasn't long before my little secret got out, thanks to the race organisers,' he explained. 'Once I'd posted off my entry forms I'd forgotten all about them until I came home from work one night and the shit really hit the fan. I was confronted by my mum and stepdad Jim, looking thoroughly miserable. I was like, "Alright? How's it goin', folks?" but Jim's response was to slap a postcard down on the table in front of me and shout, "What the hell is this?" It was the confirmation of my race entries written on a bloody postcard for the whole world to see! Shit.'

> *Dear Steve, just to confirm we have received your entry for this year's Manx Grand Prix . . .*

'I thought, *Fuckin' hell, I've been rumbled here.* Jim went absolutely apeshit, screaming at me, "How can you do such a thing to your mother?", giving it all that guilt-trip bollocks. I explained it was just something I had to do and defended myself as best I could, but it was obviously falling on deaf ears. My mum and Jim continued arguing and then she said something I'll never forget. He was rattling on about me bringing more grief into the house after Garry had already brought enough, when my mum shouted, "Why the hell should Steve live his life in the shadow of someone else?"'

Hislop was deeply moved by his mother's support. 'It was a brave thing to say,' he acknowledged. 'I mean, I know I'm a selfish person for doing what I do – as I think all bike racers must be – but my mum saw beyond that and recognised my real passion for racing. Jim hated the idea of me racing, but I never expected him to understand, and I didn't care about his opinion anyway. But I really appreciated what my mum said, because she obviously realised it was unfair to deprive me of something I wanted so badly just because my brother had been killed doing the same thing. We don't stop driving cars because someone else has an accident, do we? To me, bike racing was no different.'

While Steve Hislop knew exactly what he wanted, and stopped at nothing to make it happen, some riders fall into road racing almost accidentally, as was the case with Davey Todd, who had run out of money in 2017 and thought his short circuit racing career was over. 'That's when I got into talks with Harry Corbett from Longshot Racing about having a go at road racing, and I thought, *Why not? I've tried everything else – why not have a go at that?*' he says. 'So, he invited me over to do the Skerries in 2017 and that was my first road race.'

Although it no longer runs, the Skerries was for many years the biggest road race in the Republic of Ireland. Situated just outside Dublin, the 2.93-mile circuit was notoriously narrow, bumpy and fast, and the jumps were spectacular. Over 60,000 people regularly packed the hedgerows to watch the action and they were never disappointed. But it was a fearsome circuit on which to make your road-racing debut. 'I didn't know anything about the Skerries – I'd never even heard of it!' Todd says. 'Everyone in the paddock was asking me what road races I'd done before, and I was like, "None!" They couldn't believe I'd picked the Skerries to make my debut, but I loved it instantly. Once I got a bit more used to it and my eyes were no longer pinned to the back of my skull, I really started to enjoy it and loved the thrill of it. There's a little bit extra to road racing that you don't get from circuit racing. Maybe it's the fear, the danger, I don't know, but I just wanted more.'

James Hillier didn't. A fantastic road racer at bigger events, he quickly discovered the Skerries wasn't for him. 'I did the Skerries one time, and that was enough!' he says.

The smaller Irish national road-race meetings didn't appeal to Lee Johnston either. While he may have been comfortable racing at the TT, the North West 200 and the Ulster Grand Prix, he drew the line at the narrow, bumpier and more dangerous courses. 'I have never done the wee roads because I don't think I'd be any good at it,' he says. 'I don't even know where the Cookstown 100 course is. I couldn't do it. I'm shit at jumping; I'm happy with my arse on the ground.'

Johnson's close friend Jamie Hamilton was forced to retire from road racing after suffering life-changing injuries in a crash at the TT in 2015, but he loved the Irish nationals.

'The Irish National races are more fun because there is no big pressure, and you just go and enjoy yourself,' he said the year before his big crash. 'I love all the little jumps and bumps at the wee races; I'm not scared to put it [the bike] on its side.'

Despite the fact that there's very little prize money on offer at the smaller races – and very little in the way of fame or glory – riders are still willing to put their lives on the line to win races: their motivation comes from a much deeper place. Southern Irish rider Derek McGee is a good example. In 2018 he had a horrendous crash at the Ulster Grand Prix that saw him fracture his pelvis and femur (he broke the ball-end off the top of his femur) and he also suffered a broken collarbone and four broken ribs as well as a collapsed lung.

It looked like his bid to win four Irish national titles in one year (a feat which has never been achieved) seemed to be over, but McGee had other ideas. Just four weeks after sustaining such serious multiple injuries, he turned up at the Killalane road races on crutches with the intention of racing. 'It was very difficult,' he admits. 'I'd been in a wheelchair for weeks and had just started to walk the day before the race. I had to change the whole bike, putting extra seat foam padding on it and lowering the footrests just to make me a little more comfortable.'

There's no painkiller like adrenaline, and once the racing started McGee showed true grit, coming through to win the Supersport race to add that championship to the Supertwin and Superbike titles he already had in the bag. 'It was great to come back and win against the likes of Michael Sweeney, Derek Sheils and Paul Jordan,' McGee says. 'I only needed to finish top ten to clinch the championship, but once the adrenaline kicked in and dulled the pain I just got my head down and went for it. We were actually on to win a fourth title in the Moto3 class, but my own bike was out of action, so I had to borrow one and was only able to finish fourth in the final race when I needed to be third. That was a pity, because nobody has ever won four titles in one year in Ireland and I only missed out by two or three points.'

Derek McGee is typical of so many road racers in that he prefers the grassroots nature of the sport and the camaraderie that's so evident in the makeshift paddocks that spring up overnight, invariably in a field next to the start line. For him – like so many others – road racing is all about family and friends. 'They all give up their time to do it for nothing,' McGee says of the help he gets from those closest to him. 'If it wasn't for them, I wouldn't be racing. I think every rider dreams of getting signed up by a big team – it would take a lot of pressure off if I just had to turn up and ride the bike – because all the other organisational stuff can really stress you out. But at the same time it's nice to be able to pick and choose what I want to do, and to go racing with a big group of family and friends is just great craic. The way we approach it is that we just try to enjoy the race meeting, and if we can get some good results then that's a bonus.'

One of the darkest days at the Skerries came on 7th July, 2018, when road racing lost one of its greatest and most popular heroes. William Dunlop had already lost his uncle Joey to a race crash in 2000, and his father Robert was killed at the North West 200 in 2008. He and his brother Michael raced on after losing their father, but by 2018

William was 33 years old and his fiancée Janine Brolly was pregnant with their second child. William was ready to retire from road racing, by then more conscious than ever of the dangers involved. He was also concerned about complications Brolly was experiencing in her pregnancy. In an almost unheard-of move, he pulled out of the Isle of Man TT in 2018, saying, 'My head wasn't in the races and my thoughts were always on what was happening at home.'

Dunlop would later issue a statement and, in his habitually humble and modest style, apologised to everyone he felt he had let down.

'This is a very difficult decision and not one I have taken lightly, I can only apologise to the team, and all of our sponsors, but I believe that continuing would be the wrong decision and would not give a true account of either myself or the team. I would like to thank Tim [Tim Martin – Temple Yamaha team boss], especially for how understanding and supportive he has been over the past few weeks. I obviously feel like I have let him and the team down, but they have stood by me throughout. I am going to head home and take some time to recuperate before making a decision on when I will be back on the Temple Yamahas.'

After much soul-searching, and still seriously considering retiring from the sport, Dunlop decided to enter the Skerries, just one month after the TT. It would prove to be a fatal decision. William Dunlop was killed during practice for the southern Irish race when oil leaked from the sump of his bike and caused him to crash at over 170mph. A jury returned a verdict of death by misadventure. Two months after Dunlop's death, his second daughter was born. She was named Willa, after the father she would never get to meet.

*

Motorcycle road racing has long had a macho image, but there are an increasing number of women who are prepared to tackle this most dangerous of sports and face all the same hazards as their male counterparts. Czech racer Veronika Hankocyová is one of them. She got her first taste of road racing in Slovakia in 2005 and was instantly hooked, despite her parents' fears. 'My friends are okay about my racing, but it was very difficult for my parents in the beginning,' Hankocyová says. 'When I first started racing my mum was always crying and always had big tears in her eyes, but now she's my biggest fan!'

Hankocyová's native Czech Republic is big on road racing, meaning there were plenty of opportunities when she decided to try her hand at the sport. She made her debut in neighbouring Slovakia, and it proved to be a baptism of fire and instantly addictive. 'My first road race was in Slovakia in 2005,' Hankocyová says. 'I had a 1977 Suzuki GS750 as a road bike and my friend from Brno was doing some classic racing and he said my bike would be perfect for that and that I should try it. He helped me get my race licence, and so I started racing. It was like a challenge for me at the time because I've always loved adrenaline sports. It didn't come easy to me, though – I crashed two times in the very first practice session! Everybody was laughing at me, but after that first race I thought, *This is for me – I need to do more of this.*'

In 2013 Hankocyová made her debut on the Irish road-race scene at the Cookstown 100. 'It wasn't even my idea!' she laughs. 'I was there with Indi [former partner and fellow racer, Michal 'Indi' Dokoupil] and I was completely scared watching him race on those roads. But a friend said there was a small team that might be able to help me with a bike to race in Ireland. I was very happy about this, but at the same time very scared, because it was like another world to me. There were some really big names racing there and it was very hard for me to take in that I could actually be lining up alongside them. But I did the Cookstown in 2013 and it was fantastic. I loved it.'

Female road racers need to be every bit as tough as the men: walls, trees and houses don't discriminate when it comes to delivering bone-crunching injuries if riders of either sex make a mistake. Hankocyová proved how tough she was not long after making her debut at the Cookstown. 'I had a big crash in the Czech Republic that put me out of action for over six months,' she explains. 'I broke my pelvis and my collarbone and some fingers and other things, but the collarbone gave me the most trouble in terms of movement, so I had to have three surgeries on that. I couldn't race for a long time, so my next Irish race was the Ulster Grand Prix – two weeks after my last surgery. I also raced at Killalane and that made me realise that I definitely wanted to do more Irish road racing.'

Hankocyová crashed out of the first Supertwin race at the 2025 TT and suffered broken ribs and arm injuries. It didn't put her off in the slightest. 'I'm on the mend and never give up,' she posted on Facebook shortly after the accident. 'I'll be back.'

Another female racer, Maria Costello, earned an MBE for her racing activities in 2009. In 2005 she stood on the podium at the Manx Grand Prix, making her the first female solo rider to take a podium in a race on the famous TT Mountain course. She would back that up with a third place in the Classic 250cc race behind John McGuinness and Dean Harrison at the Classic TT in 2011.

But it hasn't always been glamour and gongs for Costello; like every road racer, she's had to suffer for her sport too. In total she has broken 24 bones, but her biggest crash came at the TT in 1999. 'I had a big crash during practice on my Honda Fireblade,' she says. 'Another rider clipped me at the bottom of Bray Hill and I rattled up someone's fence. I was thrown from the bike and knocked out, so I don't remember it – and I don't want to remember it either! I broke my pelvis, my leg was in a plaster cast, I popped my shoulder out, but popped it back in, and I took all the skin off my knuckles.'

That wasn't the only occasion that tested Costello's mettle. 'I had another crash at the TT on the same Honda RVF400 that I got a podium with at the Manx,' she continues. 'I crashed on oil at Keppel Gate in practice and ended up in the heather with Dan Kneen's dad picking me out of it [Dan Kneen was a top TT competitor until he lost his life at the event in 2018]. I broke my femur and my scapula in that one. Because it was the neck of the femur – the angled part – I was out of action for six months. Wasn't even allowed to put any weight on it for three months.'

Anita Buxton made history in 2004 when she became the first woman to win an international road race. She took victory in the 400cc race at the Ulster Grand Prix, leading a humbled Joe Phillips over the line by a mere 0.1 seconds, having led the entire race.

Another female racer, Carolynn Sells, made history in 2009 when she became the first woman to win a race on the TT Mountain course. Her victory in the Ultra-Lightweight Manx Grand Prix fulfilled her lifetime ambition and she retired happily afterwards, her mission accomplished.

One year later Jenny Tinmouth became the fastest female racer in history at the TT. Beryl Swain had been the first solo female competitor at the TT in 1962, and the pioneering Londoner lapped at 48.3mph on her tiny 50cc machine before her racing licence was revoked due to a new ruling that banned all women from competing in the TT.

Curator of social history for Manx National Heritage, Matthew Richardson, says the decision was a sign of the times. 'Having a male racer injured or killed on the TT course was one thing, but the organisers were just not prepared to take the risk of that happening to a woman.'

Some 48 years after Swain's heroic debut, Jenny Tinmouth, on an infinitely more powerful Honda Fireblade, posted an average lap time just short of 120mph, making her the fastest woman ever to compete in the TT. She still is.

It wasn't until 1978 that the sexist ruling banning women from racing at the TT was finally rescinded. That year, Hilary Musson became only the second woman to compete in a solo race at the TT (after Beryl Swain) and finished in a highly credible 15th place, just one position behind her racer husband John Musson. Hilary raced at the TT until 1985, and after retiring continued to support the event by becoming a marshal. In all her years of racing the worst injury Musson had suffered was a bruised wrist, but in 2007 two spectators and a rider were killed when the rider lost control of his machine on the Mountain section of the TT course. The same bike also struck two marshals, one of whom was Musson. She awoke six weeks later in a hospital bed to discover that her life had changed forever. She had sustained breaks in her legs, ribs and spine, as well as suffering a burst spleen. She had also survived her femoral artery being severed, but the injuries to her left leg were so severe that it had to be amputated above the knee. In a 2007 interview with the *New York Times* Musson said, 'I still find it difficult to accept it, even now, because it wasn't my fault. I still feel it was a bit cruel, I'd say.'

The horrific incident was proof that spectating or marshalling at a road race is not without risk either. Hilary Musson sadly passed away in 2023 and remains a much-missed member of the racing community, as well as a true TT trailblazer.

Jenny Tinmouth only competed at the TT in 2009 and 2010 due to lack of funds and support, but her bravery – both on short circuits and the roads – cannot be doubted. That very lack of funding during her racing career meant she had to grit her teeth even more than most. 'I'm okay with the whole pain thing,' she says. 'I managed to get my leathers off myself when I broke both wrists at Anglesey. I wouldn't let the doctors cut them off because I couldn't afford new ones! It was the same at Cadwell Park in 2003 when I broke my collarbone, ankle and wrist – I still managed to get out of my leathers.'

For Tinmouth, like most riders, pain is not the worst part of having injuries – the boredom of recuperating is far worse: 'I do get bored sitting around the house waiting to get better,' she said while still racing. 'All in all, I've broken both wrists – one of them twice – my arm, my collarbone and my ankle, and I've also dislocated my collarbone. When I first started racing I actually *wanted* to break something because I'd never broken a bone before! I was like a kid at school wanting a plaster to look cool. I was chuffed when I had to get a plate in my wrist – I was like "Yeah, check this out!"'

While female riders are still in the minority, they are more commonplace than in the past, and they're every bit as tough, gritty and determined as their male counterparts and deserve just as much respect.

*

Despite its popularity with both riders and spectators, Irish road racing has been in big trouble in recent years, and its very existence has been under threat. It's one thing when a rider dies – they know the risks and willingly accept them – but it's another thing altogether when spectators are killed. After 100 years of spectator safety at the Isle of Man TT, a rider and two spectators were killed in the same incident during the Centennial TT in 2007. In the very first running of the Armoy Road Races in Northern Ireland in 2009 a 75-year-old spectator was killed after being struck by an out-of-control race bike. Three years later, a rider and two more spectators were killed at the TT, and at the Southern

100 in 2023 a rider and a flag marshal lost their lives when a bike crashed into them.

Spectator deaths usually involve considerable financial compensation, meaning public liability insurance for road-race events has rocketed in recent years to such an extent that the Motorcycle Union of Ireland (MCUI) announced that there would be no road racing held in Ireland at all in 2023 as insurance costs were simply too high.

Crowdfunding (and a very generous local businessman) helped to save the North West 200 that year, and after a new insurance deal was agreed other Irish road races also went ahead, but it had been a close-run thing and many of the smaller events no longer take place.

The Tandragee 100 is a good example of the problems road race organisers face in the modern world. First held in 1958, the Tandragee took place over a 5.3-mile circuit near the village of Clare in County Armagh, and it has attracted many big names over the years, including Joey, Robert, Michael and William Dunlop, Guy Martin, Phillip McCallen and Ryan Farquhar, but the event ran into trouble in 2020 and has been struggling ever since.

After two years of being cancelled due to the Covid pandemic in 2020 and 2021, the event was then cancelled in 2023 due to insurance costs and again in 2024 due to the condition of the roads. The circuit, like every road circuit, has had issues with safety precautions too. In 2008 one of the most popular Irish road racers of them all, Martin Finnegan, lost his life at the event after suffering brake failure and crashing into a grass bank.

At a preliminary hearing in 2011 looking into Finnegan's

death, coroner John Leckey questioned whether racing should even take place on pure roads circuits. 'A country road circuit is a very different creature to an F1 circuit or a short circuit,' he said. 'And if it cannot be made safe to a requisite standard, then the question has to be asked: should the motor racing take place at all?'

Finnegan's fatal accident occurred at Marlacoo corner; the only corner on the Tandragee course that didn't have either a slip road or air fencing to protect the riders. A married father of one, Finnegan had won the opening race of the day before the tragedy occurred. Two spectators were injured in the accident, once again highlighting the issue of public liability insurance at road races.

And yet, even in his raw grief, Finnegan's father Jim stood by the sport. 'If you were to talk to any of the riders, they always know that there is a possibility that they could be killed,' he told *News Letter*. 'Martin knew this, but the riders love the sport and that is the reason they do it – because of the sport. My feelings are very raw, but Martin loved the sport; I love the sport and have lost my son to it, but my views have not changed – absolutely not.'

The Tandragee 100 made a successful return in 2025 after resurfacing work had been completed and the course was deemed safe to race on again. Boosted by the presence of 33-time TT winner Michael Dunlop, the resurrected event was a resounding success, and its return must be seen as a good sign for road racing.

Tragedies like Finnegan's death, and the death of spectators, are the biggest threat to road racing because of the insurance implications, but there was good news for the sport in 2025 – in the south of Ireland, at least – when it was thrown a lifeline by a breakaway group called Road Racing Alliance Ireland (RRAI) who negotiated a new insurance deal to run seven races in the south. One of the founders of the group, Paul Power, explained: 'There was no prospect for road racing in 2025. A number of clubs decided that if Motorcycling Ireland [MCI, the governing body of the sport in the Republic of Ireland] couldn't get insurance, then we should start looking for ourselves. It wasn't done to put two fingers up to MCI – the only driving force was that if we didn't do it our road racing would be consigned to the history books. We thought it was better to do something and fail than to do nothing.'

The deal ensured the return of the Walderstown, Athea, Munster and Faugheen road races, along with three others (which were still to be confirmed). Southern Irish racer Derek McGee believed this was an encouraging sign. 'The more clubs that run events, the cheaper the insurance is for everyone because it's amalgamated between all the clubs,' he says.

Sadly, the Road Racing Alliance Ireland initiative failed. In June of 2025 it was announced that the Irish government insisted on recognising just one national governing body for the sport and the MCI won out. 'We have come to the end of the road,' said an RRAI representative and, with that, the resurrection of road racing in Southern Ireland came to an abrupt end. For the time being, at least. A statement from the RRAI read:

'The RRAI would like to thank each and every one involved in the sport of road racing for their support

and messages since last year. Those words did not go unnoticed and were greatly appreciated, especially as we were ensuring that no stone was left unturned in the pursuit of getting back between the hedges, and to sincerely apologise that sadly we did not achieve the desired outcome of getting the events back up and running. It wasn't due to the lack of hard work, commitment and belief that our sport could return, and we all could get back to watching what is part and parcel of our motorcycling heritage.'

Whether the MCI can ever come up with an insurance package to allow races to be run in the future remains to be seen, but the signs are not encouraging. As we have seen, every attempt to either start a new road race (the Isle of Wight races, the Welsh road races) or to resurrect a once-traditional race meeting (Walderstown, Athea, Munster and Faugheen) have come to naught. Various reasons have been given, but could the real reason be that the authorities are simply no longer prepared to sanction such dangerous events? Is the very future of road racing under threat? Will it become just another part of motorcycling history? The two biggest events – the TT and the North West 200 – seem to be secure, but that's because they generate so much money for the Isle of Man and Northern Ireland economies respectively. The smaller races, it would seem, are doomed. In 2025 just four road races took place in Northern Ireland while none at all were staged in the south. Even the Skerries – traditionally the south's biggest road race – was cancelled. Due to insurance issues, the once-mighty meeting was cancelled in 2023 and was reduced to a much safer and sanitised sprint event in 2024. A sprint race has a start point and an end point – in this case just 0.8 miles/1.4km – meaning there's no bike-to-bike racing, no overtaking and no laps to allow riders to increase their speed through repetition. A sprint is just a short run from one point to another and is about as far removed from racing as it's possible to get. The Skerries sprint took in part of the old course but bikes were limited to 600cc, and the spectacle and thrill of full-on races is now a thing of the past. In 2025 there wasn't even a sprint event; instead, the organising club (Loughshinny Motorcycle Supporters Club) laid on a family fun day and chat show. The demise of the once-great Skerries 100 seems to be yet another nail in the coffin of Irish road racing.

Which begs the question of how even the mighty Isle of Man TT can hope to survive if there are no smaller road races to act as feeder events and to help young riders get a taste of road racing without jumping straight in at the deep end. Is the clock ticking on *all* road races, even the TT?

It's clear that organising and funding a road race isn't as easy as it once was, which is why the sport enjoyed a golden era in the 1970s when health and safety concerns and insurance cover weren't such big issues. It was a much simpler time, and the rise of two rival groups of Irish riders at that time provided a spectacle that drew tens of thousands to every event. The era of the Armoy Armada and the Dromara Destroyers was one of the greatest ever seen in road racing.

CHAPTER 13

THE ARMOY ARMADA

'I had a copy of The Road Racers *on tape as a kid, and I used to watch it over and over again. Joey and Ray McCullough and the boys racing so hard around those little Irish road circuits.'*
CARL FOGARTY

Jim Dunlop looks, and speaks, uncannily like his late brother Joey. Five years younger than the road racing legend, Jim was no mean rider himself back in the day and was one of the famous 'Armoy Armada' in the 1970s, alongside Joey, Frank Kennedy and Mervyn Robinson.

Irish road racing in the 1970s may have been hugely popular but it was also even more dangerous than it is now. Jim lost his close friend and fellow Armoy Armada rider Frank Kennedy following a crash at the North West 200 in 1979, and his brother-in-law Mervyn Robinson at the same event the following year. In just 12 months, the Armada's membership had been reduced by half, and the Dunlop brothers saw little point in carrying on. 'When Mervyn was killed, Joey just abandoned the whole thing,' says Jim. 'We had a meeting and that was it, finished. People say Joey was close to quitting racing then, but I don't think that would ever have happened.'

Joey Dunlop didn't stop racing – he went on to become the most successful TT racer in history with 26 wins to his name; a title he held for 24 years. It was only in 2024 that his nephew Michael Dunlop took the honour from him by claiming a 27th win, then a 29th and a 30th.

Jim says his late father Willie was one of the brothers' inspirations when it came to their obsession with bikes. 'When I was young my dad had a BSA, and he'd take me and my sister Linda to school on it. I sat on the tank and my sister sat on the pillion seat. There were always old bikes about when we were growing up.'

Mervyn Robinson was another source of inspiration to Joey Dunlop. 'Mervyn had raced before meeting my sister but had given it up,' Jim says. 'When he started courting Helen he started racing again and he got Joey into it. They both had road bikes and the two of them used to race each other coming home from work. There was some S-bends on a local road, and we used to go up after school and lie on the bank to watch Joey and Mervyn come round flat out. Merv would win sometimes, and Joey would win other times – they were pretty evenly matched.'

It was this impromptu racing on normal public roads that stood the Dunlop brothers in such good stead in later years, but it didn't always go to plan, as Jim explains. 'Me and Joey raced down the road one time. I had a 200cc Suzuki and Joey was on our dad's Honda Super-Six. I followed him down the wee back roads, just sitting on his back wheel. Eventually we stopped and turned round, and Joey said he'd follow me on the way back. I set off as fast as I could, knowing he'd be right on my back wheel, but at the very first corner I ran onto the grass and crashed. I threw myself down in a ditch because I knew Joey was right behind me and thought he would crash into me, but he made it round the corner safely. Then the big problem was getting home with just one bike. I wouldn't sit on the back with Joey, and he wouldn't sit on the back with me, so we were stuck. We eventually came to an agreement that he would ride halfway home, and I'd ride the other half. When we got to the house my dad was waiting in the drive, shaking his head saying, "I knew this was going to happen."'

The Dunlop brothers' need for speed soon found an outlet on the racetracks of Ireland, and together with Merv Robinson and another local rider Frank Kennedy they became known as the Armoy Armada, in response to a rival group of riders from 60 miles south: the Dromara Destroyers. Consisting of Ray McCullough, Brian Reid, Ian McGregor and Trevor Steele, the Destroyers would provide the Armada with a perfect counterpart for some epic clashes over the next three years.

By 1977, fans at racetracks were divided like football fans (without the mindless violence) in their loyalties, but the riders were great friends as well as rivals. 'It was all good fun,' Jim says. 'We once did a fundraising event along with the Dromara Destroyers where we had to eat raw onions or see who could get changed into a boiler suit the fastest – just different bits and pieces, you know? Drinking a pint of

Guinness with a sausage in it – it looked like someone had crapped in your pint. There might have been a bit of needle, just for the craic, but there was nothing serious about it – it was all good fun.'

The spirit of those years can still be seen in David Wallace's documentary *The Road Racers*, which followed the Armoy Armada throughout the 1977 season. The film has since become a motorcycling classic but not one that Joey Dunlop ever watched, according to his brother. 'I don't think Joey ever watched it because of what happened to Merv and Frank,' Jim Dunlop says. 'I've only seen it a couple of times myself. It's a good enough film to watch, but when you're involved in something maybe you don't look at it in the same way that other people do. I'm glad they made it, though.'

Being five years Jim's junior, the third Dunlop brother, Robert, was too young to ride for the Armoy Armada, but even when he did start racing he showed no sign of being the brilliant rider he would later become, as Jim recalls. 'I remember when he started, I took him round Kirkistown and said, "Just follow me and I'll show you the way round." I was going as slow as I could, and after a lap or so I looked round and he was nowhere to be seen. I said to Joey, "He'll never make a racer – he's fuckin' useless." And so he was at that time, but he went on to prove me wrong.'

They may have taken time to develop, but all three brothers clearly had exceptional talents on two wheels. Jim may be the least known of the three – chiefly because he retired from racing so early – but he was more than a match for Joey on occasion in the early days. 'I remember one particular 250 race against Joey somewhere in England,' he says. 'The likes of Ron Haslam and Steve Tonkin were there, and I beat Joey that day. Another lap and I would have beaten Haslam as well. Tonkin came off in front of me and I had to go onto the grass to avoid him. I caught Joey on the last lap but ran out of time to catch Haslam.'

Brothers they may have been – and Joey had helped his younger sibling out immensely by giving him bikes and helping him work on them – but they still wanted to beat each other. 'My bike had been handling terribly in that race and the tyres felt they were going to let go on every corner,' Jim says. 'After the race, Joey said to me, "You've got the wrong tyres on," and he told me what ones I should have had on. But he only told me that *after* the race – not before. That was Joey.'

Jim's racing career was extremely short compared to those of his brothers. He only raced from 'about 1976 to 1982', not because of any lack of talent (he was leading the Newcomers' race at the Manx GP in 1978 before his bike broke down), but because of a dire lack of money. In a last-ditch attempt to attract some backing, Jim hatched a plan but, as things turned out, it failed miserably. 'I had no moncy, so I thought if I stopped racing somebody would come and offer me a bike, but it never happened. I had two bikes, but I couldn't afford to run them.'

An early retirement is something that Dunlop says he now regrets, but that regret is tinged with a stark realisation that his enforced exit from racing is probably the only reason he's still alive today, when the rest of the Armoy Armada and his brother Robert (killed at the North West 200 in

2008) are no longer with us. 'I do regret it, but if I hadn't stopped racing then I might not be here either,' he says. 'You know, there were three of us all racing from the one family, at the one time, and the law of averages said that one of us was going to get hurt at some stage or other.'

As Joey's career went stratospheric following the demise of the Armoy Armada, Robert Dunlop also started to make a name for himself. Yet as brothers, they were very different men: Joey was shy, mumbling and unkempt, while Robert was outgoing, articulate and, usually, that bit more dapper. Jim offers an explanation. 'Robert always had to go begging a lot for sponsorship and was always having to chat to people to try and get a pound or two, so he sort of had to be more outgoing. Joey got in with Honda early on and didn't really have to do that. He never had to go looking or talking to people for sponsorship. Robert had to do whatever he could to get some backing, so he had to shout that bit louder than Joey.'

Jim Dunlop no longer rides himself, not even a road bike. A steel erector by trade, it seems that he was able to settle into a life after racing, unlike his brothers who just couldn't envisage a life without bikes. 'I wouldn't doubt that Joey would still be at it if he were here today,' Jim says. 'He'd probably be racing some of these old classic bikes or something. He owned the pub [Joey bought what is now Joey's Bar in 1984], but he wouldn't have been content sitting in there, you know? I would say he would have been racing at some level.'

Robert, too, couldn't seem to give up the habit, despite carrying horrendous injuries from a 1994 TT crash. In 2005 he took a year out following yet another operation to fix the leg he mangled in that incident, and many thought he would then call it a day. But still he came back for more. Robert lost his life during practice for the 2008 North West 200 meeting. 'Hindsight's a wonderful thing,' Jim says, reflecting on his younger brother's death. 'When Robert had a year out getting his leg fixed – you'd have thought that would have been enough, you know? He had the young boys to look after, so he could have retired from racing himself and just looked after them. But it wasn't to be.'

As previously mentioned, David Wallace's classic documentary *The Road Racers* stands as a memorial to the Armoy Armada. Carl Fogarty almost wore his copy out when he was young. 'I had a copy of *The Road Racers* on tape as a kid, and I used to watch it over and over again,' he says. 'Joey and Ray McCullough and the boys racing so hard around those little Irish road circuits.'

Shot in the summer of 1977, the film followed a then-unknown Joey Dunlop, together with Mervyn Robinson and Frank Kennedy, as they raced the Irish roads on a shoestring budget. Using pioneering techniques such as on-board cameras, *The Road Racers* has become a cult classic among bike-racing fans, and it perfectly captures the spirit of Irish road racing in its 1970s heyday.

'Most people's image of bike racing at that time was of Barry Sheene and all the glamour that surrounded him with the Brut adverts on TV,' says director David Wallace. 'It was 1977, Sheene had won his second 500cc world title and enjoyed a playboy lifestyle more reminiscent of a rock star than a motorcycle racer. He had the Rolls-Royces, the helicopters, a Penthouse Pet hanging on his arm and the world's press eating out of his hand. Sheene had it all, and his success had made bike racing more popular than it had ever been in Britain.'

But there was another side to bike racing in the 1970s, and David Wallace was determined to capture it on celluloid to complete the picture. As he says, 'Joey Dunlop was unlikely to be offered an aftershave advertising contract! I took some photographs in 1976, and his hair was so unkempt you could barely see his face when he was working on the bike.'

Even after becoming a five-time TT Formula 1 world champion (the largely roads-based championship that ran from 1977 until 1990), Joey Dunlop didn't have too much time for appearances, but when Wallace worked with him in 1976 and '77 he was a real diamond in the rough, living on the dole in a council house and digging peat to keep his young family warm in winter. Yet even then, the unkempt Irishman showed signs of the greatness that was to come. 'There was no doubt about it that Joey was the one who was really focused,' Wallace says. 'I think his ability to concentrate singled him out. He was completely into what he was doing, and he was going to do it as well as he possibly could. When I was taking photos at the Mid Antrim in 1976, I asked a spectator where the bikes would land from the jump, as I needed to get my camera focused. He said, "Well, they land all over the place – apart from Joey. Wherever you see Joey land on lap one, you could put a coin down on the spot and he'll hit it on every lap after that." That summed Joey up. He was disciplined.

He was very fast and he was very fearless, but he didn't fall off that often. Merv and Frank did most of the falling off.'

'Merv and Frank' were Mervyn Robinson and Frank Kennedy, the other two members of the Armoy Armada in 1977 (Joey's brother Jim would not join the group until later). It was a serendipitous meeting with a relation of Robinson's that led to the trio becoming the subjects of Wallace's first film. 'My neighbour was a man called Quentin Robinson,' the director explains, 'and when I mentioned to him that I wanted to make a film he said his nephew Mervyn was a bike racer, so he arranged an introduction. I didn't even know about the Armoy Armada at the time. So, I met Mervyn first. He was the most open, humorous and impish of the three – he was a lovely warm character. Frank was a bit more serious but fantastically friendly and helpful. Then Mervyn took me along to meet Joey because they were related [brothers-in-law] and Joey was quiet, as you would imagine – he didn't speak a great deal. He never said anything negative, but you got the impression that being in a film was probably the sort of nuisance he could live without.'

It was clear that even in the early days Dunlop was not comfortable in front of cameras – a trait that would continue throughout his career. 'To be honest, I think that Joey thought the others wanted the film to happen, so he went along with it,' says Wallace. 'He probably didn't realise just how much of an imposition it is having a film made about you. He managed to keep the nuisance value down by keeping a bit of distance, but he was never unfriendly. If you said you wanted to come and film in his garage the night before a race, that wasn't a problem. You could film what you liked and stay as long as you liked but, for example, if you were shooting and you missed something happening and asked if you could shoot it again, he'd say, "Look, it'll make all our lives easier if we just get it right first time, every time." With the other riders you could do as many retakes as you liked, but with Joey you just had to be that bit more efficient. He always got his part right first time, so it was almost as if he was saying, "Look, I can do it, why can't you?" Of course he would never have said that, but it was difficult to ever really know what Joey was thinking.'

The film was made on the tightest of budgets using borrowed equipment and a great deal of goodwill. Wallace's background was in making short educational films for the BBC's schools department and he really wanted to make a feature-length documentary of his own, though bike racing wasn't the first idea he pitched when he approached the Northern Ireland Arts Council for funding. Thinking they would want something 'arty' he offered up ideas on the local harvest and on Irish poets, neither of which stirred any interest in Brian Ferran, the man holding the purse strings. 'I only had the motorbike idea left,' Wallace says, 'so I pitched that, promising it would be very artistic because I thought that was what he wanted to hear. He looked up and explained that his family used to have a summer house in Portrush [the North West 200 course runs through the coastal town] and as a boy he'd run out to the front gate to watch these motorbikes rushing past at 100mph. It had clearly left a big impression on him, and he wanted to know how it all happened – how bikes could be raced on public roads. And that was *exactly* what I really wanted to make a film about.'

Wallace left with a £4,000 grant, though it wasn't nearly enough. After securing various other sponsors and ploughing around £4,000 of his own money into the project, he had a total budget of £9,000. It was just about enough to shoot the film, and he would worry about post-production later. Wallace took three weeks' leave to shoot the documentary, primarily with one camera, though others were borrowed from time to time as favours were called in. 'I paid the cameraman, the sound recordist and the production assistant £50 a week out of my own pocket, and I provided accommodation for them by hiring a little cottage,' Wallace says. 'The riders didn't get paid anything. The BBC didn't pay people for documentaries back then and, up to a point, they still don't. At that point, I was nearly as poor as the guys were.'

Yet necessity is the mother of invention, and Wallace didn't allow a shortage of funds to cramp his innovative style. *The Road Racers* featured stunning on-board camera work years before it became commonplace. Wallace explains: 'I bought a gun camera that had been used on fighter planes [gun cams were synched to the aircraft's machine guns to record any hits] and our sound engineer made all the bracketing to fit it to the bikes. We got the guys to do one meeting each with the camera. Joey was up first, doing the North West 200. The camera itself was quite small but the battery was bulky, so it had to be strapped somewhere else, like under the seat. In Joey's case we had a problem, and Joey didn't like problems. He didn't like complications – he just wanted things to work. When he came for his bike, we had the camera fitted but the battery still wasn't attached, and Joey didn't want to wait. I said we were going to have to forget it, but Joey asked what the problem was. When I told him we hadn't mounted the battery he said, "Is that all? That bit of metal?" When I said yes, he jumped on the bike and put the battery between his legs and rode off! The only thing holding that battery on during a lap of the North West 200 at racing speeds was Joey's knees!'

The opening shot of the film shows Mervyn Robinson illegally testing his race bike on small country lanes, scattering sheep in all directions. The shot perfectly summed up the maverick spirit of Irish road racing in the seventies. Wallace explains how the idea came about. 'I had asked Joey what it was like testing a race bike late at night on country roads, and was he ever worried about the police? He said, "I'm far more worried about the sheep," so that's where the idea for the opening shot came from. We set the shot up, so it was just a timing thing. We had to be sure the farmers could get the sheep off the road before the bike arrived at speed. I think the health and safety brigade would have had something to say about that now!'

Had they existed back then, the health and safety brigade would have been in an even bigger flap over the impromptu methods used to get the aerial shots seen in the film. 'They were filmed by an NBC war cameraman who had done Vietnam and the Israeli wars,' Wallace says. 'We had both been in the university air squadron and had been taught to fly by the RAF. He said he could get an aerial shot, so I gave him the camera and he and a friend who had a plane took off to get some shots of the bikes racing along the coast road at the North West. Unfortunately we hadn't thought it through properly, as the door was on the pilot's side, so the cameraman couldn't hang out to get the shot. They couldn't change seats in the air, so they landed, changed seats, and my friend, who hadn't flown for about five years and probably didn't have a pilot's licence at that point, took off and flew the plane back up to the circuit. He then hung out of the pilot's door to get the shots while the other guy reached over and held the controls! The tricky bit came afterwards, when my mate – who also hadn't *landed* a plane in five years – had to land it all by himself, but somehow he managed without mishap.'

A native Ulsterman himself, Wallace had no problem understanding Dunlop, Robinson and Kennedy's accents, but it wasn't quite so simple for others. 'When I showed the film to people in the UK they said they couldn't understand a word they said – they had no idea what they were talking about. So I explained the problem to the riders, and they all agreed to be interviewed again and to speak in what they called their "Sunday-go-to-meeting" voices. It's still their voices, but it would have been more fun for me if we could have used their natural accents.'

Although all the footage was shot at the Cookstown 100, the Carrowdore 100 and the North West 200 in 1977, the film didn't get aired until 1980, again due to budget and time constraints. 'I had to persuade editors to give their time for nothing, and they had to find spare time to do the editing,' Wallace says. 'One of my in-laws provided an editing machine – you couldn't just do it on a laptop back then, you needed an editing machine and an editing room.'

Four years after the project was begun, *The Road Racers* was finally aired on BBC Northern Ireland in 1980 before being transmitted to the rest of the UK on BBC2, and it continues to sell to this day in various formats, even though the original film no longer exists. 'All the film was destroyed,' Wallace says. 'It was standard practice back then; it wasn't exactly a prized film.'

It's a prized film now, providing, as it does, not only a perfect snapshot of Irish road racing in its 1970s heyday, but also unique early footage of Joey Dunlop before he became a superstar. It also became a tribute to Frank Kennedy and Mervyn Robinson who both died in separate incidents at the North West 200 (in 1979 and 1980, respectively) while the film was still going through the long, drawn-out post-production process. 'After Frank was killed, we talked about what we were going to do with the film,' Wallace says, 'but I don't think we ever considered *not* finishing it. I mean, it would have been easy to have had an instantaneous reaction and feel that it was no longer in good taste, but of course it *was* in good taste. I've met Mervyn's son Paul Robinson, and lots of other people since then, and most of them consider that it was a good thing to have that recording of Frank and Mervyn.'

Joey could never bring himself to watch the film; it was too painful a reminder of the loss of his two great friends. Tragically, he too would lose his life in a racing crash many years later in Estonia in 2000. By that point, David Wallace was a BAFTA-award-winning filmmaker who travelled all over the globe shooting documentaries. Such was Dunlop's fame by then, Wallace could not escape the sad news of his death, no matter where he was filming. 'I was doing a series called *Conquistadors* about the Spanish conquest of South America, and I think I was in the Amazon at the time. My wife had heard the news about Joey on the radio and the next time I spoke to her on the phone she told me about it. It was a huge shock. I didn't make it back in time for the funeral, but I saw pictures from it in the strangest places because it was such a momentous event.'

So, 20 years after his film was first aired, it's three subjects had all been killed in racing accidents. Understandably, David Wallace now has mixed feelings about road racing. 'I totally admire road racers and part of me thinks it's wonderful, but there's another side of me that says it's illogical and that surely someone's going to put a stop to it sooner or later. I don't have a fixed opinion – I still can't make my mind up. If I ruled the world, would I ban road racing? Probably not – I'd probably just leave it up to others to decide. But I'm not as gung-ho about it as I was when I was younger. I'm in two minds about road racing now: one says it's completely daft and the other says it's absolutely wonderful.'

One thing Wallace isn't in any doubt about is his lasting admiration for Joey Dunlop. Another of his successes as a filmmaker was the four-part series *In the Footsteps of Alexander the Great*. Wallace draws an interesting contrast between the Macedonian king and the quiet hero from Ballymoney. 'There's a wonderful Greek song about Alexander at the end of the film that says, "Alexander, you conquered the whole world, but you lost your soul." That's one thing you could never say about Joey – he conquered the world, but he absolutely kept his soul.'

CHAPTER 14

OCCASIONAL ROAD RACERS

*'Why bother, when it's so much easier just to shoot
yourself and get it all over with?'*
BARRY SHEENE

Not all road races are alike, and while some riders are happy to race at one event it's not a given that they would race at others. Motorcycle racers, like everyone else, impose levels of acceptable risk upon themselves, and some deem certain events to be just too dangerous. Although he loved racing at the TT, the North West 200 and the Ulster Grand Prix, Ian Simpson never competed in the smaller Irish national road races. 'It's not that I was afraid of them,' he says. 'I had raced at Beveridge Park in Scotland and that was as hairy as it got, so I would have been quite happy to ride at the wee Irish road races, but I never had enough time as I was doing so much short circuit racing, and that's where I saw my future lying, and I didn't think that racing around Kells or the Tandragee was going to help my short circuit career. I love all those wee road races, though. I'd rather go and watch a race at the Tandragee than Knockhill any day.'

Although he never officially competed at the Skerries road race outside Dublin, Simpson did find himself in an impromptu race while touring Ireland with some friends. 'Me, James Whitham and Niall Mackenzie decided to do a few laps, just to have a look at the place, and we started getting faster and faster and faster. It got to the point where we realised that we were either going to be arrested or end up in a hedge, so we had to pack it in.'

Some road races are seen as safer options than others and therefore attract more short circuit riders who would normally never consider taking on a race on public streets. The Macau Grand Prix has always attracted some of the greatest pure road racers in the world, from John McGuinness to David Jefferies and Steve Hislop to Michael Rutter – names that would normally be associated with the Isle of Man TT, the North West 200 and the Ulster – but it has also been known to tempt short circuit stars and even Grand Prix legends.

The most notable of these was 1993 500cc Grand Prix world champion Kevin Schwantz, who won on the Macau street circuit at his first and only attempt in 1988. In fact, Schwantz was so dominant and had such a huge lead that he spent most of the race on the back wheel of his Pepsi Suzuki RGV500, showboating to the crowds.

Former factory 500cc Grand Prix rider and triple TT winner Rob McElnea says that top short circuit riders can easily adapt to the roads because they're used to riding much closer to the edge. 'I was so much sharper than the average

TT rider because I was running at the front in short circuit races in the UK and had done some Grands Prix,' he says. 'So I was obviously going to be faster than the guys who just do the TT and maybe a few other races a year. If a top MotoGP guy went to the TT now and only rode at 80 per cent of his ability, you'd be amazed at how fast they could get round. They're just operating at a much higher level. Kevin Schwantz did the Macau road race just for fun and blitzed everybody.'

Although they would never dream of racing at the TT, MotoGP racers hold TT racers in a kind of startled awe. Danny Webb spent nine seasons in the Grand Prix paddock while racing in the Moto3 class before deciding to enter the TT. 'In the Grand Prix paddock I always said I'd love to do the TT when people asked me about it, and they always thought I was crazy,' he said before making his debut. 'I don't think any of them actually thought that I'd go ahead and do it, but I've committed myself now. A lot of people in the Grand Prix paddock have wished me well with it and seem to have big respect for me for doing it, so it's nice to know that. Valentino Rossi and Jorge Lorenzo respect the hell out of John McGuinness and the other top TT riders, so if I could gain a bit of that respect it would be like a dream come true for me.'

John McGuinness says even Formula 1 drivers have been known to lose the plot when they see the TT for the first time. 'The TT blows MotoGP and British Superbikes out of the water completely as a spectator experience,' he says. 'They're different trades – BSB is real close wheel-to-wheel racing, and MotoGP is the pinnacle of prototype two-wheeled sport, like F1 is in the car world, but we all know that F1 can be a bit average to watch. When [F1 drivers] Mark Webber and Martin Brundle came to watch the TT, they were annihilated – they just couldn't get their heads round what they were witnessing. Valentino Rossi was the same.'

Although he raced closely with the likes of Marc Márquez in Moto3, Danny Webb thinks road racing is *real* racing and he seems to hold the competitors in higher esteem. 'It's just completely different, you know? I mean, when I first watched John McGuinness and those guys going down Bray Hill at the TT, I suddenly didn't even feel like a real motorcycle racer. I had so much respect for those guys as I watched them, and I want to earn some of that respect too. I'd love people to look at me in the same way as they do those guys – that's what appeals to me the most.'

Former racer turned TV presenter James Whitham agrees that road racers are seen as a different breed among motorcycle racers. 'As a rider at the TT you know you cannot afford to make one single mistake,' he explains. 'I was prepared to risk breaking arms and legs when I was racing, but my biggest fear was fear of failure – of not being able to get the results I was being paid to get. Now, someone like Marc Márquez has that pressure and so does John McGuinness, but John also knows that he's got to do his job perfectly or he might not be coming back. And not every rider is prepared to face that kind of challenge. Márquez might be able to control a bike right on its limits better than McGuinness, but who's the bravest of the two? You've got to say McGuinness.'

Even TT riders themselves get scared when they're unable

to ride and have to spectate instead. 'I remember watching the Superstock race at the bottom of Barregarrow in 2014 because I didn't have a Stocker that year,' Ian Hutchinson says. 'When the first bike came past me at Barregarrow I thought, *Fuck me!* It looked so bad, I immediately thought, *I don't think I can do that again.* But the next year I went out and won the Superstock race. It's probably not a good idea for a TT racer to watch a race – it looks so much worse from the side of the track than it feels when you're on the bike. Every time I go through Barregarrow now, I picture what it looks like from the outside.'

Rob McElnea only raced at the TT for three years but picked up three wins in that time, usually having to beat Joey Dunlop in his prime to do so. Again, he says it was down to his short circuit racing skills. 'I never rode the TT as hard as I rode in Grands Prix,' he explains. 'I knew the course and I just rode well within myself. I mean, I was on the front row in Grands Prix at that time, so my riding level was so high. I was so focused and sharp that the TT felt like a doddle to me compared to how hard I was having to ride in Grands Prix.'

Kevin Schwantz is not the only established short circuit star to have tried his hand at road racing. For all his criticism of the Isle of Man TT (he raced there once in 1971 but fell off in the wet while leading and vowed never to return), Barry Sheene counted the treacherous, tree-lined Oliver's Mount circuit in Scarborough as one of his most successful hunting grounds. It might sound hypocritical to criticise the TT on safety grounds yet love racing at Scarborough, but Sheene's real beef with the TT was that it took too long to learn, that it was not 'real racing' (since it was racing against the clock) and that riders should not have been forced to compete there for world championship points (this was at a time when the TT counted as the British round of the Grand Prix world championship).

But Sheene was no stranger to dangerous tree-lined circuits that were based on real-world roads. He raced at places like Spa-Francorchamps in Belgium and Imatra in Finland before both were struck off the world championship calendar for being too dangerous, so he certainly couldn't be accused of being afraid of all but the safest circuits – he just didn't like the TT. 'The Mountain Circuit did not frighten me in any way,' Sheene said. 'No circuit frightens me. I just couldn't see the sense of riding around in the pissing rain, completely on your own against a clock. It wasn't racing, to my mind.'

On the dangers of racing at the TT, Sheene was even more forthright: 'Why bother, when it's so much easier just to shoot yourself and get it all over with?'

Despite his anti-TT attitude, Sheene was a demon road racer when he set his mind to it, as his fierce rival from the 1970s, Mick Grant, testifies. 'The way he rode on pure road circuits – like Scarborough and Imatra – there was no way that he couldn't have done the TT. I mean, bloomin' hell, Scarborough requires all the road-racing skills you'd ever need, and he could do it. He certainly wasn't slow round there.'

Another former 500cc world champion who competed in several road races was Wayne Gardner. It's a little-known fact that the 1987 500cc Grand Prix world champion took part in the Ulster Grand Prix in 1982 when he was riding for Honda Britain. He finished third in that year's Formula 1 race behind Ron Haslam and Joey Dunlop, a fact that made his later statements sound – like Sheene – somewhat hypocritical. In 2010, Gardner called for the TT to be banned following the death of two riders, Paul Dobbs and Martin Loicht. 'The rewards are just not worth the annual cost in lives,' Gardner said, 'and the whole event needs to be consigned to history.'

Wayne Gardner was one of the grittiest and toughest motorcycle racers ever, so he can never be accused of being risk-averse or 'soft'. Yet he renewed his calls for the TT to be banned in 2022, saying, 'I stand by my opinion that the TT is insane, outdated and should be banned. If being alarmed about unnecessary death makes me a "knob" or a "moaner", as some have suggested, then that's fine. Remember, there's a key difference between closed-circuit racing and the TT, and that's this: the TT virtually guarantees bodies in boxes *every* year.'

Gardner also revealed on his website that he had come very close to entering the TT early in his career. He spent a week on the Isle of Man ahead of the 1981 event, learning the course with the intention of racing there for Honda Britain. 'I was young and naïve and had been tempted by the offer of substantial start money,' he revealed. 'But at the last minute I got a call from Moriwaki [Mamoru Moriwaki – founder of Moriwaki Engineering], asking me to come to Japan to race at Suzuka instead. Thankfully, I was never tempted to roll the dice at the TT again.'

Another Grand Prix legend, Randy Mamola – a

contemporary of Gardner's – also raced on the roads, having taken part in the Whanganui Road Races in New Zealand as a teenager in the 1970s. The annual races take place on Boxing Day on the ominously titled 'Cemetery Circuit', so named because it bisects the town's cemetery, with gravestones flanking both sides of the track. The one-mile circuit also incorporates a railway crossing and a railway bridge. American Grand Prix star, Pat Hennen, enjoyed tremendous success on the circuit in the 1970s when it was the centrepiece of the now-defunct Marlboro series: a big-money championship that attracted famous riders from around the world. In later years, riders like Simon Crafar and Aaron Slight would also cut their teeth on the Cemetery Circuit before carving out successful careers in Grands Prix and World Superbikes. Even more recently, British riders Peter Hickman and Richard Cooper won the event in 2018 and 2019, respectively.

The most successful rider around the Cemetery Circuit was New Zealand's own Robert Holden, who competed in the event for 19 consecutive years up until 1995. Sadly, he was killed at the Isle of Man TT in 1996. On Boxing Day of that year, Holden's ashes were laid to rest at the Cemetery Circuit's Flower Garden Corner. The Flower Garden itself has now become a traffic island, and the corner has been renamed Robert Holden Corner. A brass plaque serves as a permanent memorial to the popular Kiwi rider for whom the term 'Cemetery Circuit' became all too literal. To this day, the feature race at Whanganui is named the Robert Holden Memorial, and the winner receives the Robert Holden Trophy. He has not been forgotten.

New Zealand's Bruce Anstey says the Whanganui races attract far more spectators in his homeland than short circuit races do. 'In the national series, on a short circuit, you only get 20 people in the grandstand and that's about it!' he says. 'On the other hand, with the pure road racing – like the Whanganui Cemetery Circuit Boxing Day meeting – you get massive crowds. There's also a February meeting at Paeroa that draws massive crowds.'

With only two road races in his homeland, Anstey was forced to move to Europe in order to make a living from the sport. Now retired, the Kiwi rider won 12 TT races, 13 Ulster Grand Prix races and ten North West 200 wins in a remarkable career. 'There was no way I could have made a living back home, so I had to come over here to do that.'

The 'Battle of the Streets' meeting ran at Paeroa from 1991 until 2018 before it was abandoned due to limited spectator numbers, meaning that the Whanganui meeting is now New Zealand's last road race.

While New Zealanders are happy to run a road race – even if it is only one – the same cannot be said of Australians. 'They used to have big races at Bathurst, which was a road circuit, but everyone's wrapped up in cotton wool over in Australia now – it's the worst nanny state country in the world,' says Australian road racer David Johnson. 'You need sunglasses because of all the high-vis vests people are forced to wear over there, so I don't think there's going to be a road race anytime soon.'

Niall Mackenzie has always been more associated with Grands Prix and British Superbikes than pure road racing, but he too has tried his hand at riding between the hedges, competing at the North West 200 in the 1980s on 250cc and 350cc machinery, and once on a Honda RVF750 in 1991. He had a best finish of second on a Silverstone Armstrong 250 in 1984 but struggled on the surprisingly uncompetitive Honda. 'When I first went to the North West I rode it 100 per cent like a short circuit,' Mackenzie says. 'That probably wasn't the right thing to do, but I was young and daft and I didn't really think about it – I loved it. It's only about nine miles long and it was mostly straights back then, so it was easy to learn. The long straights and slow corners make it a bit safer than most road courses.'

Mackenzie's motives for tackling the North West were simple: 'It just fitted in because it was a quiet time in May,' he says. 'The organisers were great, and they talked me into it a bit, and my Silverstone Armstrong team were keen to go too. The TT means having a big plan – it's two weeks – but the North West was just like going to another short circuit meeting over a weekend. You got your ferry and accommodation paid, you got decent start money and the whole weekend was just great craic.'

Mackenzie was blissfully ignorant about the North West when he turned up to race there in 1984. 'I didn't know much about the course, but I'd heard that it wasn't as dangerous as some of the other pure road circuits, even though the lap record averaged around 115mph,' he says. 'It's mostly long straights and slow corners, which isn't as bad as having lots of fast corners lined with trees.'

As things turned out, the Royal Ulster Constabulary proved to be more of a threat to Mackenzie's wellbeing than the North West course. 'I almost spent the whole weekend in a police cell!' he laughs. 'I was walking down the street in Portrush when I spotted the guys from Dunlop Tyres through the glass front of a restaurant. Instinctively, I dropped my trousers and pants and gave the boys a big moony, and then the whole world went dark. I didn't have a clue what was going on, but it turns out that the local Royal Ulster Constabulary police saw me moonshining, threw a blanket over my head and bundled me into the back of a police car. I thought it was the Ku Klux Klan or something, until I got to the station. Eventually, the Dunlop boys came down – after wetting themselves laughing – and vouched for my character, so I was released in time for the races.'

Despite the sustained high speeds experienced on the North West course, Mackenzie practically yawned his way through practice. 'I remember being really bored in practice because there was too much time to think on those long straights,' he says. 'It was getting tedious, just holding the throttle to the stop and going in a straight line. But apart from being boring it also gave me too much time to think about things that could go wrong. What would happen if the gearbox seized? What would happen if the engine seized and I couldn't get the clutch in? I was thinking about all that sort of stuff in practice, but the actual races were great fun, slipstreaming all the other riders for miles, flat out. I treated the course like a big, short circuit because I didn't know any different. I didn't know how you were supposed to ride a pure road race properly, and I suppose I still don't, but I did all right, finishing second to Kevin Mitchell in the wet 350cc race then coming home fifth in the dry 250cc event. I had been in second place and was dicing with Steve Cull but landed in a hedge on the last lap and remounted for fifth.'

As most riders will testify, the carnival atmosphere at the North West 200 is a big part of its appeal as an event. 'The best thing about the North West was the atmosphere,' Mackenzie testifies. 'We practised in the evenings then we all went out and got drunk and slept in late in the mornings. It was brilliant, and the Irish hospitality and the fans were just fantastic – everybody bought me drinks from the moment I arrived!'

Despite enjoying the North West, Mackenzie was never tempted by the TT. 'It wasn't because it was dangerous,' he says. 'As a young rider I honestly didn't care about getting hurt, and I never thought it would happen to me anyway. I just wanted to get into Grands Prix, and I knew that the TT wasn't the way to go about it.'

Mackenzie's point about riding roads courses with the same flat-out aggression used on short circuits is a significant one. It seems that racers only know one speed and, if they've got it, they'll use it. 'I remember Kevin Schwantz said he fancied having a go at Macau one year,' Mackenzie says. 'He said he was just going to go and have a wobble round and see what it was like, but it's very difficult for any racer to go out on a track and just ride round. Schwantz might have *thought* that's what he was going to do, but when he got there he went as fast as he could and ended up winning the race by a mile. And I think he would have done the same had it been the TT, the North West or anywhere else.'

With short circuit racers taking their full-on aggressive riding styles to the unforgiving roads, where there's no margin for error, are they a danger to themselves? Double British Superbike champion Josh Brookes doesn't think so. Speaking before his TT debut in 2013 (when he became the fastest newcomer in the history of the event at that time) he said, 'You have to start off slowly and build up to speed. So, it's not so much how I'll adapt my speed to the course, it's more the other way round: it's like, how will I bring my speed up after I've started off slow? Fear and self-preservation are going to stop you from going fast, so the question really should be, how are you going to get yourself up to speed? And the way I'm going to do that is by learning the track and having as much knowledge as possible. The more knowledge you have, the faster you can go.'

British Supersport champion Stuart Easton was another top short circuit rider with an occasional history on the roads. A three-time Macau GP winner, he also regularly contested the North West 200 but never competed at the TT. 'I thought about it over the years,' Easton says. 'I'm a big fan of the TT and really like it as an event, but for me the British Championship was top of my list. I had ridden for certain teams in the past who were never keen on taking me to the TT because I'd have to go as a newcomer and serve my time and it takes such a long time to learn. The North West and Macau are two road tracks that you can easily learn on your first visit, and if you're good enough, you can be successful straight away. The TT requires a big apprenticeship and obviously takes a lot more learning. I would have liked to have done it, and I flirted with the idea many times, but eventually realised that if I really desperately wanted to do the TT then I'd have done it already, so I left it at that. But I enjoyed the North West at the start of the year and Macau at the end of the year, and they didn't interfere with my championship seasons. You can earn a few bob, too, and both events are great fun, so it worked nicely for me.'

Armco barriers aside, Easton says the 3.8-mile Macau course is surprisingly like the short circuits he was more accustomed to racing on. 'It's the most short circuit-type road race of them all,' he says. 'The surface is really good because the cars lay down so much rubber and clean the track, so it's really smooth and grippy. If you took the barriers away it would just be like any other normal short circuit.'

But that didn't mean Easton rode Macau the same way as he would Donington Park or Brands Hatch. It's long been assumed that, in order to survive, road racers only ride at about 80 per cent of their abilities, but according to Easton this isn't quite the case. 'The best way I can describe it is that you always ride at 100 per cent when you're racing, but that 100 per cent is relative to the circumstances you're in. I think your mind subconsciously pulls back a bit anyway – it knows that there's a big barrier or a stone wall looming, so self-preservation kicks in. You feel like you're riding at 100 per cent but you'd never be pushing the front, for example, like you would in British Superbikes. You can afford to crash in BSB, but you can't at Macau. Ultimately, that's the difference between road racing and short circuit racing.'

As well as getting more of a thrill from road racing, Easton also gained more satisfaction from it than from short circuit racing. 'If I came away from a British Championship meeting with a fourth place I'd be disappointed, but if I came away from a road race with a fourth place after a close battle I could be perfectly happy with that, just because of the nature of the race and the fact that it's a lot more dangerous. Just competing at somewhere like Macau or the North West 200 is an achievement in itself, and it gives you a good feeling when you're on the way home or down the pub after the race – you just get a better sense of satisfaction.'

Although he later became famous as a TV presenter and commentator for bike racing, Keith Huewen was a great racer himself in the 1970s and 1980s. His problem with road racing was that he couldn't trust himself to approach the roads with the caution they demanded. 'I was good at Scarborough and good at the North West, but never really gelled with the sheer length of the TT course – I couldn't settle back into that rhythm that you needed for it,' he says. 'And I couldn't do the homework, either. I could name every corner and knew what was coming and in what sequence, but I could never steady myself back enough to just slowly but surely work away and learn the place. I was attacking it like a short circuit and realised I wasn't going to live for very long if I kept doing that!'

Huewen was under a lot of pressure during his TT debut, as in 1981 he had won the North West 200 at his first attempt just two weeks before the TT started. 'By winning the North West I had made a bit of a name for myself, and I put too much pressure on myself and just couldn't cope with it, really,' he admits. 'I never scared myself, though; funnily enough, I never got scared back then. I maybe got scared for other people, but never for myself. It's weird, but I'm more scared for people now than I ever was for myself when I was racing. And racing was a lot more dangerous back in my day.'

Ulsterman Jeremy McWilliams is another occasional road racer, only competing at the North West 200. A former 250cc, 500cc and MotoGP rider, McWilliams is one of the greatest motorcycle racers to ever come out of Northern Ireland. When he made his road-racing debut at the 2012 North West 200 it caused a few raised eyebrows, because 12 years earlier he had called for all road racing to be banned. Speaking shortly after Joey Dunlop's death in 2000, McWilliams told the *Belfast Telegraph*, 'I don't care who I upset, it's long past the time for road racing to be stopped.'

McWilliams was clearly still grieving for his countryman and friend Joey Dunlop at the time and that may have affected his attitude, but he cited a spate of other recent deaths as a wake-up call. 'I've lost too many friends – good friends – to the sport,' he continued. 'Seven top riders have been killed in the past year, including Joey Dunlop. If it goes on like this we won't have any top riders left. Just how many more young riders have to be killed before people see sense and build a purpose-built track like Silverstone or Brands Hatch in Northern Ireland?'

Now 61, McWilliams continues to race at the North West 200, despite his earlier objections, and has racked up three wins there in the Supertwin class.

McWilliams isn't being a hypocrite by racing at the North West 200; many riders view the event as a sort of halfway house between circuit racing and road racing. The course is wide and open, and it's relatively short, which makes it easier to learn. Much of the course is made up of straights, and many of the corners are purpose-built chicanes, not unlike those on short circuits. With an astonishing 29 wins, Alastair Seeley is the most successful rider in the history of the North West 200, yet it's the only road race he has ever contested and is ever likely to. Seeley has always focused on short circuits but clearly views the North West as a relatively safe way of going road racing. Jeremy McWilliams appears to feel the same way. Richard Cooper is another lifelong short circuit rider whose only forays into road racing (with great success) have been at the North West. The event occupies its own niche in the racing world and, as such, attracts riders who would never dream of competing in smaller, more dangerous road races.

Motorcycle racers are (usually) free to decide what races they enter, and should big-name riders occasionally turn up at a road race, so much the better for all involved. Equally, if they feel other races are just too dangerous, their decisions must be respected; they're the ones taking the risks, after all. Road racing isn't for everyone.

CHAPTER 15

WIN, LOSE OR DIE

'You've got to be able to accept what can happen – you've got to be able to accept the consequences.'
DAVID JEFFERIES

Like all road racers, David Jefferies knew the risks he was taking and fully accepted them. He approached each race with his eyes wide open, knowing it might be his last. He had seen his fair share of tragedy firsthand. During Jefferies' first TT in 1996, Robert Holden and Mick Lofthouse both lost their lives, and in 1999 he witnessed the death of Simon Beck. But road racers must learn to compartmentalise fear. 'I don't think you can let it affect you,' Jefferies said. 'I saw Simon Beck go down, and as I rode past him I thought, *I'm going to give him some grief about that when I get back*, but I never did, you know? To race the TT, I have to be able to accept that I go there at the end of May and that might be it – I might not come back. If you can't sit and openly discuss that with someone, if you can't accept that that might happen, you shouldn't be racing there. I think you've got to be able to accept what can happen – you've got to be able to accept the consequences.'

Jefferies had little tolerance of outsiders calling for the TT to be banned, believing it was none of their business. 'I get really annoyed with all these do-gooders saying, "Ban the TT! It's bloody disgraceful!" Blah, blah, blah. Nobody is forced to go to the Isle of Man. People get injured doing rugby or fencing, you know? There are so many other sports which are dangerous, but I've chosen to do the TT. No one is forcing me to go there. Yeah, people might say that I'm thick, a bloody silly bastard for riding at the TT, but that's what I want to do. And at the minute I'm the best in the world at it.'

Irish rider Jamie Hamilton also knew and fully accepted the risks, so when he suffered a life-changing crash in 2015 he already had the mental armour in place to help him deal with the trauma.

Hamilton had smashed into a lamp post at 170mph during the 2015 TT. He was left in a critical condition with severe injuries to his arm and leg as well as suffering memory loss. He would need to wear an external fixator cage on his leg for months and still suffers great pain from his injuries, but he knows he really shouldn't be here at all, and wouldn't be had it not been for an off-duty critical care nurse who happened to be spectating at the spot where he crashed and rushed to help. Ali Bunn gave Hamilton four pints of blood while waiting for the air ambulance, and in doing so saved his life.

'I knew what I was getting myself into,' Hamilton told BBC Sport on the tenth anniversary of his crash. 'I knew the odds were massive for possible death or serious injury, but your life is laid out for you and I was chasing my dreams. It just wasn't my time to go.'

One tragic incident in particular made Hamilton acutely aware that while road racing is undeniably dangerous so are many other activities: even driving a car. 'I had a friend who had always said to me, "Jamie, don't go road racing, you could possibly die, so you should never do it,"' Hamilton said. 'She was killed in a car crash when I was on the Isle of Man learning the course. That changed my outlook on it.'

Every road racer has their own ways of coping with the dangers of what they do. They need to protect themselves as much as they can, not only physically but mentally. Like all road racers, Kettering's James McBride has lost friends to the sport. 'Yeah, I've lost a lot of mates along the way,' he says. 'Maybe not close pals, but certainly people I spent time with and raced against, like Paul Shoesmith, Darran Lindsay, Richard Britton and Martin Finnegan. Martin was my teammate at the Macau Grand Prix in 2006, and I learned so much from him. He wanted to stop racing, but he couldn't. He got carried along with it; the next race was coming up, then the one after that. Riders at his level have so much support and there was money coming in from sponsors, too, so they can feel responsible for the people supporting them and keep on racing, even though they would maybe rather stop.'

Every racer knows where fatalities have occurred on different courses in the past, and those spots can serve as potent reminders of the risks involved in the sport. 'When you race on the roads for long enough, the fatal crash site locations start building up, and you're very aware of them,' McBride continues. 'You're going round all these corners, knowing who was killed there. Those corners are like scars, and you lose muscle control when you go through them. You remember what happened and your throttle hand just backs off a bit, almost of its own accord.'

One of McBride's defence mechanisms when faced with tragedy was to try not to look. 'You need to learn to ride as if you have blinkers on,' he says. 'When there was an accident in front of me at the TT in 2007, and there was carnage all over the road, as if a bomb had gone off, bits of bikes everywhere, and marshals tending to bodies lying on the road, I raised my head so that I could only see out through the bottom of the visor to see where I was going and to avoid all that was around me – exactly like a horse with blinkers on. I rode through in an instant because I didn't want to absorb anything. That was the crash when Jun Maeda collided with Seamus Greene and Jun lost his life. I wasn't ignoring what had happened – I was still taking it in – but I just didn't need to see it. It's the only way you can cope. I've heard graphic reports from other riders about fatalities that they witnessed, but yeah, I don't need to see that.'

Steve Hislop was one of the greatest road racers of all time, yet he wasn't killed in a motorcycle crash at the TT or the North West 200; he was killed when the Robinson R44 helicopter he was piloting came down in poor weather conditions in the Scottish Borders on 30th July, 2003.

Mike Hailwood – still regarded by many as the greatest

motorcycle racer of all time – retired safely in 1979 but was killed in a car crash two years later when a truck driver performed an illegal U-turn in front of him, leaving Hailwood with nowhere to go. The driver was fined £100.

Despite all the injuries he suffered during his illustrious career, the great Barry Sheene also retired safely but died of cancer in 2003 at the age of 52. Former 500cc Grand Prix star Norick Abe was killed on a scooter; 2006 MotoGP world champion Nicky Hayden lost his life on a pushbike; 14-time world champion Ángel Nieto was riding a quad bike when he was hit by a car and killed; two-time world champion Fausto Gresini succumbed to the Covid-19 pandemic . . . The list is endless, but the message remains the same – there are many other ways to die, aside from racing motorcycles. Yet road racing in general – and the TT in particular – tends to be singled out as presenting unacceptable levels of risk in the modern world: a world in which the authorities take a dim view of any kind of risk or danger.

Speaking at Steve Hislop's funeral service, the Reverend Neil R. Combe said, 'We live in a world where McDonald's is sued because it makes coffee hot, where a jar of peanut butter has a label on it saying "Warning: May Contain Nuts". Someone like Steve opens our eyes to a bigger world; to a world of exciting possibilities for those who are willing to take that calculated risk.'

As part of an article on health and safety for highspeedtraining.co.uk in 2015, Liz Burton-Hughes wrote: 'It's a common trend in primary schools to stop children from engaging in potentially harmful activities to keep them from ever harming themselves. A primary school in Thame,

Oxfordshire, prohibited children from using monkey bars without supervision. Another banned the sack and three-legged races from sports days. And another the use of yo-yos – all on the grounds of health and safety.'

Burton-Hughes also noted that, 'In 2014, a primary school barred the use of ladders due to "health and safety reasons", so staff had no choice but to balance precariously on chairs when accessing high places.'

In a 2018 article for the *Independent*, Emma Elsworthy pointed out that, 'Not being allowed to give a colleague a paracetamol, filling out a form to use plasters, and a ban on birthday cake candles are among Britain's most bizarre health and safety rules. A survey of 2,000 workers also found one in five are not allowed to change light bulbs in their workplace.'

Set against a backdrop of such nanny-state laws it can be little wonder that many people view motorcycle road racing as being an unacceptably dangerous sport. After all, if changing a light bulb is considered a dangerous activity, then hurtling between stone walls at 200mph on a motorcycle is unlikely to meet with the approval of those who believe that relentless legislation is actually capable of consigning accidents to history. Accidents will happen, no matter how draconian the legislation – they're simply unavoidable. Always have been, always will be.

The unforeseen side effect of such suffocating health and safety legislation is that more and more people are turning to extreme sports such as motorcycle road racing as an act of rebellion; a chance for people to make up their own minds what constitutes acceptable risk, rather than having those decisions made by an overly interfering government. The TT is generally oversubscribed every year.

It's worth remembering that motorcycle racing isn't the only dangerous sport or pastime in existence. Writing for the *Horses Only* website in 2025, Beth Mallory pointed out that a 2021 study on American horse-riding injuries found that the risk of hospital admission from equestrian injuries is higher than motorcycling, skiing and football. It's estimated that around 710 people die from horse-riding accidents every year, yet no one calls for horse riding to be banned.

It's a statistic that wasn't lost on David Jefferies. 'The people that keep saying that road racing is dangerous are all these arty-farty bastards who live in the bloody countryside and ride horses. And when you look at the amount of people that get hurt riding horses – which no one tells you about, because society says horse-riding is wonderful for the establishment – that really winds me up.'

According to Alpine police in Austria, an average of 110 mountaineers are killed every year in the Alps. In the Himalayas, over 340 people have died climbing Mount Everest alone. To narrow things down even further, to one single rock face, in fact – the north face of the Eiger – some 64 climbers have perished in the attempt to conquer it since 1935.

But those deaths pale into insignificance when compared to the fatalities in the sport of angling. Data specialist website pew.org reports that some 100,000 anglers lose their lives every year. While it's true that many more people pursue angling as a hobby than race round the TT course, the statistics stand as evidence that life itself is dangerous, and that no amount of legislation will ever remove that hard fact. There are millions of ways to die.

It's important to realise that those who call for road racing to be banned have usually never experienced the pure elation that the sport offers to those who take part in it. Leanne Harper lost her partner Dan Kneen at the 2018 TT but has never turned her back on the sport or criticised it in any way. On the contrary, she knows exactly how much it meant to Kneen and exactly why he raced. 'While fans might see road race winners spraying the bubbly and grinning on the podium, they don't get to see the true euphoria those riders experience for weeks after an event,' Harper says. 'Only those close to the competitors get to see the sheer joy and sense of fulfilment the sport gives them when things are going well. Most people don't see the sheer euphoria that the riders get out of the TT – only their families get to see that. Dan lived the equivalent of three lifetimes in the short time he was here.'

Television presenter Craig Doyle spent many years as anchorman for TV coverage of the TT, and despite having covered many different sporting events he says road racing is like no other sport on earth – and that includes the multi-million-pound world of MotoGP. 'MotoGP and pure road racing are completely different sports in my eyes,' he says. 'It's like football and rugby – they both involve using your legs, but that's kind of where the similarities end. I'm always trying to explain the TT to my mates, and I say it's like going to a rugby match at Twickenham except no one leaves when the game's over. Imagine everyone just camping on the pitch and having a big barbecue and a few beers and waiting for another match the next day! And then doing it for a whole week – awesome! The TT is like nothing I've ever experienced in my life.'

Doyle is also impressed with the friendliness of the sport and the approachability of its stars. 'You see a lot of the same faces each year, so there's a real sense of community and the riders are so approachable,' he says. 'You're watching them race – they're your heroes for a couple of hours – then you go to the paddock and can just talk to them so easily, and the public can do the same thing. It would be like 80,000 people at a rugby match going into the changing rooms afterwards and asking the players how the game went for them. It's just such pure, brilliant sport. MotoGP is a completely different world to that. Those guys are almost untouchable – they're different kinds of stars.'

Doyle recognises that road racers simply aren't like the rest of us. 'They're pretty special guys, and they live life very differently to the rest of us, and they think differently too,' he says. 'They don't really give a damn what people think about them, and I really envy them for that. I think that's an amazing trait, and it must be really cool to be like that. It certainly leads to some unusual interviews!'

The late Keith Flint – former frontman of The Prodigy – ran a successful road-race team for several years before his untimely death in 2019. He spoke eloquently about the sport he loved so much. 'The TT is one of the greatest races still out there and one of the greatest challenges for a racer to undertake,' he said. 'They must be some of the bravest men on the planet. It's a cliché, but they're like modern-day gladiators. A photographer once told me that he'd been taking pictures of fighter pilots just before they took off from the flight deck of an aircraft carrier during the Gulf War. He noticed that the look in their eyes, through their visors, was *exactly* the same as that of TT riders as they prepare to blast off down Bray Hill. He said it was very obvious that the bravery and the controlled fear was exactly the same. And I think that fear is crucial – if you don't have an element of self-preservation then you're not coming home.'

But despite the dangers and the associated fears, Flint believed it was crucial for the human spirit to preserve events like the TT. 'If someone went to a government today and said, "We're going to set up a road race and this is how it's going to be," it would never happen,' he says. 'So, events like the TT are precious – we need to not be told what to do all the time. We need to be able to make our own decisions to go and do stuff, even if it has an element of danger attached to it. Otherwise, we're just going to live in a nanny state, wrapped in cotton wool, and lives won't be worth living.'

There can be no denying that motorcycle road racing is dangerous. No one tries to cover this up: not the race organisers, not the teams, not the riders, not the fans. But while the media seems to relish reporting on deaths in road racing (a sport the mainstream media very rarely covers *except* when there are fatalities), there is never any mention of the untold millions of safe racing miles completed by the racers. That's not news. That doesn't sell newspapers or generate clicks on websites.

Despite the fact that so many deaths occur in different sports and pastimes, there are never any calls for horse-riding or mountaineering to be banned. Not so with road racing: almost every year around TT time, articles are published protesting the 'insanity' of the event. They make triple TT winner Ian Simpson angry. 'If you ban the TT, then where do you draw the line?' he questions. 'Riders get killed in the British Superbike Championship and in MotoGP and World Superbikes, so you'd have to ban them, too, because they also carry an element of risk. And mountaineering. And horse-riding. And so many other sports and pastimes. It seems that every single day the government comes up with some ridiculous fucking pish, saying we can't do this and we can't do that. I think we should celebrate the TT while it's still there and admire the heroes who do it. If you don't like it, don't watch it.'

Michael Dunlop, now the most successful TT rider of all time, feels the same. 'Nobody asks any of us to race at the TT – we don't have to do it,' he says. 'And people don't have to watch it, either, if they don't like it. This job has its ups and downs, that's for sure, but nobody's holding a gun to my forehead to make me do it.'

The current TT lap record holder Peter Hickman agrees. 'As to those who say road racing should be banned, it's usually people that don't understand it and haven't experienced it,' he says. 'If they want to have an opinion like that then they should go to some races and speak to the riders and teams and realise how passionate everyone in the paddock is about racing – see what it's all about before expressing an opinion on something they don't understand.'

Road racing offers such a rush that riders often struggle to give it up. The parallels with drugs are obvious.

Charlie Williams retired in the 1980s but struggled to deal with life after road racing. His words show just how much the riders get out of it, and why they're prepared to take any amount of risk to get their fix. 'Anyone who suggests that the TT should be stopped wants to race around the place before they make such comments,' he says. 'When I retired from the TT it left a huge gap in my life, and I've never been able to replace the thrill I got from riding there. I was tempted to make a comeback just to get that rush again, because I got terrible withdrawal symptoms for years after I stopped. It took about four to five years before I could accept the fact I was just a spectator and not a racer anymore.'

Road racers want to race; they live to race; they sacrifice everything to race. The sport is everything to them. So long as road racing is permitted to continue, so long as human beings are willing to push the boundaries of what's possible and strive to achieve new heights, so long as the human spirit refuses to be fettered by endless government legislation and regulations, there will be no shortage of riders lining up to test themselves in one of the world's most dangerous but thrilling and exhilarating sports, whatever the eventual consequences: win, lose or die.

ACKNOWLEDGEMENTS

A huge thank you to the riders who have granted me fresh interviews for this book, and to those who have granted me interviews over previous years, excerpts of which have been used throughout:

Bruce Anstey, Josh Brookes, Roger Burnett, Maria Costello, Conor Cummins, Gerald Davison, Cameron Donald, Geoff Duke, Jim Dunlop, Michael Dunlop, William Dunlop, Stuart Easton, Adam Evans, Ryan Farquhar, Carl Fogarty, Mick Grant, Dave Greenham, Jamie Hamilton, Veronika Hankocyová, Dean Harrison, Peter Hickman, James Hillier, Steve Hislop, Ian Hutchinson, Keith Huewen, Paul Iddon, Glenn Irwin, Louise Jefferies, Tony Jefferies, David Johnson, Lee Johnston, Gary Lingham, Niall Mackenzie, Guy Martin, James McBride, Derek McGee, Adam McLean, Rob McElnea, John McGuinness, Don Morley, Neil Morris, Paul Owen, Steve Parrish, Steve Plater, Michael Rutter, Tony Rutter, Ian Simpson, John Surtees, Barry Symmons, Jenny Tinmouth, Davey Todd, Neil Tuxworth, Jack Valentine, David Wallace, Danny Webb and James Whitham.